Financial Innovation and Technology

Series Editor
Thomas Puschmann, Swiss FinTech Innovation Lab, University of Zurich, Zurich, Switzerland

The book series 'Financial Innovation and Technology' features scholarly research on the latest developments in the world of finance such as AI, FinTech startups, Big Data, Cryptocurrencies, Robo-Advisors, Machine Learning, and Blockchain applications among others. The book series explores the main trends and technologies that will transform the finance industry in the years to come. The series presents essential insights into the financial technology revolution, and the disruption, innovation, and opportunity it entails. The books in this series will be of value to both academics and those working in the finance industry.

Thomas Puschmann
H. S. H. Prince Michael of Liechtenstein

Financial System 2030

Digitalization, Nation States and (De-)Regulation as Drivers of Change

Springer

Thomas Puschmann
Global Center for Sustainable
Digital Finance
Stanford University
Stanford, USA

Global Center for Sustainable
Digital Finance
University of Zurich
Zurich, Switzerland

H. S. H. Prince Michael of Liechtenstein
Industrie- und Finanzkontor
Vaduz, Liechtenstein

ISSN 2730-9681 ISSN 2730-969X (electronic)
Financial Innovation and Technology
ISBN 978-3-031-55699-9 ISBN 978-3-031-55700-2 (eBook)
https://doi.org/10.1007/978-3-031-55700-2

This Springer imprint is published by the registered company Springer Nature Switzerland AG
The registered company address is: Gewerbestrasse 11, 6330 Cham, Switzerland

Prologue

The financial system is currently confronted with tremendous challenges from the global economy, trade, politics, demographics, and most recently enormous technological advancements. These developments have the capacity to change the existing financial system fundamentally. This topic was the subject of a series of ten two-day roundtables with high-level experts on the future of the financial system from 2018 to 2023, which will be continued in the forthcoming years. In these roundtables, we had the privilege to welcome 78 participants from five continents in Liechtenstein and online during the COVID-19 pandemic. We want to cordially thank all these individuals who contributed to the discussions and who represent a comprehensive view on the future of the financial system. All views expressed in this book are those of the authors, and not the named roundtable participants, unless expressly identified as such. The participants joined us from the following organizations:

- *Supranational institutions:* Bank for International Settlements (Morten Bech), International Monetary Fund (Kenneth Kang), United Nations Capital Development Fund (Aiaze Mitha).
- *Central banks:* Bank of Canada (Francisco Rivadeneyra), Bank of England (Michael Kumhof, William Lovell), Bank of Japan (Masaki Bessho), Central Reserve Bank of Peru (Milton Vega), European Central Bank (Philipp Hartmann, Andrea Pinna), National Bank of Cambodia (Serey Chea), People's Bank of China (Changchun Mu), Swiss National Bank (Thomas Moser).
- *Commercial banks and providers:* Deutsche Bank (Paul Achleitner), Citi (Andres Wolberg-Stok), BBVA (Alvaro Martin), ING Group (Teunis Brosens), JPMorgan Chase (Manuela Veloso; Emerita Carnegie Mellon University), Mastercard (Jesse McWaters), Private Client Bank AG (Ivan Adamovich), Société Générale (Claire Calmejane, Anne Marion-Bouchacourt), Standard Chartered (Kahina van Dyke).
- *Regulators:* European Commission (Helen Köpman, Lukas Repa, Pēteris Zilgalvis), Financial Conduct Authority (Ravi Bhalla), Monetary Authority of Singapore (Sopnendu Mohanty), US Securities and Exchange Commission (Commissioner Hester Peirce).

- *Startups and technology companies:* Aave (Stani Kulechov), Autpay (Andrzej Anton), BankServAfrica (Chris Hamilton; now Hamilton Platform), Circle (Dante Disparte), Melonport (Mona El Isa; now KR1), Google (Victor Bergmann), Ripple (Jeremy Light; now pingNpay, Antony Welfare), wefox (Julian Teicke).
- *Ventura capitalists:* 1k(x) (Diana Biggs), DFJ & Draper Associates (Tim Draper), Haun Ventures (Tomicah Tillemann), Matuschka Group (Albrecht Matuschka).
- *Universities:* Aix Marseille University (Elisabeth Krecké), Chinese University of Hongkong (Marlene Amstad; now FINMA), Duke University (Steven Schwarcz), IMD (Frédéric Dalsace), Loerrach University (Heike Walterscheid), London Business School (Michael Jacobides), MIT (Alex Pentland; Ali Robleh; now Wadagso), Nottingham University (Meryem Duygun), Politecnico Milano (Filippo Maria Renga), Singapore Management University (Heng Wang), Stanford University (Darrell Duffie), Tel Aviv University (Jacob A. Mendel), University of Pennsylvania—The Wharton School (Itay Goldstein), University College London (Iris Chiu), University of Berne (Dirk Niepelt), University of California Irvine (Tom Boellstorff and Bill Maurer), University of Cambridge (Robert Wardrop), University of Hong Kong (Douglas Arner), University of Oxford (Nir Vulkan), University of Toronto (Joshua Gans), Université du Luxembourg (Dirk Zetzsche), University of Zurich (Thorsten Hens), Yale University (Gary Gorton).
- *Think tanks, foundations, and visionaries:* Alliance for Innovative Regulation (Jo Ann Barefoot), Atlantic Council (Martin Mühleisen), Avenir Suisse (Jürg Müller), Bill & Melinda Gates Foundation (Konstantin Peric), Cardano Foundation (Frederik Gregaard), David Chaum (Inventor of DigiCash and xx network), Digital Dollar Foundation (J. Christopher Giancarlo), Industrie- und Finanzkontor (Gisela Bergmann, Princess of Liechtenstein), Longevity Institute (Joanna Bensz), The Finality Project (Jean-Marc Bonnefous), Pindar Wong (veriFi).

During these roundtable sessions we developed potential scenarios for the financial system 2030. We believe that there might be not only one possible outcome but different pathways, depending on geopolitical and economic developments and other global events which we cannot foresee. We think that the knowledge of these experts serves as an excellent source for this book on the "financial system 2030" which aims at summarizing the discussions in a structured way. In the roundtable discussions we could reflect various views on the financial system and discussed them in detail. We learned that the different views not always overlap and might hold the potential to take different directions. This uncertainty clearly showed us the need for an internationally oriented book that sheds light on the various drivers, as this provides a huge opportunity. For example, the financial industry in the USA employed around 6.72 million people in June 2023 (U.S. Bureau of Labor Statistics) and in 2022 contributed a gross output of $14.19 trillion to the economy, which equals 7.72% of the country's total gross output (U.S. Bureau of Economic

Analysis). But, since the financial sector is also an enabler for all other economic activities, its relevance goes far beyond an isolated view of the sector. Therefore, the book targets all readers with an interest in the future of the financial system and the economy, including:

- Financial institutions, utilities, and companies which rely on financial services
- Regulators and supranational institutions
- Policy makers
- Entrepreneurs, venture capitalists, think tanks, and visionaries
- Researchers and teachers
- Individuals with a general interest in economics and finance

Prince Michael of Liechtenstein
Thomas Puschmann

Acknowledgement

We would like to thank everyone who contributed to this book, especially the excellent organizers of the roundtables Luca Clavadetscher, Lisa Lüdtke, and Jürgen Moosleithner and the outstanding staff, headed by Karin Marxer, who hosted us in Liechtenstein. Without them, the discussions and the book wouldn't have been possible.

Contents

List of Abbreviations

AI	Artificial intelligence
AML	Anti-money laundering
API	Application programming interface
ASIC	Australian Securities and Investments Commission
ATM	Automated teller machine
B2B	Business-to-business
B2C	Business-to-customer
BAT	Baidu, Alibaba, Tencent
C2C	Customer-to-Customer
CAGR	Compound annual growth rate
CBDC	Central bank digital currency
CFT	Counter-terrorist financing
CHAPS	Clearing House Automated Payment System
CHIPS	Clearing House Interbank Payments System
CHF	Swiss franc
CLS	Continuously Linked Settlement
COSMOS	Customers, Operations, and Services Master Online System
DAO	Decentralized autonomous organization
dApp	Distributed application
DeFi	Decentralized Finance
DID	Decentralized identifier
Digital ID	Digital identity
EBA	European Banking Authority
ERMA	Electronic Recording Method of Accounting
EU	European Union
EUR	Euro
ECB	European Central Bank
FCA	Financial Conduct Authority
FINMA	Swiss Federal Financial Market Supervisory Authority
Fintech	Financial technology

FMI	Financial market infrastructure
FSA	Financial Services Authority
FSB	Financial Stability Board
GAFA	Google, Amazon, Facebook, Apple
GDP	Gross domestic product
GFIN	Global Financial Innovation Network
HD Wallet	Hierarchical Deterministic Wallet
ICO	Initial coin offering
IMF	International Monetary Fund
IPO	Initial public offering
Insurtech	Insurance technology
IoT	Internet-of-Things
IT	Information technology
LLM	Large language model
ML	Machine learning
NFC	Near-field communication
NFT	Non-fungible token
P2P	Peer-to-peer
PBoC	People's Bank of China
RegTech	Regulatory technology
RFID	Radio frequency identification
RTGS	Real-time gross settlement systems
SME	Small and medium-sized enterprise
STO	Security token offerings
SWIFT	Society for Worldwide Interbank Financial Telecommunication
TVL	Total value locked
W3C	World Wide Web Consortium

List of Figures

List of Tables

Chapter 1
Introduction

Discussing scenarios for the financial system 2030 should obviously start with "money," as the significance of money is relevant in all economic transactions. Although historically both economic and financial systems developed in parallel, in 1608 the foundation of the Amsterdam Stock Exchange marked the separation of the two systems. With this, financial products that are part of the financial system could be traded without being directly involved in economic transactions of the goods and services they represented. Since then, as a means of exchange, a store of value, and a unit of account, money has been subject to continual change and has been the object of numerous innovations. Especially the current transformation through technology paired with the ongoing economic and geopolitical change of the global landscape already has and will continue to have a huge impact on the financial system in the forthcoming years and decades. Digital currencies, digital assets, and digital financial market infrastructures are only the most recent terms of this fundamental redesign—one that goes far beyond previous innovations like automated teller machines (ATMs), credit cards, or mobile payments. When money is detached from its carrier systems, this also has direct implications on the entire financial system.

But what characterizes a financial system? In general, a macro and a micro perspective can be distinguished. The macro perspective defines the financial system as the system that facilitates the transfer of resources from savers to those who need funds, from payors to payees and from creditors to creditees (Boot & Thakor, 1997). In other words, the financial system describes the interaction between the supply of and the demand for the provision of capital and other finance-related services (Schmidt & Tyrell, 2003). The micro perspective, on the other hand, defines the financial system as one sector of the economy that offers and provides financial services to other sectors of the economy. This book aims to describe the macro perspective which itself distinguishes at least four different sub-perspectives (see Table 1.1; Schmidt & Tyrell, 2003). First, the institutional perspective focuses on

T. Puschmann, H. S. H. P. M. of Liechtenstein, *Financial System 2030*, Financial Innovation and Technology,
https://doi.org/10.1007/978-3-031-55700-2_1

Table 1.1 Different perspectives to analyze financial systems

Perspectives	Institutional perspective	Intermediation perspective	Functional perspective	Systemic perspective
Key characteristics	Institutions such as banks, insurance companies, etc.	Term transformation and lot size transformation	Transfer economic resources, provide payment system, pool resources, control risk, manage asymmetric information	Complementarity and consistency

the different financial institutions and utilities, including central banks, commercial banks, non-bank financial institutions, and regulatory and supervisory institutions. Second, the intermediation perspective aims to solve the challenges of direct financing between those who need capital and those who provide it, since both parties have different needs and preferences. For these, intermediaries provide term transformation and lot size transformation. Third, from the functional perspective, the financial system provides functions to transfer economic resources, provide payment infrastructures, pool resources, control risk, and manage asymmetric information. Fourth, the systemic perspective differentiates a set of complementary and consistent elements. For example, two systems are complementary to each other if the positive effects reinforce each other, and the negative effects mitigate each other.

Just recently, there have been discussions about how the financial system might look like in the future in the context of digitalization (e.g., Cecchetti, 2014; Heckel & Waldenberger, 2022; BIS, 2023; Gąsiorkiewicz & Monkiewicz, 2023); Carstens and Nilekani 2024. For example Carstens and Nilekani (2024) mention interoperability, evolvability, modularity, scalability, division of labor and competition, inclusiveness and accessibility as well as security and privacy as design principles for a future financial system. From an institutional and intermediation perspective there has been an intense debate, whether financial technology (fintech) startups will disintermediate the incumbent financial institutions or even make them obsolete. From a functional perspective, the payment systems are currently undergoing a fundamental transformation. Non-cash payments increased in Sweden from around 50% in 2011 to almost 90% in 2021, in Britain from around 50% to almost 90%, and in the USA from around 50% to around 75% (Economist 2023). In parallel, in emerging markets open payment systems like GoPay in Indonesia and GCash in the Philippines emerged and provide an alternative path between the bank- and card-centric systems of the developed countries and the Chinese bigtech fintech world with Alipay and WeChat Pay. From a systemic perspective, especially the recent crypto and decentralized finance (DeFi) wave, which evolved as a novel system in parallel to the incumbent financial system, challenges the status quo of the current system. However, crypto and DeFi have not yet proven to make the entire existing financial system more efficient (except for some use cases like cross-border payments). Instead, they have woken up central banks which now work on central bank digital currencies (CBDC) to complement, or even replace their existing cash-based money system by a digital one.

But despite all these technology-enabled innovations, a more comprehensive view of what might shape the future of the financial system, and which involves different stakeholders and disciplines as well as geographical perspectives, is a missing component in the current debate. This book aims to contribute to this discussion by providing an overview of the impact of digitalization on the financial system. Obviously, this impact is enormous given the information-based character of the financial system which is all about collecting and processing information. However, the revolution driven by digitalization is not new. The financial industry was among the first to leverage IT for digitalizing stock exchanges or cashless money transfers between bank accounts (Bátiz-Lazo, 2015). This made the financial system a core driver of globalization, as cross-border financial transactions could be performed in real time. Now the emergence of various new technologies like blockchain, artificial intelligence, etc. and their convergence pave the way for another, probably even more fundamental transformation of the financial system which is enabled by the full digitalization of money and assets, the decentralization of its functions, and the redefinition of the existing roles.

The remainder of this book is structured along the following chapters which together form the "Vaduz Architecture of the Financial System 2030" (see Fig. 1.1):

- *Chapter 2* discusses which information technologies are currently emerging and how they might affect the financial industry and the financial system as a whole. A special focus will be on selected technologies like artificial intelligence, blockchain, etc. as well as the convergence of these technologies.
- *Chapter 3* deep dives into the role of nation states by outlining how central bank digital currencies, novel digital payment infrastructures, etc. foster the emergence of peer-to-peer ecosystems and digital communities. In addition, the role of nation states in an ongoing digitalization process, in which physical entities and roles must be matched with digital ones, is discussed.

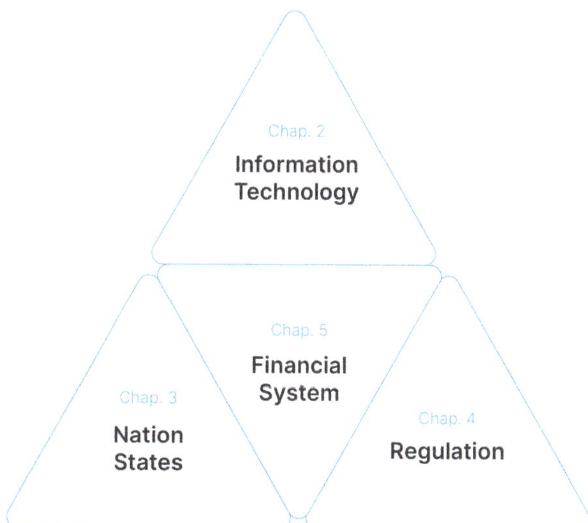

Fig. 1.1 Vaduz architecture of the financial system, 2030

- *Chapter 4* describes the developments in the regulatory field by outlining the impact of novel technologies on regulation, by showing how the right balance between innovation and regulation could be achieved, and by looking at the potentials of RegTech as a novel instrument for regulators to become part of this new financial system.
- *Chapter 5* focuses on the impact of digitalization, nation states and (de-)regulation on the financial system and shows how bigtech companies transform the financial system, how decentralized finance, stablecoins, novel financial market infrastructures, digital ecosystems, and sustainable digital finance might lead to new market structures and reshape the future financial system.
- *Chapter 6* summarizes the findings and provides an outlook on potential future developments.

Chapter 2
Information Technology

Information technology (or short IT) describes all general technical developments and advances enabled by computers (Boaden & Lockett, 1991). IT has been a key driver of innovation over the past decades with many new companies that emerged during this era. Examples are Alphabet, Amazon, Apple, Meta, Nvdia, and Microsoft, which together with Tesla form the so-called magnificent seven and which currently head the list of the most valued companies in the world. IT has accelerated the process of digitalization across society and all sectors of the economy as well as government services. The term's predecessor is the concept of "informatization" which was introduced in 1979 by Simon Nora and Alain Minc (Nora & Minc, 1979). It describes the social process of generating and using information to be able to generate further information from it. While many relate it to the invention of computers, the original concept also describes double-entry bookkeeping or parts lists. However, the term is usually used in a more specific meaning: the permeation of all areas of life in society. Today, the term "digitalization" is often used to describe this phenomenon.

2.1 Digitalization

Digitalization dates at least back to as long as 1679 when Gottfried Wilhelm Leibniz developed a mechanical calculator which was based on the binary system. The binary system was even invented before the development of this calculator. However, the term digitalization it self was used only as late as in the 1950s with the advent of computers. For example, in 1955 Bank of America was among the first banks in the world to introduce a computer with the Electronic Recording Method of Accounting (ERMA) which was used for automated check processing. In 1960, American Airlines launched the Sabre flight-reservation system which was able to

T. Puschmann, H. S. H. P. M. of Liechtenstein, *Financial System 2030*, Financial Innovation and Technology,
https://doi.org/10.1007/978-3-031-55700-2_2

process 84,000 telephone calls per day and store 807 megabytes of reservations, flight schedules, and seat inventory. FedEx's Customers, Operations, and Services Master Online System (COSMOS), which was introduced in 1979, digitized the management of people, packages, vehicles, and weather scenarios, allowing real-time updates on delivery status. All these examples show that digitalization is not a new phenomenon. Especially the financial industry has been among the pioneers to use computers as it is an information-centric sector which means that most of its products and services are based on data rather than on physical goods (Tallon, 2010).

The term "digitalization" has been used excessively in media over the past few decades and has left many confused about its real meaning. In general, digitalization refers to two basic concepts: (1) Digitization as a technical transformation approach which means the conversion of text, image, sound, or other analogue signals into digital ones (e.g., a payment slip which is scanned using a smartphone camera and then automatically transferred to) and (2) digitization as a social transformation process which aims to convert all kinds of government-, business-related, etc. processes and business models into digital ones (Matt et al., 2015, 340ff.). While the first one was used in the early times of computer application, the latter one was only used lately in the context of IT-enabled business models, technology firms, and startups (e.g., fintech startups). However, both approaches rely on each other. For example, IT-enabled business models are not possible without the availability of digitally converted signals into data. This is the basis for what we currently can observe as being the major driver of a fundamental reorganization of the entire economy and society caused by digitalization which is often termed as the "digital economy" (Tapscott, 1996). In this context, many studies identified the digital economy as the main driver of economic growth in both developed and developing countries (Pradhan et al., 2019). The digital economy can increase capital and labor productivity and obtain goods and services at lower prices. For example, IT can foster economic growth in countries with relatively low levels of productivity and can increase the output by facilitating technology innovation, improving the quality of decision making, and reducing production costs.

Digitalization is also not a new phenomenon in the financial services industry and dates back to the 1950s when many banks first started to use computers for their operations. From then on, the digitalization of the industry can be aligned to three phases (Puschmann, 2017). The first phase (1950s–1970s) focused on internal business processes and covered innovations such as the ATM which was first introduced in Arlington/Ohio in 1959. The second phase had its focus on the further evolution of business and personal computing. Part of this phase, for instance, was the introduction of home banking in 1981 from Citibank and Chase Manhattan as well as the development of major core banking applications (1980s–1990s). The third phase included the fintech evolution and saw the emergence of mobile payment applications, robo-advisors, peer-to-peer lending platforms, etc. (2000s–2010s). Finally, the still ongoing fourth phase concentrates on the digitalization of the whole financial system and includes IT innovations like blockchain, AI, etc. which is also referred to as the "internet of value" (since 2020s). Of course, these phases overlap, and recent phases do still develop further.

2.2 Exponential and Converging Technology

An exponential technology is characterized by an exponential advancement in terms of quality of care, size, speed, and manufacturing/delivery cost. In 2001, Ray Kurzweil, an entrepreneur and former Director of Engineering at Google, stated that "An analysis of the history of technology shows that technological change is exponential (…). So, we won't experience 100 years of progress in the 21st century—it will be more like 20,000 years of progress (at today's rate)" (Kurzweil, 2001). Exponential (information) technology is connected to Moore's Law, which says that the number of transistors on a microchip doubles every two years, though the cost of computers is halved. Moore's law also states that we can expect the speed and capability of our computers to increase mostly every year. Drawing on this, Kurzweil analyzed that Moore's law had been at work not only since the computer was invented, but at least since 1900. He estimated the number of calculations performed by analog machines, by mechanical calculators, and later by the first vacuum tube computers per second per $1000 and extended the same calculation to modern semiconductor chips. He established that this ratio has been increasing exponentially for the past 109 years. It is sometimes difficult to recognize exponential technologies as potential disruptors, as they typically go through an initial disappointment phase (benign neglect; see Fig. 2.1), where the technology is bulky, is expensive, and does not compare favorably with existing systems. An example is quantum computing, which is still too complicated, too large, and too expensive to be used on a broader scale. However, the predictions of its future performance are enormous. While some of these technologies are already widely used (e.g., blockchain), some are still more in an experimental phase (e.g., quantum computing).

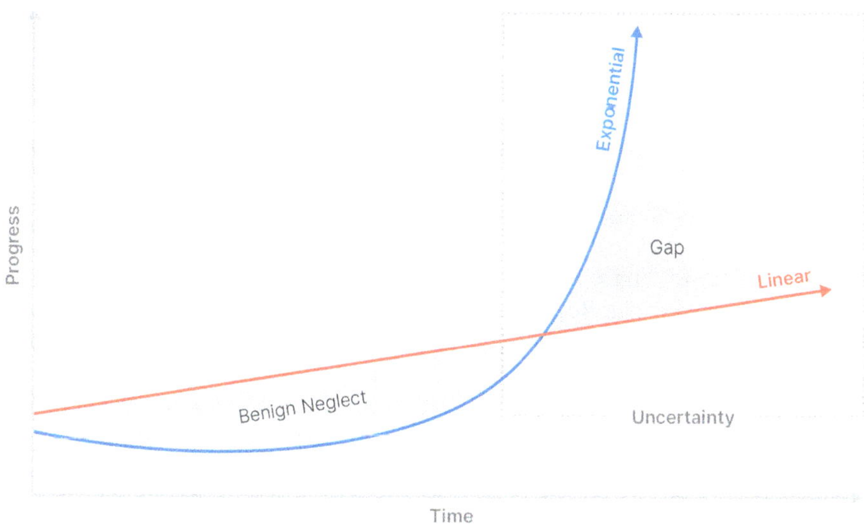

Fig. 2.1 Exponential technology (according to Azhar, 2021)

A strong driver for exponential technology has been the convergence of various technologies, which often leads to exponential growth (Alt, 2021). An example for this is triple/quadruple play with the convergence of the previously separate sectors of communication, data processing, and entertainment technologies. This shows that with convergence, two or more formerly independent technologies integrate and form new outcomes (i.e., telephony, Internet, TV, media). It is also closely connected to the convergence of functions and content formats on devices such as smartphones or smart TV sets. Another area of convergence is the combination of social, mobile, analytics, and cloud technologies. While social media platforms have created new forms of interaction and led to peer-to-peer models also in the financial industry (e.g., social trading, crowd lending/–funding), mobile technologies like Internet-of-things (IoT) technologies replace barcodes with intelligent devices such as RFID or NFC for contactless payments. The most recent field of convergence combines developments in blockchain, AI, metaverse, and quantum computing.

2.3 Financial Technology

IT expenditures typically make up around 15–20% of all costs in financial institutions, only surpassed by personnel expenses which account for 55–60%. In comparison with other industries, banks spend around 7.3% of their revenues as IT costs compared to 3.7% as an average of other industries (Gopalan et al., 2012). Overall, the total IT expenditures of the banking industry have increased from $603 billion in 2021 to $652 billion in 2022 (Gartner, 2023). For example, in 2019 JPMorganChase had a $11.4 billion technology budget, Bank of America $10 billion, Wells Fargo $9 billion, and Citigroup $8 billion (Business Insider, 2019). But of course, the overall IT costs are only one important measure for how important technology is for the financial sector. Another measure is the percentage of those expenditures that are spent on innovations rather than on maintaining existing applications. Estimations are that only around 20–25% of those investments are spent on innovations and 75–80% on maintenance of existing IT. These numbers also show that most banks still operate many legacy applications, while fintech startups have a different starting position.

While the use of IT in financial institutions has a long history, the term “financial technology” (short “fintech”) was most likely only coined in the early 1990s by Citicorp’s chairman John Reed in the context of the foundation of the “Smart Card Forum” consortium (Kutler, 1993). However, the link between finance and technology was already mentioned in the book *The Economic Consequences of the Peace* by John Maynard Keynes (Keynes, 1919). In its modern form fintech stands for innovative financial solutions enabled by IT and is also often used for startup companies that develop such solutions. However, it also very often refers to financial institutions’ and technology companies’ digital services. A more fine-grained perspective distinguishes fintech approaches according to their innovation degree, object, and scope (see Fig. 2.2; Puschmann, 2017):

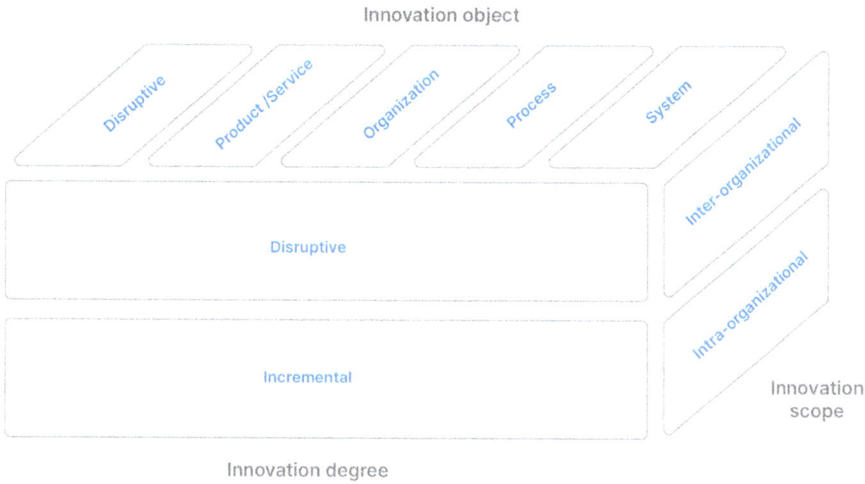

Fig. 2.2 Innovation dimensions of fintech solutions (Puschmann, 2017, 74)

- *Innovation object.* In this dimension, the five different objects business model, product and service, organization, process, and system can be distinguished. An example for the first category is a blockchain-based DeFi solution for lending like MakerDAO, which works without financial institutions (see Sect. 5.4). An example for the products and services object is a digital asset platform. An organization innovation might be the use of a decentralized autonomous organization (DAO) based on a blockchain platform (see Sect. 5.4). Process innovations either digitize formerly paper-based processes (e.g., account opening) or redesign existing processes (e.g., clearing and settlement of securities on blockchains). Finally, system innovations focus on novel technology infrastructures like distributed applications (dApps).
- *Innovation degree.* Technology, and especially exponential technology, can have a huge impact on existing business models, products and services, organizations, processes, and systems. The innovation degree distinguishes whether this effect is incremental or disruptive (Foster 1986). For example, incremental solutions only improve existing solutions in their quality, time, and/or cost. On the other hand, disruptive technologies in most cases feature inferior performance in the early stages of their evolution, but in their later development might lead to fundamental changes of the entire value chain (Bower & Christensen, 1995). An example for the first one is enhanced mobile banking functionality while a disruptive innovation would be a blockchain-based insurance model which completely changes the entire existing value chain.
- *Innovation scope.* Fintech innovations can either address intra- or inter-organizational applications. While intra-organizational ones provide internal solutions, the latter ones focus on macro structures with an impact on value chains or even entire industry structures. Intra-organizational solutions are, for example, electronic b2b marketplaces for which banks open their APIs to third-

party developers. An inter-organizational application, for example, is a new multi-currency CBDC platform established through cooperations of central banks, commercial banks, etc.

Fintech innovations relate to specific customer needs and processes (see Table 2.1). They usually focus on activities in the areas of advice, payments, investments, financing, or cross-processes (Alt & Puschmann, 2012; Puschmann, 2017):

- In the field of *advice*, this encompasses services like online community-based advice (e.g., Wikifolio), use of digital channels for expert advice (e.g., text-based online chats), and personal finance management (e.g., Personal Capital).
- The *payment* area includes novel payment methods like mobile payment (e.g., Stripe) as well as Bitcoin credit card payments (e.g., Wirex).
- In the *investment* area, robo-advisors enable the management and execution of transactions on a deposit of securities (e.g., Wealthfront) and increase transparency for the customer through "covesting," in which investors disclose their portfolios to others (e.g., InteractiveAdvisors).
- The *financing* area is characterized by a tendency toward disintermediation, i.e., the handling of existing service providers in consumer and real estate loans via crowd platforms (e.g., Zopa) or SME lending (e.g., Finpoint).
- The *cross-process* area is assigned to a variety of solutions including for example loyalty points marketplaces (e.g., PointsPay) or electronic data safes (e.g., SecureSafe).

Over the past few years, fintech firms have emerged as competitors to the incumbent banks. For example, by 2020, the fintech startups in the payment sector had a market capitalization of 10% compared to around 70% of the incumbent banks and approximately 20% of those of other payment firms. While the share of the fintech firms and the payment firms is growing steadily, the banks' share is decreasing (Economist, 2020). The "unbundling of banks" is a metaphor that has been used in this context for many years. Although outsourcing has already had a big impact on banking value chains, the core activities are still performed by banks and competition in these services is rare. But with the advent of fintech, the division of labor

Table 2.1 Non-bank fintech examples along the banking processes (according to Alt & Puschmann, 2012; Puschmann, 2017)

Interaction type	Banking process				
	Advice	Payments	Investments	Financing	Cross-process
C2C	Community-based advisory (Wikifolio, AUT)	Mobile Payment (Stripe, USA)	Covesting (Covestor, USA)	Crowdlending (Zopa, UK)	Loyalty points marketplace (PointsPay, CH)
B2C	Personal finance management (Personal Capital, USA)	Cryptocurrency Payment (Wirex, UK)	Online Portfolio management (Wealthfront, USA)	Corporate credits (Finpoint, GER)	Electronic data safe (SecureSafe, CH)

Fig. 2.3 Unbundling of banks (CB Insights, 2015)

among clients, banks, and non-banks has already begun to change. Although fintech startups developed solutions for all areas of the banking business (see Fig. 2.3) competition remained low as the startups started to cooperate with banks due to restricted access to clients and limited economies of scale.

Of course, this development varies by country. This has, among other factors, also to do with cultural differences. The Inglehart-Welzel Cultural Map[1] (see http://www.worldvaluessurvey.org/WVSContents.jsp), for example, shows how traditional values (e.g., religion) and secular-rational values (e.g., divorce) as well as survival values (e.g., physical security) and self-expression values (e.g., environmental protection) impact a society and economy. Islamic finance, for example, has different foundational pillars than the banking sector in the Western world (e.g., Mudharabah (profit sharing), Wadiah (safekeeping), Musharakah (joint venture), Murabahah (cost plus finance), Ijar (leasing), Hawala (an international fund transfer system), Takaful (Islamic insurance), and Sukuk (Islamic bonds)).

In the meantime, the incumbents themselves started to launch new services such as pro-privacy post-trade settlement (e.g., R3, Quorum, ASX, etc.), international payments (e.g., Swift's nostro POC), new asset class trading (e.g., SIG, DRW, Goldman Sachs), and exchange functions (e.g., CME, CBOE, ICE), CBDCs (e.g.,

[1] The "Inglehart-Welzel Cultural Map" was invented by the two political scientists Ronald Inglehart and Christian Welzel. It proposes that there are two major dimensions of cross-cultural variation in the world: traditional values versus secular-rational values and survival values versus self-expression values.

Bahamas)). Functions that could but might not necessarily face a near-term change are custody, correspondence banking, clearing houses, and trade finance as the substitution of banks is more obvious in these areas while the areas that are closely related to risk management might remain or even become more important for the banks as their core expertise. But with the changing nature of the firm, the regulatory regime that will evolve might be to effectively treat all companies as public companies and design digital governance mechanisms accordingly (Casey & Wong, 2017).

While the customer behavior obviously demonstrated a clear shift toward digitalization, on the other hand, the fintech industry is also showing a similar trend. Compared to 2020, global investments in fintech startup companies have increased from \$124.5 billion to \$238.9 billion in 2022 but faced a stronger headwind with a decrease to \$164 billion in 2022 and the first and second half of 2023 (see Fig. 2.4, KPMG, 2023).

The 2021 increase can be argued with COVID-19 as a strong driver of digitalization. A global survey of 1428 startups shows a very positive impact of COVID-19 on new customers (+22%), and the retention of existing customers (+29%) compared to the pre-pandemic level (Ziegler & Zhang, 2021, 28). Surprisingly, the fintech startups' market performance during the pandemic in developing and emerging countries does not differ significantly to the one in high-income countries. For example, although the latter group has increased their customers by 20%, the former group has increased them by 24%. This increase can also be observed across almost all verticals including Digital Custody (36%), Digital Asset Exchange (33%), Digital Savings (26%), WealthTech (24%), and Digital Payments (21%), while Digital Lending is the only vertical which shrank by 8% (Ziegler & Zhang, 2021, 29). In addition to this sharp increase in numbers, 60% of the 1428 startups surveyed have implemented or introduced new products or services, and a further 32% will soon do so. This especially applies for value-added non-financial services (e.g., information services) with 31% currently working on the introduction of such

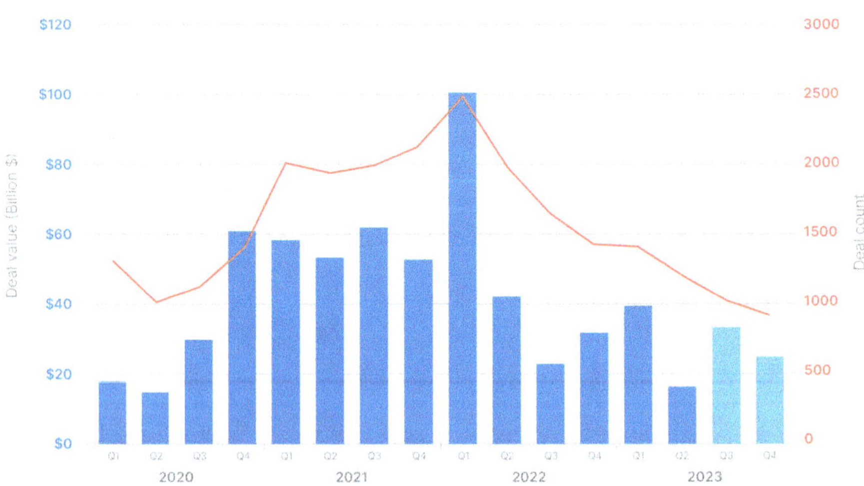

Fig. 2.4 Investments in the fintech sector from 2019 to 2022 (KPMG, 2023)

services. Among the examples of such services is a portal in India to help low-income female entrepreneurs to understand the financial products that the platform offers, and how best to use them as well as a lending platform in Uganda that created a website to connect unemployed professionals to SME owners. The following

Case Study: Société Générale

- Société Générale has around 138,000 employees located in 62 countries. The bank serves around 29 Mio. customers in the three core business areas: Retail Banking France, International Retail Banking, Insurance and Financial Services and Global Banking and Investor Solutions. The company has a strong digital adoption in its retail customer segment with 60% digital clients at group level.
- The bank follows an open innovation approach and has set up a portfolio of 27 internal and external startups. In addition, it participates in 9 consortia and 6 venture capital funds and 1 incubator program (see Fig. 2.5).
- Société Générale has 250 AI uses cases in four areas in production: (1) personalizing and automating advisory services and pricing to maximize customer engagement and sales efficiency, (2) improving response time and pertinence in customer exchanges, (3) improving fraud detection and risk and compliance management, and (4) increasing operational efficiency through the systematization of automated document analysis.
- Another focus of innovation is on green commodity trade finance through "komgo," a consortium of 29 financial institutions, 146 corporates, and 1000 registered users. By digitizing 36 documents which are usually exchanged among different stakeholders for commodity trade finance, errors and fraud could be decreased in 25,000 letter of credits and 3000 messages per month. With this, transactions can be monitored in real time and by optimizing logistics routes the carbon emissions can be decreased.
- Société Générale focuses on three strategic pillars for its future development: client centricity, corporate and social responsibility, and efficiency. For this, it has defined priorities in 9 areas: (1) leading the energy transition (e.g., acquisition of Luno, a crowdfunding platform for renewable energy projects), (2) supporting SMEs and entrepreneurs (e.g., investment in Shine, which is a responsible Neobank for freelancers and SMEs in France), (3) financial inclusion and education (e.g., Yup offers mobile money services without a bank account), (4) diversity (e.g., 25% of financed startups have to be founded by women), (5) employee reskilling and job mobility (e.g., internal initiative to identify future roles and skills), (6) responsible use of new technologies (e.g., sustainable IT Charter), (7) sustainable mobility (e.g., ALD automotive), (8) client experience (e.g., kwiper digital wealth management), and (9) promoting transparency in the financial system (e.g., Forge tokenized securities platform).

Source: Société Générale

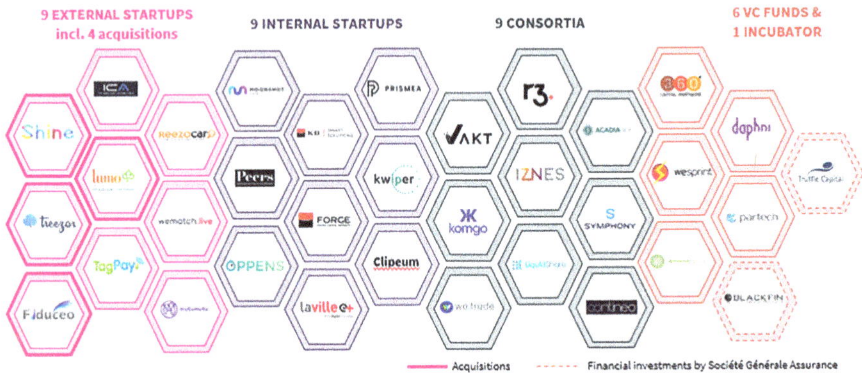

Fig. 2.5 Société Générale's open innovation approach

case study from Société Générale shows how fintech is used as an instrument for innovation across all customer segments and business areas.

In addition to fintech, insurtech has developed as an additional field of innovation since around 2012 when Aviva was piloting a telematics app for private auto insurance (Braun & Schreiber, 2017). The field may be interpreted as a subset of fintech for innovative, technology-driven startup companies in the insurance sector. But the insurtech sector has only grown most recently, as the industry is one of the most complex businesses. However, the insurance industry with global premiums more than \$5 trillion is also a very attractive business. That's why the global insurtech market revenue was valued at \$5.48 billion in 2019 and is expected to reach \$10.14 billion by 2025, growing at a CAGR of 10.80% during the period from 2019 to 2025. For example, compared to 2020, 2021 saw a 90% increase in insurtech funding and a 21% increase in deals. From the total insurance market, investors see the greatest potential in health insurance, followed by auto, life, specialty, home/renters, and travel insurance (Milken Institute, 2019). The key areas of innovation through insurtech are:

Insurance intermediation and distribution models. In developed insurance markets, insurance intermediation is traditionally an agent/broker or bancassurance model. However, startups are increasingly focusing on new distribution models for less developed insurance markets in Asia and Africa, where the conventional intermediation model may not be efficient or effective. Examples of such solutions are from BIMA, Friendsurance, or InsPeer.

Sharing economy. The sharing economy services with platforms like Airbnb, Uber, etc. are increasingly required to have insurance coverage for certain aspects of their businesses. For example, some insurers are addressing the uniqueness of ridesharing and AirBnB provides insurance protection for hosts through its platform.

Robo advice and AI. Policies are often complex and must be aligned with the needs of customers. An approach to tackle this is solutions for financial guidance, which tailor policyholders' income and needs with greater automation through AI. With this, robo-advisors support organizations in better understanding client needs, proposing policies, implementing policies, and monitoring and adjusting policies. It is expected that AI will change insurance in the next few years fundamentally (Duygun & Xu, 2021).
Data aggregation and analytics. IoT, hand-held devices, and data analysis software allow firms to collect more data and analyze it with more precision. While insurance has traditionally relied on quantitative data to manage risk decisions, data analytics goes beyond that and can even be controversial at times. For example, in the past auto insurance relied on internal data sources and is now enriched with behavior-based credit scores from credit bureaus (e.g., people who pay their bills on time are said to be also safer drivers) and driver data from pay-as-you-drive or pay-how-you-drive solutions. And in the field of life insurance, open data from governments as well as other data sources such as face recognition technology are used to support insurance underwriting more accurately. One example is the marriage of longevity data and face recognition technology, which can predict factors such as smoking habits and body mass index, thereby increasing life expectancy.

To analyze the impact of insurtech on the industry, the same framework from the banking industry can be used but structured along the insurance processes (advice, non-life, life, claims management, risk management, cross-processes). Among the examples are pay-as-you-drive solutions (non-life), where drivers share their vehicle usage data with insurers and in return receive a reduced insurance premium based on an individual risk evaluation, or drone-based claims analysis (claims management), where drones are used for claims inspection instead of humans. Other important areas are the use of big data analytics, for example in the case of the analysis of industrial accident insurances (risk management), to offer more personalized premiums and automated policy management (cross-process). Compared to banking, most of the solutions in the insurance industry currently focus on b2c, while c2c services are still rare.

Summarized, the potentials of insurtech can be aligned to at least four areas:

- *Empowered customers*. As digital natives more and more become the most relevant customer group, this group uses insurances services not only digitally but also in a context-based way. An example is on-demand insurance services for AirBnB travel or mental health insurance, especially for the younger generation.
- *Simplified processes*. Insurance products and processes are often very complex. Insurtech enables automation and simplification of both processes and products.
- *Custom-tailored services*. Insurtech enables the migration from one-size-fits-all products and services to custom-tailored ones. By collecting more individual data and analyzing customer needs more properly, insurtech solutions can provide individualized solutions.

- *"Exciting" products*. The insurance industry claims that there are no attractive products and services that customers want to buy. Since approximately 40% of all costs related to insurance products can be assigned to marketing and sales, it becomes clear that this is a field of optimization.

A more recent field of innovation in insurtech is DeFi insurance (see Sect. 5.4). One example is the startup Unslashed Finance, which offers protection for various DeFi risks, such as centralized exchange hacks. Other examples of DeFi insurance are Risk Harbor and Nexus Mutual.

2.4 Blockchain

The basic technologies for blockchains emerged in the 1960s as part of research projects of the US military. For example, the RAND Corporation focused on the development of novel IT architectures which allowed IT systems to still communicate, even when a military strike would destroy large parts of the communication network. At that time, mainframe computers hosted the entire functionality and data and were only accessible by stations that allowed to log into these computers (see Fig. 2.6). However, if the central mainframe computer was not functioning, the whole system collapsed. This changed with the introduction of client/server architectures in the 1980s that allowed a decentralized approach. This approach was also used by the Internet in the 1990s. Blockchains go even a step further and belong to the group of distributed network architectures where every node of the network hosts the full set of data. They emerged with the introduction of Bitcoin (2007) and

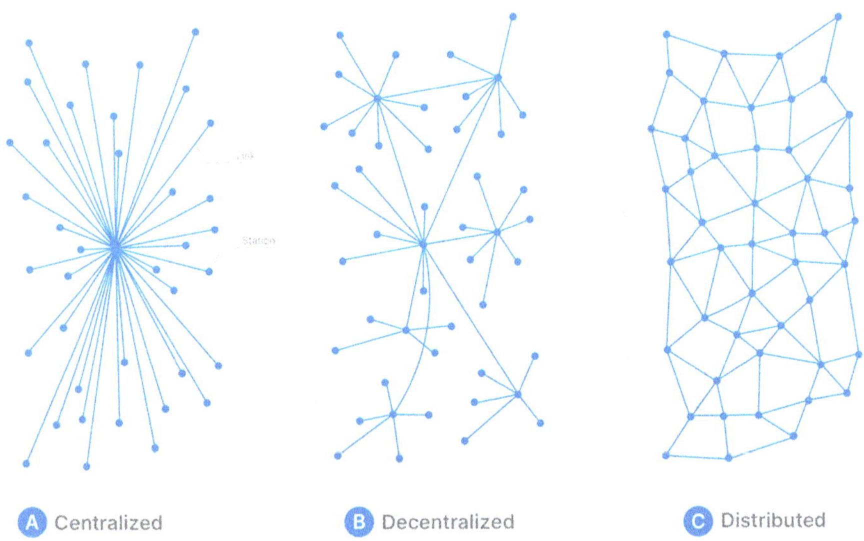

Fig. 2.6 Distributed communication networks (Baran, 1962)

other protocols (e.g., Ethereum, etc.) in the 2000s and 2010s. The development of these architectures is still ongoing.

There is no common standard definition which describes a blockchain comprehensively. The most used term is that they represent a "distributed ledger of transactions" (Halaburda, 2018, 28). Blockchains aim at reducing verification costs and verify the performance of obligations. An obligation is a specific action by an agent, which is created if a specific state arises. A state may be an event, an outcome, or the performance of another obligation. To create an obligation, states/transactions must be recorded, to become verifiable. Obligations are often part of contracts. In today's economy, usually the instrument of courts is being used for the verification of obligations. But courts can usually not be attended online. A good example is international trade where the involvement of courts is often challenging and, in many cases, almost impossible. The key innovation of blockchain in contrast to this is that instead of using courts, it uses (digital) consensus mechanisms and (digital) smart contracts which ensure that trust is being established among anonymous stakeholders. Blockchain and smart contracts can help to implement an improved contract infrastructure which is more reliable and more efficient.

In this context, blockchains can be defined as (1) digital records of who owns what, with no central storage but via copies of the ledger at each participating node. (2) A consensus mechanism ensures that each node's copy of the ledger is identical to each other node's copy. (3) The write access is organized by miners or validators using a consensus mechanism and cryptographic signatures.

A blockchain can either be open or closed. The latter one describes a blockchain which is either private permissioned or used only by a limited set of authorized members (e.g., a consortium of companies), while public ones can be used by anyone (e.g., Bitcoin). While private blockchains were often praised in the past to be more secure, just recently one private permissioned blockchain had stopped operations. On November 29, 2022, A.P. Moller – Maersk, an integrated logistics company, and IBM announced the discontinuation of TradeLens, a blockchain-enabled global trade platform built on a private blockchain. The development of a global industry collaboration for supply chain management could not be achieved. In another announcement by the Monetary Authority of Singapore (MAS) on October 19, 2022, however, just a few weeks before TradeLens discontinued its operation, Project Guardian was officially initiated. The project is a collaborative initiative with the financial industry that seeks to test the feasibility of applications in asset tokenization and DeFi while managing risks to financial stability and integrity. Project Guardian, in contrast to TradeLens, is built on a public blockchain. Table 2.2 shows the different forms of blockchains. While in the case of open blockchains anyone can "read" their content, the "write" and "commit" function is restricted to authorized members for public permissioned ones.

Using blockchain in the financial system would mean to distribute functions and applications from central institutions to a decentralized community of individuals and institutions that directly perform processes among each other regarding payments, investments, and financing. Although many banking services were already

Table 2.2 Types of blockchains

Blockchain	Type	Operations			Example
		Read	Write	Commit	
Open	Public permissionless	Anyone	Anyone	Anyone	Bitcoin
	Public permissioned	Anyone	Authorized members	All or subset of authorized members	Sovrin
Closed	Inter-organizational permissioned	Authorized members	Authorized members	All or subset of authorized members	Partior
	Intra-organizational permissioned	Authorized members	Network operator	Network operator	Allianz captive insurance

Table 2.3 Benefits of centralized and decentralized approaches

Benefits of a centralized approach	Benefits of a decentralized approach
• The *security and integrity* of the data is high because banks have strict regulations regarding data security. • The *costs* are in many cases (still) lower today, since the decentralized models often do not scale, while the centralized model uses, for example, freemium models. • The *user-friendliness* is high because these systems have been developed over many decades. • The model has *economies of scale* since scalability is very high.	• *Layer unbundling* allows services to be shared between multiple service providers. • *Data transferability and interoperability* increase because individual interfaces from individual providers no longer must be considered. • The verifiability of data and transactions increases since every authorized person can view them *transparently*. • The incentives for open protocols are increasing because of *network effects*. • *Risk diversification* increases because of the layer unbundling since this is now distributed among several providers.

decentralized to clients, such as payments with online banking, the existing financial system is in many parts centered around financial institutions and currencies like the US dollar as the dominant currency. A system based on blockchain, as for example, Ripple's RippleNet, aims to decrease the complexity and costs for such processes. But, however, both systems, centralized and decentralized, have their benefits and risks (see Table 2.3). Thus, a general recommendation, whether a service should be centralized or decentralized cannot be given, but instead the benefits of reach approach must be weighed depending on the usage.

In addition, a distinction between technical/architectural decentralization and organizational decentralization must be made. While the technical approach allows to decentralize (technical) transactions, in many application fields, a centralized organizational governance approach is required which abstracts from this perspective. For instance, a permissioned blockchain solution may require a permissioning authority. Currently, many concepts for decentralized blockchain applications, such as real estate ownership records, voting, or digital identity, are developed. However, many of these approaches show the challenges that arise when using blockchains instead of centralized models. There is no "one-size-fits-all" approach for all applications and many questions are not yet solved such as the question of governance: the trust in delegating to a centralized entity is not given in the context of decentralized structures; instead, computed consensus algorithms shall solve this problem.

Whether decentralized or centralized design principles will dominate the financial system may also depend on how strongly the guarantees from governments and central banks protect incumbents and foster centralization. These guarantees are in effect government subsidies for incumbent "too-big-to-fail" institutions and provide incentives for market entrants to cooperate with these institutions. For example, p2p lending in the USA quickly transformed into a new form of marketplace lending; an initially decentralized business model was re-intermediated and integrated into the banking institutions, where banks play pivotal roles on both sides of the market. The past experiences with financial innovations in the shadow banking sector have forcefully demonstrated that regulation and government guarantees are shaping financial innovation. Therefore, it is important to reconsider the role of financial regulation (see Chap. 4) and government guarantees so that the market structures emerging from the digital transformation are both efficient and resilient (McMillan, 2014).

2.5 Artificial Intelligence

AI is "concerned with the development of computers able to engage in human-like thought processes such as learning, reasoning, and self-correction" (The New International Webster's Comprehensive Dictionary of the English Language). More specifically, the term is used to measure the intelligence of computers in contrast to natural intelligence from humans or animals. Thus, it is applied when a machine mimics "cognitive" functions that humans associate with other human minds, such as "learning" or "problem solving." One definition therefore depicts it as "(...) activity devoted to making machines intelligent, and intelligence is that quality that enables an entity to function appropriately and with foresight in its environment." (Nilsson, 2010).

The Dartmouth Summer Research Project of 1956 on AI was initiated by a proposal, co-authored by John McCarthy, Marvin Minsky, Nathaniel Rochester, and Claude Shannon in 1955, which included seven specific fields. It is often referred to as the event that initiated AI as a research discipline and is said that one of the participants, John McCarthy, to have been coining the phrase "artificial intelligence" (AI) (Moor, 2006). However, the 1956 summer research project didn't hold up to its original expectations, and there was no agreement on a general theory of the field. However, the project was followed by an AI boom which led to a variety of new discoveries like the General Program Solver, a computer program created in 1957 by Herbert A. Simon, J. C. Shaw, and Allen Newell from the RAND Corporation, which should work as a universal problem-solver machine, or the programming language LISP which became the most important AI programming language in the following years.

Although AI has often been predicted to be the "game changer" for many industries, it has had many fallbacks, which is called the "AI winter" (see Fig. 2.7). This AI winter appeared when promises and expectations outpaced reality. For instance, predictions in the 1980s that ten million self-driving cars would be on the road by 2020 could not be fulfilled. Surprisingly, the first driverless car was developed during that phase by Mercedes Benz in 1986 as a van that was equipped with sensors and cameras and could drive up to 55mph. But although those high expectations in the early AI days could not be fulfilled, in recent years, hardware and software increased in their performance leading to a wider adoption of AI across many industries. This led to an explosive growth phase with big data, neural language models, deep learning, transformers, and the emergence generative AI models most recently.

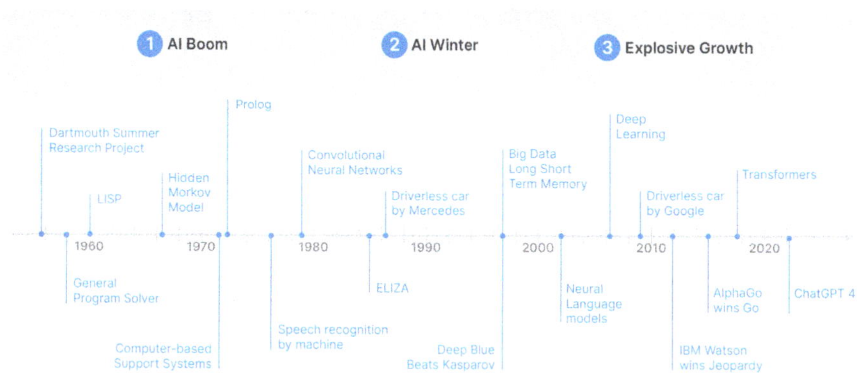

Fig. 2.7 Selected milestones in the history of AI

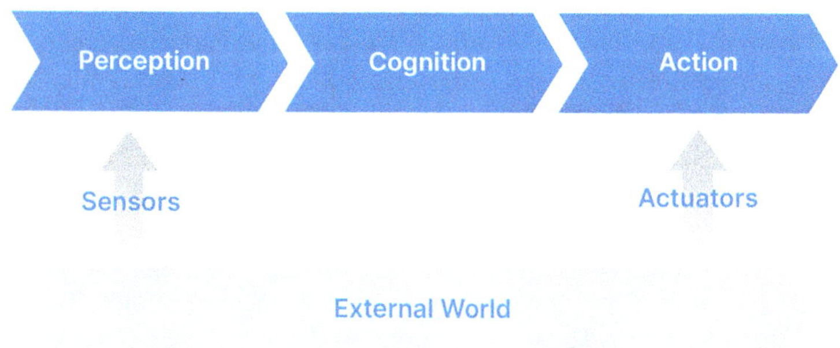

Fig. 2.8 AI processes

AI consists of at least three building blocks, comprising data, decision making, and action as well as the external world (see Fig. 2.8):

- *Data.* Data is the key "ingredient" of AI and can be collected in the form of written text (natural language processing, NLP), verbal language (speech recognition), and images (computer vision).
- *Decision making.* Decision making is based on the data that fuels the decision process. In AI algorithms, such as search, planning, learning from experience, multi-agent reasoning, deep learning, time series, optimization, and knowledge representation, all support this decision-making process.
- *Action.* Decision making will ultimately lead to actions in the real world. This can be execution of decisions in the form of processes (e.g., from robots), human–AI interaction (e.g., chat bots or virtual call center agents), or continuous learning.
- *External world.* Data can either be from internal sources and/or from external sources. Actions can either trigger intra- and/or inter-organizational processes.

In that system, AI collects data from the external world through sensors and aims at closing the loop of perception (processing, understanding of sensory data), cognition (knowledge representation, planning, learning), and action (motion, manipulation, speech).

Data has become a primary means of production, just like capital, labor, and land. While institutions have been in place for those for many years, there are no such institutions for data yet although there are still many concerns regarding privacy, security, etc. But over the past few years, novel technologies and novel ways of organizing data have been developed which allow us to solve these issues. The traditional way of data analysis was to pool all data in one place (i.e., in a database) which comes along with various challenges like data leakages, data security, etc. Another way to organize this is to share flows and statistics and not individual data. This, for example, allows us to implement zero-knowledge proofs which then allow the validation of requests without sharing and without owning the data. An example would be the request if a specific amount like a person's income is above a certain value. Earlier such examples are from credit card providers that also use such methods. In the USA, for example, most of the bank accounts now run on such a federated system. For instance, if a customer buys something with a credit card with the mobile phone, the mobile phone generates a one-time routing number which carries the purchase to the bank and either approves or denies it sending back a "yes" or "no" without sharing the bank account, the name of the bank, the purchased good, etc.

While data is an important element for AI, it is often unstructured. An example of how AI works is provided in Fig. 2.9.

During the cognition process, AI tries to find a linear separator (H3) between different classes (here, black and white circles in the left figure). Here, H1 does not match this task, and although H2 is very close, a generalization might be too difficult. However, many classes are not of this nature and can't be separated with linear separators. That's why neural networks are used. Neutral networks (NN) develop layers of data transformations until they can be separated into classes (see right figure). By identifying various hidden layers, AI can help identify patterns in images and other objects (see layered separation and deep learning in Fig. 2.9).

In the field of natural language processing, for example, AI technology has already outperformed humans (see Fig. 2.10; Perrault et al., 2019). An example which demonstrates this is GLUE, the "General Language Understanding Evaluation" benchmark. GLUE tests AI systems on nine distinct tasks: two on single sentences (measuring linguistic acceptability and sentiment), three on similarity and paraphrase, and four on natural language inference, including the Winograd Schema Challenge. The performance of available AI systems crossed the one of non-expert human performance already in June 2019. That's the reason why the inventors of GLUE developed a new, more challenging model called "SuperGLUE." Other areas of technical performance are images (classification, generation, semantic segmentation), video (activity recognition), and image language (visual question answering).

The following case study shows some exemplary application areas of AI in financial services at the Spanish bank BBVA.

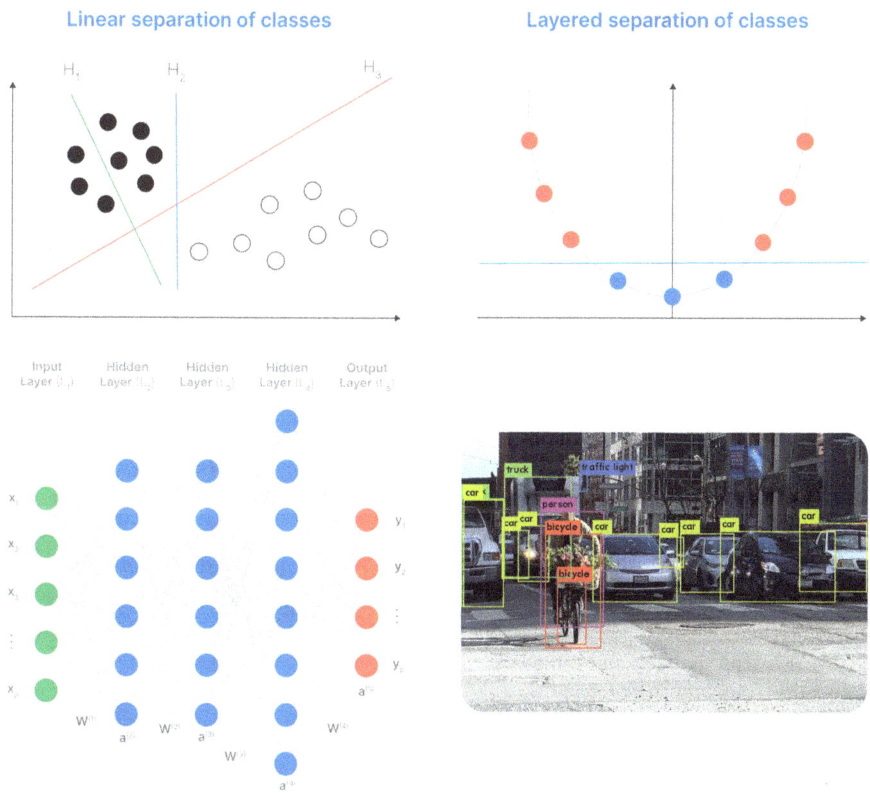

Fig. 2.9 AI classification models

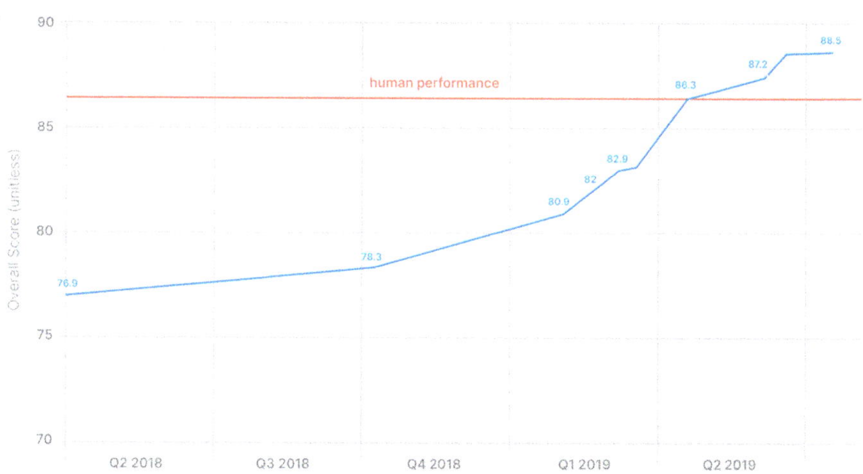

Fig. 2.10 Natural language processing technology performance (Perrault et al., 2019)

Case Study: BBVA

- BBVA runs more than 1500 advanced analytics and AI models and adds around 200 models every year. A typical retail client is subject to around 40 analytical inferences every day in its relationship with BBVA.
- The time-to-value or lead time, i.e., the time which is required from defining a business problem to using a data model in production, takes up to one year and covers the phases of planning and designing the solution, obtaining the necessary data, developing the analytical model, and bringing it to full production. Sometimes the data that is required is not available or exists under various functional definitions (e.g., an account balance might exist in several forms, depending on the nature and specificities of the process that consumes it).
- "Traditional machine learning" (supervised ML) typically reaches a limit independent of the amount of data used at a certain point (see Fig. 2.11). In a bank setting, this especially applies to structured data, which needs to be complemented with new sources of data to increase data variety. When this involves unstructured data, labeling is usually required. Labeling puts unstructured data in a specific context and meaning and makes it easier to process. In contrast to that, deep learning does not require labeling because it learns by itself in an unsupervised way.
- An important milestone in the use of deep learning is the rise of foundational models. These foundational models are built on extremely large, not annotated datasets. These foundational models can be adjusted and fine-tuned to perform successfully in environments in which only smaller specific datasets are available. As an example, it is possible to train a large language model on publicly available sources and later generate language outputs that can be used in other environments (e.g., customer service). While traditional, supervised learning models require large amounts of labeled data, foundational models can work with less specific inputs and can be implemented much faster. Other advantages are frequent updates, higher robustness, lower resource-intensiveness, and lower technical expertise to use the foundational models.
- Currently, large language models (LLM) for generative AI solutions like ChatGPT are being increasingly used in all kinds of applications. GPT-3 is a foundational model with around 175 billion parameters and 195 billion training words (web crawling, books, Wikipedia, etc.). Some estimates point that GPT-4 has then 100 trillion parameters and was trained with 300 billion words.
- Banks are at the forefront in the use of machine learning applications, followed by insurers. For example, in the UK, most application areas are in customer engagement, risk management, and compliance as well as other areas like HR and legal (Bank of England, 2022).

- The use of AI by the industry is raising technical, social, and political concerns. The AI Act in Europe was the first relevant regulation to address these issues across sectors for example, in the case that a client is not treated fairly by an automated AI model, or if a hiring decision is made based on the output of an AI model. This clearly requires internal quality assurance processes and further transparency. The same applies for certain relevant decisions, such as credit admission, which will also have a particular focus under the AI Act.

  Source: BBVA

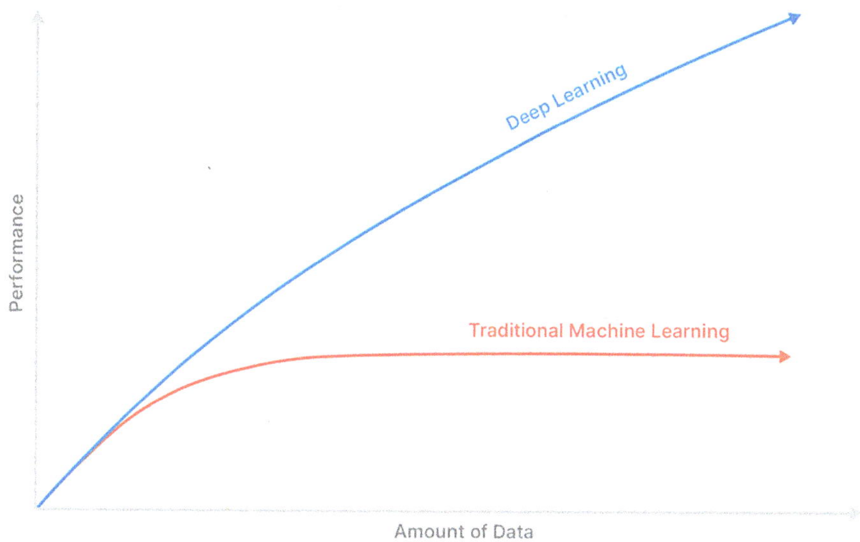

Fig. 2.11 Relationship between the amount of data and the performance of AI models

AI has been among the top domains of venture capital investment in recent years. In 2022, venture capital investments in AI startups reached $52.1 billion, down from $89.6 in 2021 due to the current market conditions (GlobalData.com). This changed just recently again. According to research by PitchBook (www.pitchbook.com), VCs invested 25.87 billion globally in AI startups in the first quarter of 2024, up from 21.69 billion in the first quarter of 2023. Especially the financial services industry has concentrated on this IT domain among others (e.g., cloud computing, blockchain, etc.) most recently. For example, the financial services sector is currently ranked in third place regarding the share of AI jobs posted in the USA. Especially also central banks showed a special interest in AI. Fintech startups as well as incumbents are moving from mainly using AI to reduce costs to leveraging its capabilities for revenue generation, albeit pursuing different AI strategies to achieve this. Most incumbents primarily use AI to enhance existing products and services, whereas many fintech startups use it to create new value propositions.

While today, risk management is the leading AI implementation area, followed by the generation of revenue potential through new products and processes, within the next 2 years AI will be primarily used for the generation of new revenues. The top three use cases from a study name AI-enabled customer communication channels, AI-enabled real-time service adjustments, and personalized risk exposure analysis (Ryll et al., 2020).

Although there is a small adoption gap between the incumbents and fintech start-ups, more financial service companies are currently implementing AI in the short term. An example for enhancing revenue generation in models of alternative finance are data-based alternative credit decisioning (ACD) models. These models represent a borrower's credit profile and thus enable not only the evaluation of the risk potential but also the best possible tailoring of the financing offer to the borrower. The use of AI in the financial services sector is being seen as a major competitive advantage. One of the most dominant benefits is that AI may lead to a so-called flywheel effect which enables competitive advantage for early movers and entry barriers for others. One of the reasons is that AI models which attract many users (customers) in the beginning fuel the system with growing data and thus increases a system's accuracy.

Albeit the potential of AI is enormous, the use of AI in business and society raises also risks and ethical questions. Estonia, for example, already began in 2017 to give a new legal status to all its AI-commanded robots. The law envisions granting "human" liabilities to these robots. The country intends to give rights to every AI system which means that if a natural person is the owner of a particular AI, it can act on behalf of this person with all the relevant duties and responsibilities. But since the European Union also started a dialogue on this topic, the Estonian approach may later be embedded in a more comprehensive European legal and regulatory solution redefining the boundaries between natural and legal persons.

Although AI holds great potential, it also raises some fundamental challenges and questions:

- *Data correctness.* One critical question is how data correctness can be validated? As of today, in most cases humans must still validate data correctness, or a specific algorithm can support humans by validating data from multiple sources, as reliability is different across different sources (e.g., Wikipedia is more trustable than social media sources). Another important application for this might be the use of diversified AI models (just as human diversity is used to evaluate approaches from different perspectives), which would allow to look at results from machine learning differently. However, such AI models are just getting started and the question remains how data correctness can be ensured?
- *Ethical bias.* Another important issue in the context of AI is ethical bias, which can only be removed by constantly teaching the algorithms to improve the outcome. But how can ethical biases be reduced?
- *Real-time and geolocation data.* The move from static data to contextual geolocation data will include more decentralized real-time data in the future, including edge technology from mobile devices. How can these data be included in AI and what challenges might this pose?

- *Market manipulation.* The example of using social media data for company evaluations shows that using such data for decision making might lead to market manipulation. How can the risk of market manipulation by using AI data be reduced to a minimum level?
- *Consumer data.* The use of consumer data for AI might raise issues in the context of consumer privacy. Some countries and regions (e.g., the EU) have outlined these risks and taken action. However, the potential for application areas such as micro finance is huge. For example, based on an individual's payment history AI systems can make better credit decisions in favor of the credit applicant. How can we then use consumer data in a way that allows us to improve financial services for consumers and limit the risks of misuse? A very practical question is how can health data be kept private but also be shared to identify people with similar rare illnesses?

2.6 Quantum Computing

Quantum computing emerged in the 1980s and gained interest only in the 1990s with the introduction of Shor's algorithm that could threaten existing cryptographic methods which were used to protect communication and data models for the first time. Quantum computers exceed classical, binary computers in their performance because their quantum bits (so-called "qubits") can not only represent the values 0 or 1 at a given time but both values at the same time (so-called "superposition"). For example, a traditional computer can only use 0 or 1 even if the value is slightly different from that. This means that traditional computers remove such errors (often called "noise") from the system. In contrast, quantum computers have a higher error rate as a qubit can be any kind of combination of 0 and 1 and thus can also have values in between. This means that the same calculation must be made several times to ensure that the output is correct. But this also means that the lower the error rate, the better the results of a quantum computer. Another important characteristic of quantum computers is that all qubits are interconnected. If one qubit changes its state the other does too, even if they are separated in space. This also has a significant improvement in terms of calculation speed. All these differences show that quantum computers require new hardware, new software, and new algorithms to harness the performance advantage over traditional computers.

In assessing where quantum computing will have most utility potential, it is important to mention that the primary benefits of quantum computing arise from its increased computing power in contrast to classical computers. As of today, no practical applications have been developed yet, despite some experiments. In general, quantum computing allows to analyze large datasets more efficiently and effectively. However, due to its multi-dimensional approach specific software for quantum computers will also enable novel ways of how problems are analyzed. With this, problems can be solved which cannot be solved with traditional computers in a reasonable time frame. But quantum problems are not programmed as traditional software is. Instead, a matrix of multiple elements is loaded into a quantum computer. The difference between the classical binary programming and the novel multi-dimensional optimization is that quantum computers require highly trained quantum experts to (1) define the problem and (2) the way how it is processed to benefit from this new approach. The situation is therefore comparable with the use of the first computers in the 1950s when financial institutions needed to hire and train staff for the use of this new technology. But, as today quantum computing is not fully developed yet, and organizations often use a hybrid approach, this means that a combination of quantum elements and classic computers takes advantage of both to solve highly complex problems.

One example is quantum sensors. Classical sensors are unable to detect quantum activities in the physical world. Quantum sensors play an important role in measuring quantum properties (through quantum entanglement, quantum interference, and quantum state squeezing). Such sensors utilize photonic, atomic, and solid-state systems to detect small-scale changes in time, gravity, temperature, pressure, magnetic fields, etc. They provide optimized precision and reliability that overcomes the limitations of current sensor technologies. Potential applications for this are weather forecasting, healthcare, seismology, etc. Another example for quantum computing is quantum communication which applies the principles of superposition to transmit the hybrid values of both 1 and 0 and transfers encoded information through networks. However, this requires repeaters to cover long distances which are vulnerable points in such a communication network. An application which is specifically important to the financial industry is quantum key distribution which aims to replace traditional key management models. In this case, quantum cryptography ensures secure key exchange for communication, identifies eavesdropping, and offers guaranteed key encryption life to withstand malicious attacks, for which different cryptographic algorithms are available (see Table 2.4). For example, a quantum random number generator (QRNG) allows for better accuracy without post-processing. Today, there is no commercial products for this yet. Based on this, the National Institute of Standards and Technology (NIST) in the USA recommends two primary algorithms to be implemented for most use cases: CRYSTALS-KYBER (key establishment) and CRYSTALS-Dilithium (digital signatures). In addition, the signature schemes FALCON and SPHINCS+ will also be standardized. Additional standardization efforts emerge from ISO/IEC 27001 and 27,002, ISO 15408, RFC 2196, etc.

Table 2.4 Impact of quantum computing on cryptographic algorithms (NIST, 2016)

Cryptographic algorithm	Type	Purpose	Impact from quantum computing
AES	Symmetric key	Encryption	Larger key sizes needed
SHA-2, SHA-3	–	Hash functions	Larger output needed
RSA	Public key	Signatures, key establishment	No longer secure
ECDSA, ECDH	Public key	Signatures, key exchange	No longer secure
DSA	Public key	Signatures, key exchange	No longer secure

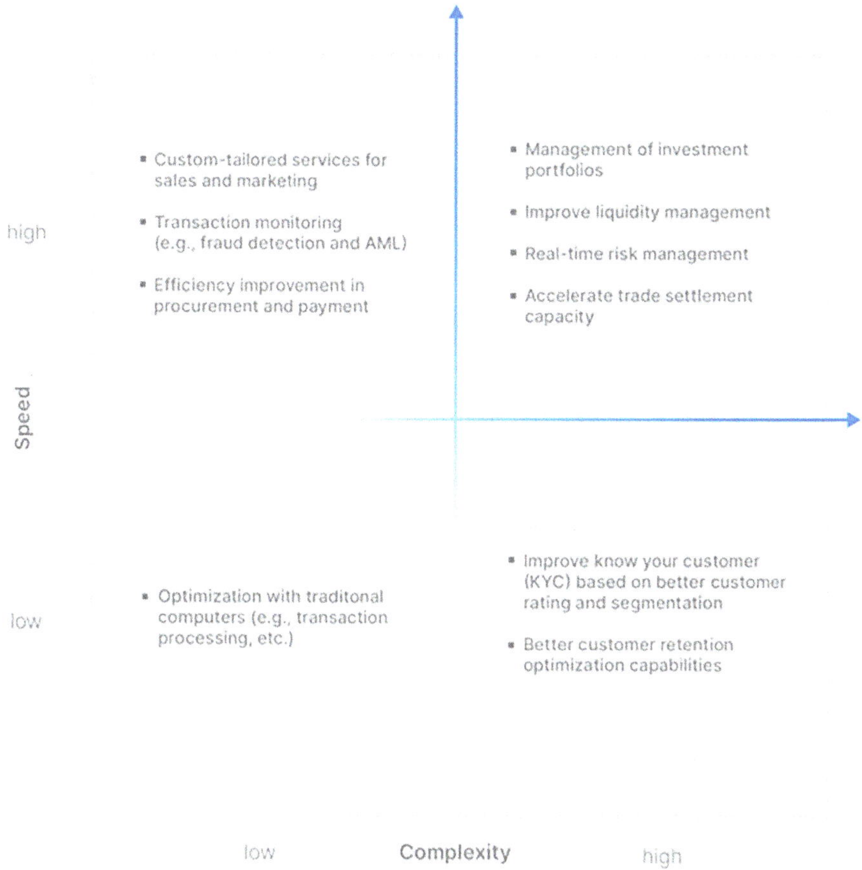

Fig. 2.12 Quantum computer use cases in finance

But what is the concrete potential for the financial system? One obvious application area is the classification and forecasting of large unstructured data, the determination of optimal investment portfolios, algorithmic trading, etc. Quantum computing is beneficial for highly complex models that require fast results. Figure 2.12 shows areas where quantum computing has benefits over traditional computers.

2.7 Web3

The Internet has evolved over different phases over the past few decades. In the first phase, which was from around 1980 to 2000, access to information became standardized by HTLM and web browsers. In the second phase from around 2000 to

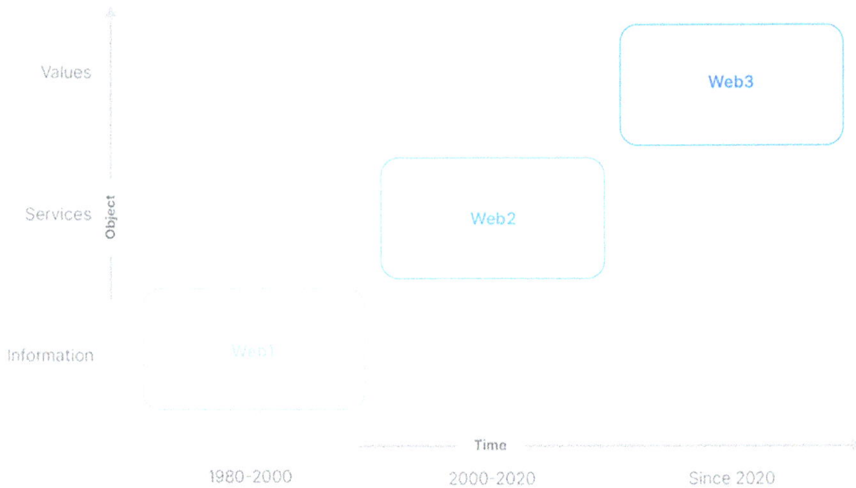

Fig. 2.13 Development of the Internet

2020, access and use of services was standardized by large platforms like Amazon, Google, etc. For many users, however, the current version of the Internet is both a blessing and a curse. On the one hand, it allows them to connect with clients, and on the other hand, the platforms that connect users charge high fees. Web3, on the other hand, allows users to interact directly with other users (clients) based on the possibility to exchange values peer-to-peer (see Fig. 2.13).

The digital transformation of the financial sector might be the spearhead of the emergence of web3, which is referred to as a group of technologies that encompasses digital wallets, digital assets, non-fungible tokens (NFTs), decentralized autonomous organizations (DAOs), and the metaverse (a16z, 2021, 4; Murray et al., 2022). It complements and renews the existing Internet protocols TCP/IP, HTTP, etc. with new ones in areas such as consensus mechanisms and smart contracts based on blockchains. Among the examples of new emerging web3 service providers are Aave (financial services), flow (arts and entertainment), or arweave (identity and personal data management). With these new solutions, for example, musicians and content creators can now transact directly with their fans over the Internet by selling unique digital artifacts, such as music and art. The "Network Flywheel" describes the value creation on web3 in five steps (see Fig. 2.14):

1. *Startup founders* launch a new application (e.g., a new blockchain protocol with an associated vision).
2. *Investors* finance the project with capital, which results in a value for the tokens and the company value.
3. *Miners/validators* provide the capital of production by validating transactions.
4. *Third-party developers* participate in the development project and contribute their human capital.
5. *End users* use the new solution.

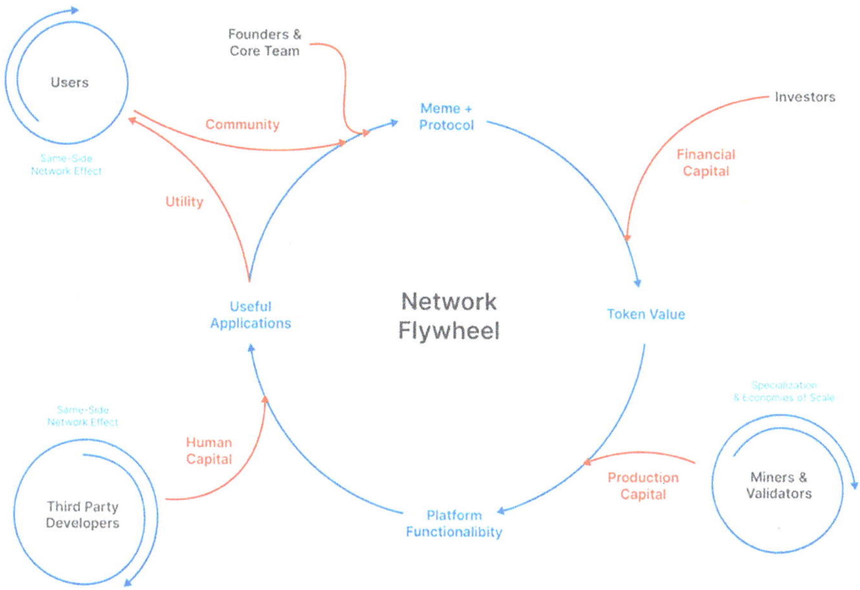

Fig. 2.14 Value creation in web3 (a16z, 2021, 28)

In the following, the elements of web3 are described in more detail.

2.7.1 Digital Wallets

The number of digital wallets is expected to increase from 3.4 billion in 2022 to 5.2 billion in 2026 (Juniper, 2022). Since most of the browsers will soon have wallets integrated, this number is expected to increase even more rapidly over the next few years. Just recently, for example, Microsoft announced that the Internet Explorer will soon be equipped with a digital wallet, too. In addition to this development, W3C in September 2022 released a standard for a payment request API which has the aim to standardize payment processes between a merchant, user agent, and payment method provider. But what connection do IDs and digital wallets have? Digital IDs will be operated via digital wallets in most cases. An example is the planned EU

Case Study: EU Data Governance Act

- The proposed EU regulation on data governance (the Data Governance Act), adopted by the Commission on November 25, 2020, aims at enabling data sharing across sectors and EU Member States.
- The EU will enable these data-sharing systems through four types of measures:

- Mechanisms to facilitate the reuse of certain public sector data that cannot be made available as open data. For example, the reuse of health data could advance research to find cures for rare or chronic diseases.
- Measures to ensure that data intermediaries will function as trustworthy organizers of data sharing or pooling within the common European data spaces.
- Measures to make it easier for citizens and businesses to make their data available for the benefit of society.
- Measures to facilitate data sharing, in particular to make it possible for data to be used across sectors and borders, and to enable the right data to be found for the right purpose.

Source: https://digital-strategy.ec.europa.eu/en/policies/data-governance-act

Case Study: EU Digital Identity

- The European Digital Identity will be available to EU citizens, residents, and businesses who want to identify themselves or provide confirmation of certain personal information. It can be used for both online and offline public and private services across the EU. Every EU citizen and resident in the Union will be able to use a personal digital wallet.
- The EU Digital Identity will be operated via digital wallets available on mobile phone apps and other devices to:
  - Identify online and offline.
  - Store and exchange information provided by governments, e.g., name, surname, date of birth, nationality.
  - Store and exchange the information provided by trusted private sources.
  - Use the information as confirmation of the right to reside, to work, or to study in a certain Member State.

Source: https://ec.europa.eu/info/strategy/priorities-2019-2024/europe-fit-digital-age/european-digital-identity_en

Digital Identity which distinguishes different roles, such as users of the wallet (1), wallet providers (2), person identification data providers (3), etc.

In contrast to digital wallets, which focus on individuals, other forms are also an enabler of the machine-to-machine economy, where machines automatically communicate with each other and conduct payments among each other. Such wallets would not be used by humans but by machines. If, for example, there would be a wallet in every device (robots, cars, etc.), these devices could communicate automatically, exchange data, and execute contracts automatically.

The following case studies show how the EU plans to roll out their data governance and digital ID initiatives.

2.7.2 Digital Assets

A digital asset is "(...) any item of text or media that has been formatted into a binary source that includes the right to use it" (Van Niekerk, 2006). In general, this includes all digital elements which are reusable. Examples for this are digital art, music, and other forms of creative content, digital documents such as contracts, certificates, licenses, etc. But it also includes digital currencies such as Bitcoin and Ethereum. While the characteristics of a digital asset primarily can be assigned to intangible goods that do not have an underlying physical object, this also creates some challenges from a legal perspective. For example, a person only purchases the right to listen to a song from Spotify, not the ownership. This poses questions like the right to listen to the song if it is being transferred to another person. Theoretically, such information could be stored on a blockchain in a smart contract but would then require the private key of the original purchaser to listen to the song.

Another category of digital assets are ones which stem from the tokenization of tangible assets that rely on physical objects. One of the key challenges here is that the issuer of such a token needs to ensure that the number of tokens is always identical to the quantity or value of the physical goods which it represents. Another major challenge is the exact assignment of the physical good to the digital asset token. For this, some methods have already been developed (e.g., a unique DNA "painting" which is applied to the physical good and allows its identification).

To create digital assets, a specific digitalization process for assets is required. This is also referred to as "tokenization." In general, there are two kinds of processes for this:

- *Tokenizing a digital asset by pegging it to an existing digital asset.* If a digital asset is pegged to an existing digital asset, the usage right is stored and, in the case of an ownership change, transferred with the existing digital asset. For example, Bitcoin transactions allow to link another digital asset in the metadata (e.g., the right to use a certain video). If this Bitcoin (or a fraction hereof) is transferred to another person, the usage right is also transferred with the metadata. Of course, the Bitcoin amount to which the digital asset, which is being transferred, is linked must be negligible compared to the value of the digital asset.
- *Tokenizing a digital asset by issuing a smart contract token.* A second way for tokenization is to issue a smart contract token. For example, Ethereum provides the possibility to issue a digital asset in the form of a token by using a standard template. In this case, the digital asset is not pegged to Ether. However, other questions arise like a dynamic token supply (e.g., the increase of tokens if a company increases its capital). An example would be a precious metal like gold or silver, for which the number/value of the tokens must be stabilized according to the value of gold/silver to which it refers to. For this, escrow accounts might be used as an instrument to keep the right balance.

2.7.3 DAOs

While Wikipedia has been an example of a nonprofit community, it has also shown limitations as it provided no economic incentive to contribute to it. Web3, on the other hand, provides economic incentives for all participating stakeholders. And even the management of web3 companies will become much easier. While cloud computing erased the need to buy and maintain large computers, DAOs now enable founders to automate legal and operations processes of a firm through code. This concept is also called "composability," and it allows users to flexibly "compose" any kind of business process. A DAO is an organization controlled by the organization's members and not influenced by a central organization or government; in other words, it is a member-owned community with no central leadership. Those DAOs are operated on blockchains which means that all organizational processes should be implemented on a blockchain. Prominent examples are from Aragon or Tezos. However, the reality of these DAOs is rather different. Table 2.5 compares these two DAOs and shows how the different governance mechanisms of coordination, controlling, and incentives are implemented. The analysis shows that, as of today, most governance-related activities are implemented off-chain. This means that only a few participants are involved in the governance of these DAOs and not the entire community.

DAOs can have different purposes and can therefore be clustered depending on their activity (e.g., functional DAO like for a specific application as Ethereum), value transfer (e.g., investment DAO for coordinating investments), and social aim (e.g., community DAO for networking) (WEF, 2022). But despite the large number

Table 2.5 Comparison of DAOs

DAOs Governance	Aragon	Tezos
Coordination	**Technology (on-chain):** Ethereum **Organization (off-chain):** The Aragon Association coordinates and decides over all suggestions for improvement based on the Aragon Governance Proposal Process	**Technology (on-chain):** Tezos through baking **Organization (on- and off-chain):** The Tezos Foundation coordinates and decides over all suggestions for improvement based on the Amendment Process
Controlling	**Technology (on-chain):** Proof-of-Stake **Organization (off-chain):** The Aragon Association controls all activities	**Technology (on-chain):** Liquid Proof-of-Stake **Organization (on- and off-chain):** The Tezos Foundation controls all activities
Incentives	**Technology (on-chain):** Monetarily through mining **Organization (off-chain):** Collection of ANTs and participation in decision-making processes	**Technology (on-chain):** Monetarily through baking **Organization (off-chain):** A baker must keep 8.25% of all XTZ tokens in their own fund

of examples and the great potential they promise, DAOs still have some challenges to overcome:

- *Procedural, lengthy voting process.* For example, the BitShares exchange faced a lack of turnout or voter engagement due to the amount of work required to review each proposal.
- *Legal vagueness.* For example, similar organizational structures have been used by the US Securities and Exchange Commission considered an illegal form for unregistered securities.
- *Structural rigidity.* A DAO's code will be extremely difficult to change once its system is up and running. This extends to trivial things like bug fixes in centralized code as well as issues of a structural nature.
- *Voter manipulation.* DAOs can be subject to manipulations that disrupt their voting structures, particularly when a concentration of tokens distorts democratic processes (a recent analysis found evidence that on average, only 3.25 voters were needed for the proposals to reach a quorum and pass, and only 2.84 voters were needed to reach 50% of the total votes (Messias et al., 2023).

2.7.4 Non-fungible Tokens

While DAOs are important for managing decentrally organized blockchains, non-fungible tokens (NFTs) are a novel instrument for digital ownership. In economics, a "*fungible good*" is one that is interchangeable: a liter of gas at one gas station is equal to a liter of gas at another, and the price can be paid in money with identical value. A "*non-fungible good*," on the other hand, is unique: Vincent van Gogh's painting "Starry Night" (1889) only exists as a single example; it is a unique creation and therefore a "non-fungible" work of art. A "*non-fungible token*" (NFT) is a non-exchangeable digital asset such as a photo, song, or video whose ownership has been authenticated and stored on a blockchain and which is collected, sold, and traded on various online platforms.

While Ethereum is the most popular network for creating NFTs, there are other smart contract-backing blockchains such as Solana, Tezos, EOS, and TRON that can be used to create NFTs. For example, the Ethereum blockchain offers two different standards: the ERC-20 token standard is used to create fungible tokens like Chainlink (LINK) and Tether (USDT), while the ERC-721 standard is used to create non-fungible tokens. Platforms like Decentraland and Crypto-Kitties, for example were developed using the ERC-721 standard.

NFTs are confronted with technical and legal challenges. Technically, there is currently no established token standard, the risk of theft of private keys is high and the data risk by deletion of the external stored data file. From a legal perspective, there are still many differences between different jurisdictions (e.g., AML, taxes, etc.) in the classification of NFTs as asset tokens and counterfeit NFTs.

2.7.5 Metaverse

While DAOs focus on the organizational element of decentralization and NFTs and digital assets on the technical part (technology layer), functions for extended reality like the "metaverse" provide new capabilities for navigating through the web (presentation layer). Such extended realities refer to augmented and virtual realities and rely either on traditional computers/mobile phones or on virtual reality glasses (e.g., Meta Quest Pro, Apple Vision Pro). The term "metaverse" was coined by Neal Stephenson in his novel *Snow Crash* (Stephenson, 1993) and was used again in 2021 by Mark Zuckerberg, CEO of Meta Platforms, to describe it as the successor to the mobile Internet that:

- *Amplifies physical world experiences*. Through mixed reality and physical world experiences, the Metaverse will amplify the sense of presence. There are currently several use cases that serve as templates for the future of metaverse applications, for example, how furniture fits, or what glasses or make-up looks like. In the future, one can imagine a world where many physical objects (e.g., TVs, computers, etc.) can be holograms designed by developers.
- *Is a space for co-creation and co-building*. Many companies will work together to build the metaverse (including corporations, entrepreneurs, policymakers, etc.). To support this, open standards and interoperability are core elements of the Metaverse, with new forms of governance likely to emerge (e.g., DAOs).

More recently the term was defined as "(…) an interconnected web of ubiquitous virtual worlds partly overlapping with and enhancing the physical world. These virtual worlds enable users represented by avatars to connect and interact with each other, to experience and consume user-generated content in an immersive, scalable, synchronous, and persistent environment. An economic system provides incentives for contributing to the Metaverse" (Weinberger, 2022). But what is the potential of such ubiquitous virtual worlds? As the financial system is mostly digital, there might be great potential and the first banks started to launch virtual bank branches in the metaverse which focus on establishing new distribution channels and offering new products. For example, one of the first banks that has set up a virtual storefront in the metaverse is HSBC, which purchased land in The Sandbox, a virtual gaming world based on Ethereum, where virtual land can be purchased for Ether, earlier this year. It will use this virtual store to engage with online sports fans and e-sports enthusiasts. JPMorgan Chase is another example of a bank that has already established a presence on the Decentraland platform. The company created a lounge area called Onyx inside Decentraland's "Metajuku" virtual mall to provide visitors information about blockchain and other technology initiatives of the bank. In total, the metaverse today brings together around 500 million users globally. Many are especially attractive for children. For example, around 75% of all children in the USA between 12 and 16 are on Roblox, a gaming metaverse. An early example of the metaverse has been Second Life, which was introduced in 2003 and which relies on the Linden Dollar as its own currency, a characteristic which many metaverses have.

The development of such metaverse approaches is in line with two major developments that the industry is currently facing, and which relate to the Generation Z's new preferences.[2] First, the shift from ownership to experience-oriented, temporary usage toward the so-called "Sharing Economy" which also influences the financial sector (Puschmann & Alt, 2016). In the banking industry, for instance, clients share information about banking products on social networks and even share their assets to jointly create new digital banking products without banks (e.g., DeFi). The second development is the shift of knowledge from providers to clients induced by AI. With digital bots that act as virtual assistants, clients now have access to almost all the information that until now was exclusively reserved for banks (reduced information asymmetry). An example in this category is the recent success of ChatGPT which allows customers to gather information about financial services and products. But also examples from other industries demonstrate the future potential of the metaverse in areas of b2c and b2b:

- *Production.* A manufacturer who buys new supplier parts does this today via physical brochures or a web shop. In the metaverse, on the other hand, users can cost-effectively test the products in a virtual environment using a digital twin or digital factory to see how robotic systems interact with the physical environment.
- *Retail.* Instead of having stores in every city, a large retailer could build a global hub in the metaverse, capable of serving millions of customers.
- *Labor market.* Workers in countries with low wage levels could take jobs (e.g., IT, back office, etc.) in Western companies without having to emigrate. Educational opportunities are also expanding, as metaverse worlds are a cheap and effective way to access training.

The second element of Mark Zuckerberg's definition of the metaverse refers to the co-creation and co-building of the required infrastructure. Different models aim to describe the architecture of the metaverse in different layers (e.g., McKinsey, 2022) where elements from hardware, platforms and content are combined to create novel marketplaces (e.g., OpenSea), avatars (e.g., mutant cats), or virtual worlds (e.g., Decentraland).

[2] The Generation Z is the demographic cohort succeeding the Millennials and preceding Generation Alpha. Researchers and popular media often use the mid-to-late 1990s to the early 2010s as the birth years of this generation.

Chapter 3
Nation States

Although IT has been a strong driver of innovation, the global money system remained very stable until now. But since digital currencies entered the arena in the 2010s it is more and more challenged by novel stakeholders and new digital forms of money. The state monopoly over money has evolved over the last few centuries and has rarely ever been questioned since then (Dowd, 1998). But this has been very different before state-controlled currencies were introduced. For example, in the US Free-Banking Era from 1837 to 1864 every city, region, or state could issue its own currency (Sanches, 2016) which was then restricted by the National Bank Acts in 1863 and 1864 and led to the US dollar as the single US currency. With the emergence of Bitcoin, Ethereum, and other privately issued digital currencies, this "natural" monopoly became challenged in some countries, especially those ones that were impacted by high inflation over a longer period. El Salvador and the Central African Republic, for example, made Bitcoin a legal tender in 2021. Inspired by the possibility to digitalize money, many nation states around the world started to experiment with CBDCs, a purely digital representation of central bank money. These experiments are not yet completed and the decision whether a country introduces a CBDC very much depends on individual conditions. The Bahamas, for example, was among the first to introduce a CBDC in 2020, as the country consists of many small islands and cash circulation is very expensive. Most other countries are still in the process of evaluation and analyze the willingness of citizens and consumers to use CBDCs and what impact this might have from a macroeconomic perspective. In addition, IT considerations also play a major role, since blockchain offers new ways to implement payment infrastructures based on CBDCs to improve efficiency and add new functionality.

T. Puschmann, H. S. H. P. M. of Liechtenstein, *Financial System 2030*, Financial Innovation and Technology,
https://doi.org/10.1007/978-3-031-55700-2_3

3.1 Citizens

Recent developments in IT have led to full "digital citizens" and to a fundamental change in their behavior induced by the emergence of "digital natives" (Palfrey & Gasser, 2016). This might result in the so-called "digital society" where today's limitations between the physical and digital world become blurred. While digitally assisted human-to-human interactions have been already used for many decades, applications for self-service human-to-machine interactions (e.g., robo-advisors and chat bots) are in place only since a few years in more complex advisory processes. Such scenarios are currently fueled by more advanced AI tools such as ChatGPT, Hugging Face, or Cohere, the new category of generative AI systems (see Sect. 2.5). The next step in this development is expected to be machine-to-machine interactions (e.g., automated payments in IoT networks or cars that communicate with smart contracts) which are predicted to become mainstream within the next few years as part of the convergence of different technologies like IoT and blockchain. Three major shifts may foster the emergence of the digital society in the forthcoming years:

- *From institutions to citizens.* Decentralized technologies like blockchain combined with AI-based systems might increase the shift of knowledge from institutions to citizens. With new services like digital IDs provided by blockchain technologies, for example, such a new system would connect billions of people without any intermediaries and thus lead to a democratization of information and value exchange among individuals (see Sect. 3.5). This especially applies to many countries in emerging areas like Africa, where many citizens are not part of the financial system today and where trust in central institutions is often low (Arner et al., 2018; see Sect. 3.4). For the first time in history, mankind could deploy a system that is able to store an "unbroken historical record" (Casey & Vigna, 2018, 260). An example of this is the messages that are written in Bitcoin transactions (just as it was the case with the very first transaction block that was created on or after January 3, 2009, including a comment on the instability caused by fractional-reserve banking; see Fig. 3.1).
- *From ownership to usage.* The second driver is a general change in user behavior which describes the shift from ownership to experience-oriented, temporary usage toward the so-called "sharing economy" or "peer-to-peer-economy" which has already and still is affecting all industries (Puschmann and Alt 2016; Sundararajan 2016). Among the prominent examples are Airbnb for apartment rental or Nextbike offering rental bike services. Examples from the financial industry are clients that share information about financial products on social networks or share their assets to jointly create new digital financial products without banks. While the evolving digital ecosystems (see Sect. 5.6) affect all areas of life such as mobility, health, education, work, etc., the underlying technologies are still in an early phase of development (see Sect. 2.2–2.7). A digital ID, for example, is currently being created in many countries as a basic infrastructure (as part of so-called digital public infrastructures, DPIs; see Chap. 6) element for

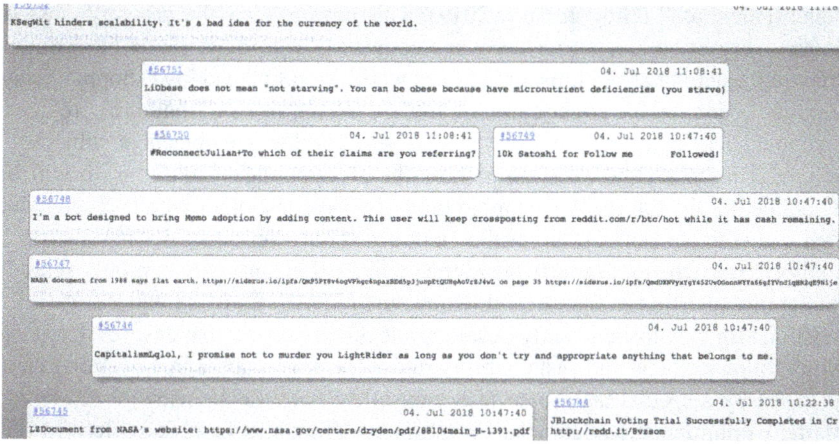

Fig. 3.1 Extract from Cryptograffiti.info (discontinued)

gaining access to all kinds of public and private digital services. This basic service enables users to access data based on the principle of "selective transparency" which means that data can be shared selectively depending on the involved actors and which ensures that data ownership remains with data owners.

- *From humans to machines.* The increased computing power and the availability of more data allows for more sophisticated services which do not require any human interaction. For example, an IBM computer called "Project Debater" communicated with humans in a competition and won this debate (Slonim et al., 2021). For the financial industry, this shift leads to a lower level of interaction between clients and advisors, which in consequence would further reduce human client advisors and branches. With digital chat bots that act as virtual assistants, clients now have access to almost all the information that until now was virtually exclusively reserved for banks and other institutions. This decreases one of the major frictions of the financial industry, the information asymmetry between providers and customers. In addition, in a digital environment, money can now "turn" something "on" or "off." For example, cars can communicate with smart contracts automatically. We know how to lend money to individuals and firms, but we don't know how to lend money to machines. Such a digital ecosystem is a complex adaptive flow network of automated obligations and enforcement between machines.

Especially, the shift from humans to machines provides some aspects for discussions from an ethical point of view. For example, in recent years, the banking industry automated its front-to-back-operation tasks more accurately and efficiently without completely overhauling existing operating systems (which still remains one of the weaknesses of the incumbents). The examples stretch along the entire banking value chain covering front office (e.g., conversational banking), middle office (e.g., fraud reduction), and back office (e.g., underwriting). These transactions very often are supported in the background by invisible human labor, called the "global human underclass" (Gray & Suri, 2019). This term reflects the growing class of humans, very often located in low-wage countries, working in fields like content reviewing, teaching algorithms, or the ones who sort, fill in, and load shopping bags for online orders by the upper class. In law, it's becoming clear that one core question about such "computational servants" is whether they are objects or subjects of contract. This raises the question of how the principal-agent relationship will be (re-)defined in the future? An example might be the question of who is responsible when a predictive policing algorithm unfairly targets an African American as a recidivism risk when a similarly positioned white defendant is not similarly scored? The liability question is an ethical dilemma and requires legal adaptations.

Estonia for example currently develops a legal framework that ensures that technology follows ethical and sustainability rules. The work started in November 2016 and is led by a special task force in a joint effort with the Ministry of Economic Affairs, Communications and the Government Office. To involve society in this process, the task force uses a special character from the Estonian mythology called the "Kratt" which is an artificial creature that has existed in the cultural space for hundreds of years and is composed of several unique features that everyone knows. Technology on the other hand is something that is complex and difficult to understand for citizens. From a technological point of view, the Kratt character has exactly the same features as an artificial robot (see Fig. 3.2).

A major driver for these developments is the so-called "millennial" generation. In the USA the generation of the "millennials" (the generation born between 1982 and 1998) is already the largest living generation withmore than 80 million in number. From a global perspective, the millennials account already for around 30% of

Fig. 3.2 The "Kratt" as an "artificial robot" (Homeless Bob Production 2016)

the entire population. The primary customer segment, therefore, shifts from the baby boomers to the millennials in the forthcoming years. Financial services, therefore, must be reflected from this perspective. Looking further ahead, millennials will control the largest share of global wealth, as they will benefit from one of the largest intergenerational wealth transfers in human history. As a major characteristic, this generation is strongly influenced by IT and thus millennials' view of the world varies greatly from that of previous generations. As such, the implications for the financial system currently hold at least three paradoxes:

- *Trust paradox.* The Millennial Disruption Index, which includes over 10,000 surveys from 73 companies in 15 industries, concludes that banks are most likely to be disrupted by the preferences of this generation in two areas: customer acquisition and customer journey (McAuley & Weiner, 2015). First, millennials are said to trust IT more than face-to-face relationships, resulting in the consequence that IT-based acquisition tools are believed to be the primary instrument which is in the second step paired with a human advisor (which in consequence has been the strategy of many fintech startups). Regarding the customer journey, millennials say that fintech startups are bridging the gap between what financial services firms currently do not offer versus what today's customers want. Fintechs have been targeting industry niche areas with superior products and services to fill gaps left by incumbents throughout the customer journey. Paradoxically, 84% of the millennials seek financial education and advice from a financial institution or a financial advisor (EFMA, 2017).
- *Privacy paradox.* Digital services rely on data and their accessibility by providers. Millennials are willing to forego privacy more so than other generations if sharing personal data gives them a more convenient service. For example, 57% would share details of their savings with family and friends, while just 32% of surveyed Baby Boomers would divulge the same information. Paradoxically, a survey of more than 2000 US banking consumers identified that 89% of them are concerned about data privacy and data sharing (The Clearing House, 2018). This paves the way for banks which in the same survey are viewed as the most trusted provider of data security and are expected to safeguard customer data.
- *Digitalization paradox.* While the use of cash is steadily decreasing in some parts of the world like in many Western European countries, it remains important in Africa but becomes less important in China, where WeChat Pay or Alipay dominate the mobile payment market. In addition, the increased use of digital finance services is leading to a decreased personal interaction of consumers with banks. For example, the number of bank branches in the European Union declined by around 85,000 branches to approx. 138,000 from 2008 to 2021 (see Statista.com). Paradoxically, still many clients prefer human advice for "big" decisions like buying a house or investing large amounts of money. In contrast to that in Africa, where fewer bank branches are available, the developments are leapfrogged by digital-only services like the mobile phone payment systems. M-PESA demonstrated this very impressively.

However, the use and impact of fintech services is different in developing countries, as the following case study shows.

Case Study: Financial Inclusion in Developing Countries

- About 1.4 billion people worldwide are still excluded from formal financial services, such as savings, payments, insurance, and credit. In developing economies, only 63% of adults have an account.
- In just the past 6 years, 1.2 billion million people worldwide have gained access to bank and mobile payment accounts (World Bank, Global Findex). But still, most payments are in cash as most people have no access to electronic payment systems. In developing economies in 2021, 18% of adults paid utility bills directly from an account. About one-third of these adults did so for the first time after the COVID-19 pandemic.
- To realize the full potential of financial inclusion, policymakers and business leaders will need to invest in the right payment infrastructure, regulatory standards, and customer activation strategies. Five key success factors seem to be of most importance:
  - Accessibility: Reach the poorest neighborhoods and smallest villages and easy to acquire and understand.
  - Reliability: Money and information need to be reliable and highly secure, protected against cybertheft and money laundering.
  - Valuability: Clear advantage for people to use digital payments instead of cash.
  - Affordability: Free of cost for all or most people.
  - Profitability: Involvement of the private sector to develop sustainable business models.
  - In most countries of the developing world, novel, mobile-based financial systems evolved as parallel infrastructures complementary to the existing ones (e.g., M-PESA in Kenya). For example, in sub-Saharan Africa in 2021, 55% of adults had an account, including 33% of adults who had a mobile money account.
- Often, these novel financial infrastructures are not or only loosely coupled to the incumbent infrastructures from banks.
- For example, to link the two separated infrastructures, the Bill & Melinda Gates Foundation developed the open-source software platform "Mojaloop" which enables payment interoperability between banks and other providers and allows the creation of digital ecosystems and the release of novel financial models like the leasing of solar battery (which are not affordable for many) and small payments.

Source: www.gatesfoundation.org

3.2 Customers

Costomer centricity puts the customer at the center of a firm's strategy. In 1954, Peter Drucker wrote in his book *The Practice of Management* that "it is the customer who determines what a business is (…) what it produces, and whether it will prosper" (Drucker, 1954, 37). Historically, firms in these times were more internally oriented, with their attention focused on manufacturing superior products, rather than concentrating on the purchasers of those products. With IT, firms could then collect and analyze data about customers and personalize their products and services. This evolutionary path also applies to the financial industry. After the introduction of punch cards, the emergence of standard software, and online banking, a new phase of digitalization emerged, which leads to a paradigm shift from a bank-centric inside-out perspective to a customer-centered outside-in view (Puschmann, 2017). This pertains to developments such as electronic marketplaces in customer contact, including comparison portals and crowdsourcing platforms as well as peer-to-peer platforms. In many respects, electronic platforms have replaced the traditionally bilateral relationship between banks and customers or service providers with one more multilateral in nature, allowing customers and service providers to use an interface (to the marketplace) for customer-centric integration. From a customer's point of view, this fosters a hybrid form of interaction, as customers use several channels (mobile, social, web, branch, non-bank, etc.) to exchange information and execute transactions relevant to banks.

Customer centricity very often shifts along a firm's life cycle. Initially, many companies are customer-centric per definition as they need to acquire new customers on a broader scale, and to gain efficiency and by putting manufacturing or service provision mechanisms over customer-centric ones, they may lose some customers. That is also the reason why the fintech startups are often more customer-centric than the incumbents in their early stages of development. As customer centricity is putting the customer at the "heart" of all activities across all dimensions of the business model, three dimensions are of high relevance (Gassmann et al., 2014):

- *Value conception (what?).* This dimension refers to the desirability of a product or service from the perspective of a customer. IT is an enabler for providing insights about customer preferences by asking customers via online channels and by observing customers how they behave and speak about a company and its products and services (e.g., social media listening and online experimenting).
- *Value delivery (how?).* This dimension refers to the feasibility of how a product or service is delivered to the customer. IT is once again an enabler to optimize and redefine this dimension. The Netflix model, for example, demonstrated a fundamental shift in how customers consume entertainment and how customers and third parties can be involved in the value delivery process.

- *Value capture (value?).* IT allows contractibility for all risks associated with the purchase of a product or service on a very fine-grained level (e.g., a car or a financial product) and thus can improve profitability. The pay-per-use model and the subscription economy are the very early signs of an "outcome economy," where customers pay for the outcome (e.g., paying not for pharmaceutical products, but for the results of a treatment for that the product is used).

To implement these three dimensions, three characteristics remain central to advancing customer-centric business models (Bonnet et al., 2021):

- *Empathy.* Customer empathy is about understanding three aspects of the human condition: (a) the cognitive part (how customers think in a given context), (b) the affective part (the emotions behind customers' choices), and (c) the behavioral part (the actions people take). Data provides a source to analyze all three areas more progressively in a real-time environment to understand and react to customer behavior and the actions.
- *Humility.* Today's customer–firm relationships are digitally mediated reciprocal partnerships. This means that these relationships are not only unilateral where firms control, but ones where customers become collaborators across the entire value chain, from product development (e.g., Austria's Erste Bank's "s Lab") to content creation (e.g., LinkedIn articles) and services (e.g., iStockphoto inspectors).
- *Audacity.* Audacity means that IT enables firms to reduce the risk for their customers. For example, a logistics service provider may purchase a truck with a guaranteed "up-time" model, but to make this model work transparently, the truck manufacturer needs to know that the vehicle will be well maintained and operated properly, which can be monitored by IoT.

The following case study shows how IT may be used to achieve increased customer centricity by constantly validating novel products and services.

Case Study: Uber's Experimentation Platform

- Experimentation is at the core of how Uber improves its customer experience. Uber applies several experimental methodologies to use cases for testing out a new feature to enhancing the application design (see Fig. 3.3).
- Uber's Experimentation Platform (XP) plays an important role in this process, enabling the firm to launch, debug, measure, and monitor the effects of new ideas, product features, marketing campaigns, and promotions.
- There are over 1000 experiments running on the platform at any given time.
- At a high level, Uber's XP allows engineers and data scientists to monitor "treatment" effects to ensure they do not cause regressions of any key metrics. The platform also lets users configure the universal holdout, used to measure the long-term effects of all experiments for a specific domain.

Source: https://eng.uber.com/xp/

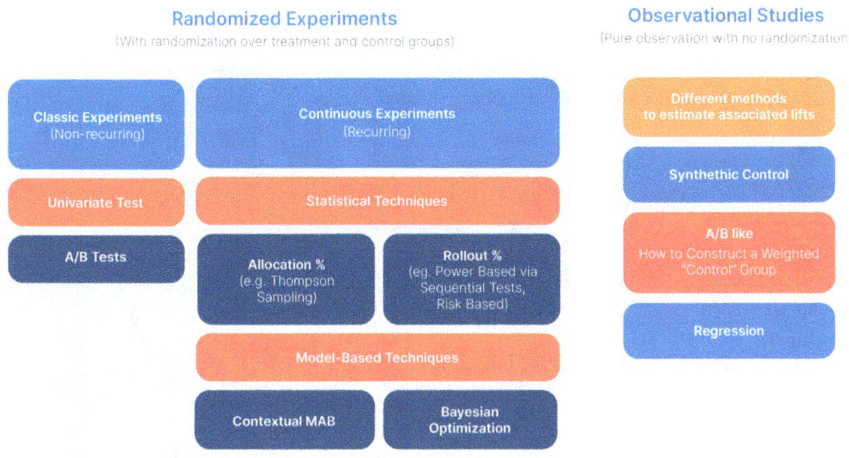

Fig. 3.3 Uber's experimentation platform

3.3 Digital Money

The impact of IT on citizens and customers is fundamental. This impact can also be observed in the context of money which currently shifts from cash money to digital money. From a historical perspective, money is based on two principles (Harari, 2019, 228): (1) it provides a conversion mechanism for goods and services (promoted by interoperability) and (2) it is an instrument for economic cooperation (promoted by affinity). In this context, one of the major requirements (and also its greatest benefit) of money is the network effect, which means that the more people trust in it and use it, the more it is accepted by even more people. There are several lessons in history that teach these two principles. First, the evolving British Empire in the nineteenth century led to the sterling as the world's reserve currency. However, the dominance was lost in the twentieth century because of its lack of interoperability, as the world became more diverse and more geographically separated. Another example is the US Free Banking Era which later led to the US dollar as a singular national currency by the National Bank Acts in 1863 and 1864 and which reduced complexity for the citizens and customers (Gorton & Zhang, 2021). These fiat currencies brought interoperability but often lacked affinity as they often led to a social divide (e.g., banked vs. unbanked). Social money like the Chinese Taobao tried to solve this issue, but its systemic risks remain unsolved. Currently, stablecoins like USDC are building on the discussions around privately issued money and government-issued money. As history has shown, private money and public money have always coexisted, clearly with a stronger focus on public money. Table 3.1 gives an overview of the development of central banks and the decision on a sovereign money monopoly in different countries starting with Sweden in 1668 and the first central bank money monopoly granted in Austria in 1816.

Table 3.1 History of the sovereign money monopoly in selected countries

Country	Central bank founded	Decision on money monopoly
Sweden	1668	1897
United Kingdom	1694	1844
France	1800	1848
Finland	1811	1886
Netherlands	1814	1863
Austria	1816	1816
Norway	1816	1818
Denmark	1818	1818
Portugal	1846	1888
Belgium	1850	1850
Spain	1874	1874
Germany	1876	1876
Japan	1882	1883
Italy	1893	1926
United States	1913	1913

The evolution of the financial system is tightly coupled with the evolution of money as an instrument for value storage, exchange, and transfer. However, in recent decades, money decoupled from physical transfer mediums like coins and banknotes and became digital in many countries. And the role of money has also changed over time, although still many ritual and religious uses of money like beliefs about lucky numbers and lotteries can be found as well as the stitching together of the lineaments of kin and social relations through money and payment whether physical or digital. An example is the digital "hong bao" or lucky red envelopes that were key success factors for the adoption of WeChat Pay and Alipay in China. Or the way people use M-PESA in Kenya to pool resources for coming-of-age ceremonies and the purchase of livestock needed to mark ritual events.

Throughout history, money was usually backed by a commodity—very often a precious metal like gold or silver. When money broke loose from commodities, inflation increased in many cases. The current financial system has its roots in a time when the evolution of global value and supply chains emerged. During that time, the production and distribution of physical goods was at the center of the global economy. As we currently can observe, a shift from physical goods to service production by humans and to robots and machines is taking place. That's why we also might need to rethink the design of the financial system. Wouldn't it make sense if the financial system would also be digitalized and automated in the same way as the production and distribution of goods and (digital) services are? But international trade is still very complicated because most countries have their own currencies, which move in idiosyncratic ways and can be held down to boost competitiveness. Jurisdictional borders is still one of the most challenging elements for the financial system.

3.3.1 Money Taxonomy

The current financial system, which is very often termed as "Bretton Woods II," emerged after World War II and has a clear US dollar dominance (Economist, 2019). But with slower and reduced global trade, the current system seems more vulnerable than ever. As money evolved in many regions and countries of the world independently from each other, a very heterogeneous world of "money" exists today, although in some regions consolidation already began (e.g., within the European Union). In parallel, a new financial system with digital, privately issued currencies and stablecoins emerged, which, in most parts, is not connected to the incumbent system.

To understand the different forms of money, a taxonomy can be helpful. One taxonomy of money distinguishes four dimensions (Bech & Garrat, 2017).

A first dimension focuses on the accessibility (Brunnermeier & Niepelt, 2019). For example, the field of privately issued digital currencies has seen an enormous increase over the past few years. The total market capitalization of these digital currencies increased from around \$13.6 billion in November 2017 to more than \$3 trillion at its peak in November 2021. The number of digital wallets increased from around 21 million in 2017 to around 3.4 billion users in 2022 (Juniper, 2022). The second dimension differentiates whether the money is electronically issued, while the third dimension defines if it is issued by a central bank or private institutions. Finally, the fourth dimension relates to the p2p transfer mechanism. Each of the dimensions can be mixed and lead to a "money flower" for which different examples can be assigned (see Fig. 3.4).

Another taxonomy is the "Money Tree" which differentiates four attributes of means of payments: type (claim/object), value (fixed/variable), backstop (private/government), and technology (see Fig. 3.5; IMF, 2019). In contrast to the money flower, this one includes the value (fixed/variable), the kind of technology used (centralized/decentralized), and the kind of stakeholder involved (public/private).

The taxonomies show that the number of forms of money has increased enormously with digitalization. This leads to a greater variation of possibilities for citizens and customers but also to a higher complexity.

3.3.2 Digital Currencies

"The value of money requires not just the belief of the public at any point in time but critically the consent of the public at all times. When it comes to money, the consent in trust of the public must be nurtured and continually maintained" (Mark Carney, former governor of the Bank of Canada and the Bank of England at the Andrew Crockett Memorial Lecture at the Bank for International Settlements, June 28, 2021). But what is the value inherent in digital money and how does this value lead to consent in trust? In recent years, especially concepts for central bank issued

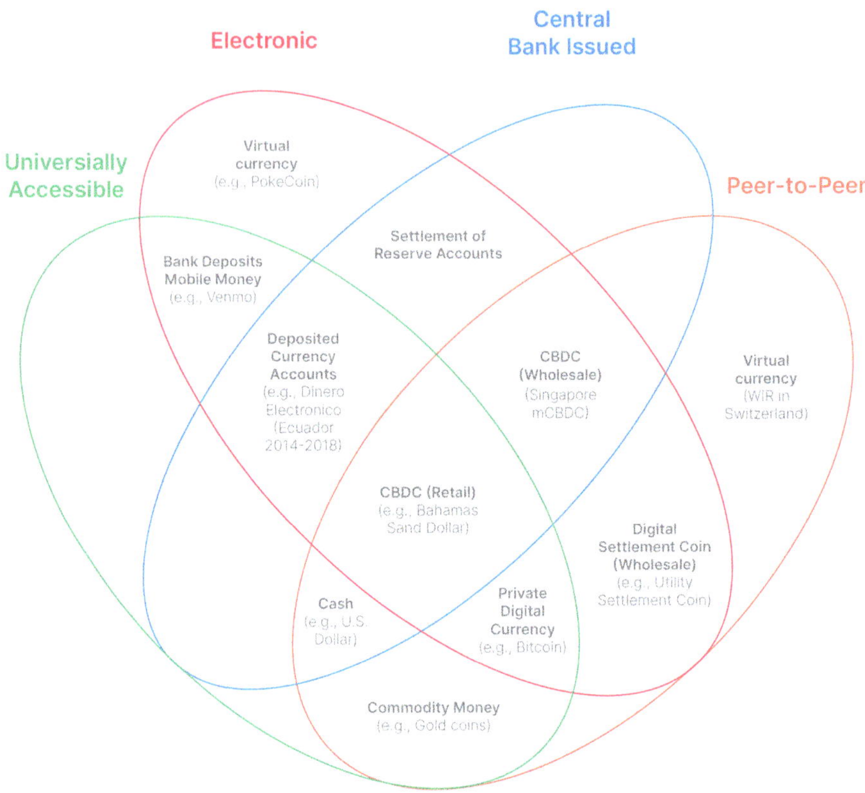

Fig. 3.4 Taxonomy of money (modified according to Bech and Garrat (2017)

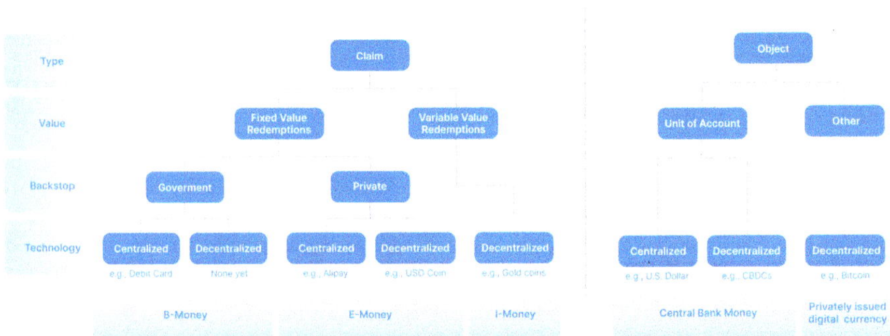

Fig. 3.5 Money tree [modified according to IMF, 2019]

forms of digital money (CBDCs) and privately issued stablecoins have evolved (BIS, 2019b, 2020b). Stablecoins already settled over 11 trillion on-chain transactions in 2022, almost surpassing the payment transaction volume of the biggest credit card providers. However, this simple differentiation between private and public money falls short. With the digitalization of money, the typical functions of money as a unit of account, a medium of exchange, a store of value, and a legal tender are increasingly becoming unbundled (Brunnermeier et al., 2019; see Fig. 3.6). For example, Bitcoin serves the function as a medium of exchange in some countries (e.g., El Salvador) of the world better than existing fiat currencies which have higher transaction costs. On the other hand, digital platforms may also lead to a re-bundling of monetary functions. Here, payment services are bundled with other services (e.g., data services). This means that we might not only differentiate between private and public forms of (digital) money but also between private and public forms of single functions of money which would ultimately lead to a higher complexity in the design of monetary functions.

The discussion whether digital currencies (especially private ones) can be seen as "currencies" in their traditional understanding evolved over the past decade since money's four core functions have not been stable over the past centuries but have also changed over time and digitalization might now change these functions again (Hens, 2020). For example, the function as a medium of exchange was first fulfilled by miniature tools out of precious metal, later from coins, then from printed paper, and most recently from plastic cards and electronic accounts. So will we now see

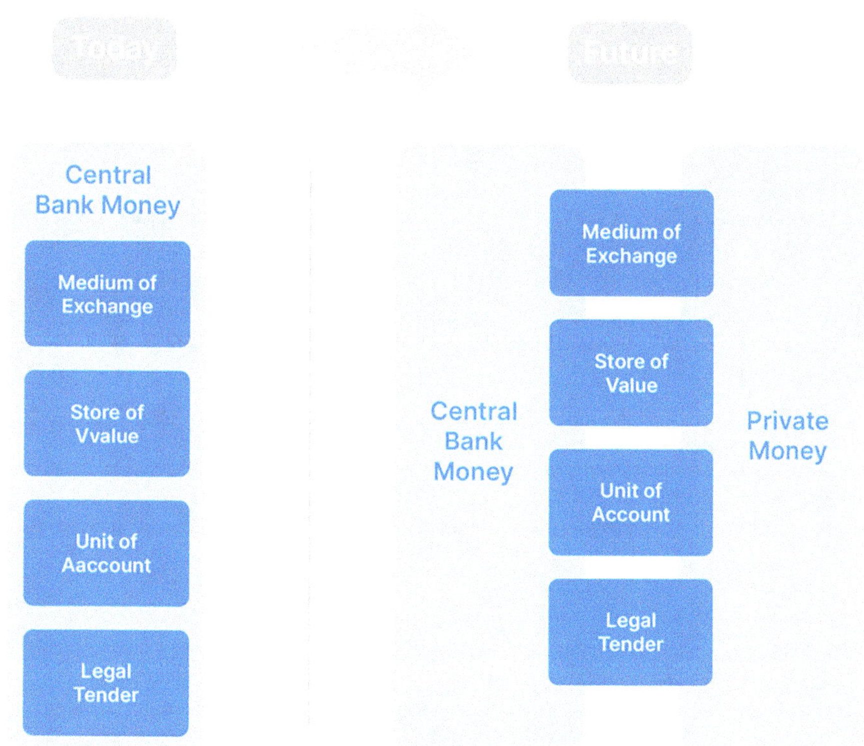

Fig. 3.6 Unbundling of monetary functions through digitalization

another shift in this development toward digital currencies, including also privately issued digital currencies? Table 3.2 provides a summary of the benefits and risks of privately issued digital currencies that come along with this development.

The discussion of whether money should be issued by public or private institutions has a long tradition. For example, this has been intensively discussed by Friedrich August Hayek's book *Denationalization of Money* (Hayek, 1976). One major argument against competing currencies is the high information cost, which means that for all payments various prices in different currencies must be calculated. This is especially critical if the exchange rates are fluctuating. But with the technological advancements, these costs can now be reduced to a minimum which would be a strong argument for the coexistence of privately and publicly issued digital money. Table 3.3 summarizes the key functions of money complemented by "identification," "incentives for issuing money," and "firearms in crises" as further monetary functions and compares public central bank money and private digital currencies. The most significant difference between privately issued digital currencies and central bank money is backing. Digital currencies have no backing from governments, and the value of the currency is only set by the market. In contrast, stablecoins are collateralized by stores of value like gold, real estate, or fiat currencies (e.g., Tether, USD Coin).

A novel type of digital central bank money is CDBCs, which can be used as an instrument for retail payments or wholesale payments (see Sect. 5.2). The number

Table 3.2 Benefits and risks of privately issued digital currencies

Benefits	Risks
• Lower cost, especially for small transactions • Financial inclusion • Cross-border financial services	• Currency substitution • Illicit financial flows • Cyberattacks, data, and privacy • Governance of private digital currencies

Table 3.3 Characteristics of central bank money and private digital currencies (Hens, 2020)

Monetary functions	Central bank money	Private digital currencies
Medium of exchange	Small charge for transfers within one country but high for international transfers	Free of charge nationally and internationally. But mining costs are a waste of energy
Store of value	Permanent losses due to inflation	Volatility due to speculation unless collateralized
Unit of account	Well established	Not yet established
Legal tender	Well established	Occasionally
Identification	High for nations and supra-nations like EU	So far only high for international cryptocurrency community
Incentives for issuing money	Generally high since monopoly power but competition internationally: "Dollarization"	Limited because of the thread of hard forks
Firearms in crises	Yes, since flexible money supply	Only if a reserve has been accumulated

of CBDC projects from central banks is steadily increasing. As of November 2023, 11 projects were launched, 21 running under pilot projects, 33 under development, and 46 researched (https://www.atlanticcouncil.org/cbdctracker). This trend is in line with the CBDC sentiment, which shows that the number of CBDC speeches globally has increased over the past few years. A recent global survey among central banks identified that 86% are actively researching the potential for CBDCs, 60% were experimenting with the technology, and 14% are deploying pilot projects (BIS, 2021).

A CBDC can be defined as a digital payment instrument that is denominated in the national unit of account and which is a direct liability of the central bank. A CBDC can therefore be understood as a digital form of central bank money that is different from balances in traditional reserve or settlement accounts. Importantly, a CBDC is not the same as "synthetic CBDCs," i.e., narrow-bank money (no direct claim) and not a liability issued by a central bank that is not in its own currency. In general, four forms of central bank money can be distinguished:

- *Central bank money in its current form.* This describes the existing form of central bank money as we know it in many countries (e.g., USD, GBP, and CHF).
- *Central bank accounts for all.* "Central bank accounts for all" is an approach where a central bank, in contrast to commercial banks, provides bank accounts for the society and business. An example is the "Dinero Electrónico," which was introduced in 2014 in Ecuador and used only until 2018, as the usage numbers were too low.
- *Central bank retail digital currencies.* This form of central bank money, also known as retail CBDC, provides digital central bank money that users can spend via a digital wallet. Current examples are the Bahamas Sand Dollar or the Digital Yuan in China (see case study below).
- *Central bank wholesale digital currencies.* Central bank wholesale digital currencies, also known as wholesale CBDC, refer to the settlement of interbank transfers and related wholesale transactions in central bank reserves. An example is the mCBDC project in Singapore for cross-border payments (see Sect. 3.4).

However, the motivations to engage with CBDC vary. Especially the emerging and developing economies have a strong focus on central bank retail digital currencies for monetary policy implementation, financial inclusion, and payments efficiency optimization, while industrialized countries focus more on wholesale CBDCs. In general, at least three kinds of motivations among different countries can be observed in this context for establishing retail CBDCs:

- *Create a new digital "store of value"* which aims at reducing cash management costs.
- *Deliver new payment functionality,* which aims at expanding financial access (e.g., facilitating government disbursement to citizens).
- *Achieve domestic political aims,* such as re-launching a domestic currency in "dollarized" markets.

However, all these CBDC projects face common challenges, including the handling of commercial bank deposits, potential disruptions to monetary policy and financial stability, as well as unintended spillover effects on other countries. For this, three major questions must be asked in the context of CBDCs: (1) Is a CBDC the best approach to achieve the goals? (2) How will a CBDC fit into the current system? (3) What role should the private sector play regarding responsibilities between the public and the private sector? Especially, the third question has recently attracted great interest, considering the discussion surrounding private stablecoins. So, what is the role of the private sector in the context of CBDCs? Table 3.4 summarizes some major retail CBDC features.

Despite all the new functionalities it is still unclear how CBDCs might be designed in a proper way. In fact, a CDBC would, through digitalization, simply turn the central bank's implicit lender-of-last-resort guarantee explicit and thus would only change the composition of bank funding (Brunnermeier & Niepelt, 2019). This seems to be obvious as central banks remain the issuer of money. But many questions are still unclear (e.g., you can exchange a banknote of which you have more than 50% in a new one but what happens if CDBCs are "destroyed"?). And what would the introduction of a retail CBDC mean from an economic perspective? Modern economies typically have a monetary system, which consists of two tiers: the first tier is based on non-financial institutions from the private sector that use deposit liabilities of banks (and claims on deposits) as payment instruments. The second tier, the commercial banks, conducts payments that are based on

Table 3.4 Retail CBDC functionality (BIS, 2021)

CBDC features	Description
Safety of funds	In normal and crisis periods, this distinguishing feature of central bank money relative to other forms of money could make a difference for users' adoption. The physical nature of cash helps support the identified difference between central bank and private money
Reduced cost	Consumers' utility is affected mostly by the transaction cost of the payment instrument. Although the overall cost of a CBDC system could increase with the complexity of its design, there should be little or no (explicit) cost to the CBDC end user
Offline	A CBDC could allow users to maintain the cash-like experience they are familiar with, together with the additional benefit of participating in the digital economy. This feature may be particularly relevant in environments where Internet availability is limited or unreliable
Security	Several factors affect an end user's overall perception of security: the reputation of (and trust in) the issuer, intermediaries, and the underlying technology; whether the involved entities are regulated; the level of fraud protection and end-user liability; and the quality of education and marketing campaigns. A CBDC might seek to adhere to a higher security standard to address these concerns
Privacy	Protecting an individual's privacy from both commercial providers and governments has the attributes of a basic right (BIS, 2021). CBDC could be designed to offer more privacy to users because the central bank would not have incentives to monetize the data
Accessibility	Accessible design is fundamental for both specific user groups (e.g., people with sensory, motor, and cognitive challenges) and the general population. CBDC end-user devices could be designed to improve on accessible digital interactions

central bank reserves (R) (as well as ςD which represents a fraction of the reserves from the deposits of the commercial banks) who themselves hold assets (A). In addition, the commercial banks hold deposits (D) and provide loans (L) to the public and private sector. However, the aforementioned design of a retail CBDC would allow a direct access of the private sector to the reserves. But what would be the macroeconomic effect of introducing such a retail CBDC?

In general, introducing a retail CBDC has an impact on both the balance sheets of both central and commercial banks (see Fig. 3.7). If some households would switch their commercial bank deposits (D) into a retail CBDC account (Δ), then commercial banks' deposits would be reduced to $D' = D - \Delta$. This means that the deposits would shift from the commercial bank to the central bank which then would hold these deposits. In addition, the reserves of the commercial bank would shrink as there is less need to hold higher reserves at the central bank due to the reduction in the clients' deposits (Δ (1 - ς)). With this, the central bank would have more available assets. In principle, these assets could flow back to the commercial banks, which could extend the loans for the commercial banks.

But what would the costs for the commercial banking sector be? As of today, a commercial bank usually pays an interest rate for the central bank reserves and operating costs for the payments infrastructure. In the case of a retail CBDC, as described above, the central bank would extend the loans for the commercial banks and the costs for the commercial banks would remain the same. However, the central banks, as they now operate the retail CBDC, would have higher costs and reduce operating costs on the commercial banking side. In a detailed calculation, Niepelt (2020) concludes that the funding cost reduction of commercial banks would have been around 0.4–0.8% of the GDP before and around the financial crisis and would have led to no reduction thereafter. Another impact of the introduction of a retail CBDC would be the increased transparency for consumers and lower taxes. Other factors like the impact of cash and the relationship between banks regarding proportions of CBDC/deposits and funding by the central bank's reserves are also questions which must be considered in such a scenario.

Despite the costs, CBDC holds a lot of potential. Among others, these are easier access to central bank money (e.g., in countries where cash declines like in Sweden) and improved resilience while at the same time imposing stability and sovereignty

Central Bank		Commercial Bank	
A	R	$R = \zeta D$	D
		L	

Central Bank		Commercial Bank	
A	R'	$R' = \zeta D'$	$D' = D - \Delta$
...	$CBDC = \Delta$	L	$\Delta(1 - \zeta)$

Fig. 3.7 Balance sheet comparison of central and commercial banks in the case of the current fiat system and a retail CBDC (Niepelt 2020)

risks. Table 3.5 summarizes potential benefits and risks of CBDCs (Bank of England, 2020, 16ff; Economist, 2021).

Current discussions are often centered around national CBDC projects. But if CBDCs are placed in an international context, they can aggravate existing weaknesses of the international monetary system. At least three challenges could arise:

- *Reserve currencies.* First, CBDCs may induce a shift in the configuration of reserve currencies. Throughout history, transitions from one dominant currency to another often took many decades. The last shift in global dominance of a currency happened from the 1940s until the 1970s where the US dollar increased its dominance as a reserve currency from approx. 10% to almost 90% ((IMF, 2020), (Economist, 2020)). This demonstrates the large inertia in reserve currency holdings which transforms in decades and centuries rather than years. While in the last few years the trade links between single countries have declined, the financial connections have risen in importance. Digital currencies could speed up the transition to alternative reserve configurations induced by CBDCs and stablecoins. In addition, geopolitical developments may lead to an even greater reserve fragmentation in the future (Burns et al., 2020). Digital money, and CBDCs, could accelerate this transition. One possible outcome is a reinforcement of the existing unipolar global reserve system centered around the US dollar. In this system, the perceived safety and trust in the reserve asset would likely persist, but liquidity provision may not significantly expand despite the lower transaction

Table 3.5 Benefits and risks of CBDCs (BIS, 2020b)

Benefits	**Description**
Access	Easier/improved access to central bank money, especially in countries with declining cash
Resilience	Additional payment method which improves operational resilience, especially for geographically remote locations. However, cyber risks provide a challenge
Diversity	CBDCs could provide a homogenous infrastructure for fragmented payment systems and thus increase the diversity of payment instruments (decreasing monopolies of payment system providers)
Inclusion	CBDCs could increase financial inclusion if embedded in a wider set of reforms in other areas (e.g., regulation)
Borderlessness	CBDCs might decrease the complexity of cross-border payments if it is designed interoperable
Privacy	CBDCs might decrease frauds due to a better balance between public privacy and reducing illegal activity
Risks	**Description**
Stability	CBDCs might increase runs (digital runs) into central bank money and disintermediating commercial banks which then could focus on wholesale funding while losing deposits. In addition, it might lead to the circumvention of rules, sanctions, and compliance requirements
Sovereignty	CBDCs (especially foreign ones from the perspective of one country) and private stablecoins use might have a negative impact on the use of the domestic sovereign currency (e.g., "digital dollarization") and could lead to the substitution of this currency

costs. Moreover, the greater risk of currency substitution may weaken monetary policy independence in some countries. An alternative is the emergence of additional new dominant reserve currencies—a multipolar scenario with regional CBDC blocs. These blocs could allow for more efficient risk sharing and a greater and more diverse supply of global safe assets. However, they could also make the system less stable if some of these CBDC blocs are fragmented due to weak interoperability. This underscores the need for cooperation across such blocs and would require supranational coordination.
- *Management of capital flows.* A second challenge posed by CBDCs relates to the management of capital flows, which are expected to be larger and more volatile with digital money, aggravating well-known instabilities of the system. Bystander countries may face the difficult challenge of integrating their currencies into this digital system while losing some autonomy of their macroeconomic policies. However, capital account restrictions could become easier to implement to help manage these flows if CBDCs are properly designed. In this design, policymakers will need to consider the trade-off between traceability and privacy protection to ensure appropriate monitoring and controls while maintaining their attractiveness to the public.
- *Reserve accumulation.* Third, CBDCs may alter the incentives for reserve accumulation. With greater currency substitution or more volatile capital flows, central banks may increase foreign reserves holdings with precautionary motives, possibly exacerbating global imbalances. The incentives to supply more safe assets may also vary among reserve issuers, who could have different policy objectives for internationalizing their CBDCs, leading to shortages or instability in the system.

All these developments call for more cooperation, more multilateralism, and less fragmentation. This requires a comprehensive policy framework with policy principles related to privately issued digital currencies, CBDCs, and the international monetary system. Potential solution approaches to these aspects are the creation of problem-solving collaborative networks, knowledge sharing and co-production, the introduction of governance structures and standards, as well as the promotion of transparency, legitimacy, and accountability. A major prerequisite for CBDCs to flourish are institution-based (linked with the institutional environment), process-based (develops from reputation and experience), characteristics-based (based on characteristics and associations with cultural elements or groups), and system-based forms of trust. For example, in the 1800s and 1900s the emergence of distance for transactions over longer distances and then later the emergence of communication networks required other forms than face-to-face based peer-to-peer transactions and led to the development of intermediaries for ensuring trust among anonymous parties. That was the time when system-based trust evolved. An example are shares that were transferred from paper to IT systems in the 1960s. However, system-based trust is difficult to establish. An example is continuously linked settlement (CLS), an alert method type that enables both investment managers and broker/dealers to populate their foreign exchange CLS instructions and publish them to their respective counterparties. CLS usually requires many years until a new currency can be used. For example, the Chilean Peso took around 3 years to be implemented. The reason is that CLS operates on netting which is ultimately based on trust. In the same way, CBDC interlinking also will require trust in such a shared settlement system (e.g., where are the IT systems domiciled?). Can this trust ultimately be established with technology (e.g., blockchain)?

The following case studies show some examples of CBDCs which not only demonstrate the different motivations but also the different ways of how they are implemented.

Case Study: CBDC in Bhutan

- The Royal Monetary Authority (RMA) of Bhutan pilots a CBDC using the Ripple CBDC Private Ledger, mainly for the purpose of financial inclusion.
- The RMA will use the CBDC for retail, cross-border, and wholesale payment use cases for a digital Ngultrum (their local currency) in phases using Ripple's blockchain technology platform.
- The CBDC project shall increase financial inclusion in Bhutan to 85% and will also be available with offline functionality.

Source: Ripple

Case Study: Stablecoin in Palau

- The Western Pacific Island State Republic of Palau aims to create a government-issued national stablecoin.
- The initial focus is on developing strategies for cross-border payments and a US dollar-backed digital currency for Palau. The next stage will see the implementation of a government-backed national stablecoin.
- The benefits to the Republic of Palau are:
  - Mint, manage, redeem, and destroy stablecoins along the complete life cycle.
  - Enable secure, anonymous transactions.
  - Bridge disparate currencies.
  - Accelerate payments.
  - Low energy use with low carbon footprint.
  - Gain trust and credibility.
- An offline version is an important feature for Palau because of religious ceremonies, power outages, etc. Currently, a paper-based version is used.

Source: Ripple

Case Study: CBDC at the **Bank of Japan**

- Japan currently explores the potential use of a CBDC. However, the decision if a CBDC should be issued will require judgment by the people of Japan.

- Nevertheless, the central bank decided to explore potential design options to help such a decision making for the future, as technologies in this field are developing very fast.
- Therefore, the Bank of Japan carries out experiments and explores policy issues:
  - Proof of Concept Phase 1: was completed in March 2022.
  - Proof of Concept Phase 2: started in April 2022.
  - Focus areas of policy exploration include allocation of roles, financial stability, privacy and AML/CFT, and cross-border payments.
- A Liaison and Coordination Committee was founded, where diverse stakeholders discussed the future of payments and published an interim report in May 2022.
- The Bank of Japan will stay committed to supplying cash, as long as public demand exists, as this payment instrument still makes up a significant part in Japan (see Fig. 3.8).
- Therefore, as of today, a CBDC could only complement other payment instruments and would coexist with cash, bank deposits, and other forms of private digital money (horizontal coexistence; see Fig. 3.9).
- As part of the vertical coexistence, the CBDC system would be divided into an "foundational instrument" and "overlay services." The foundational instrument is created as a public good, provided by the central bank

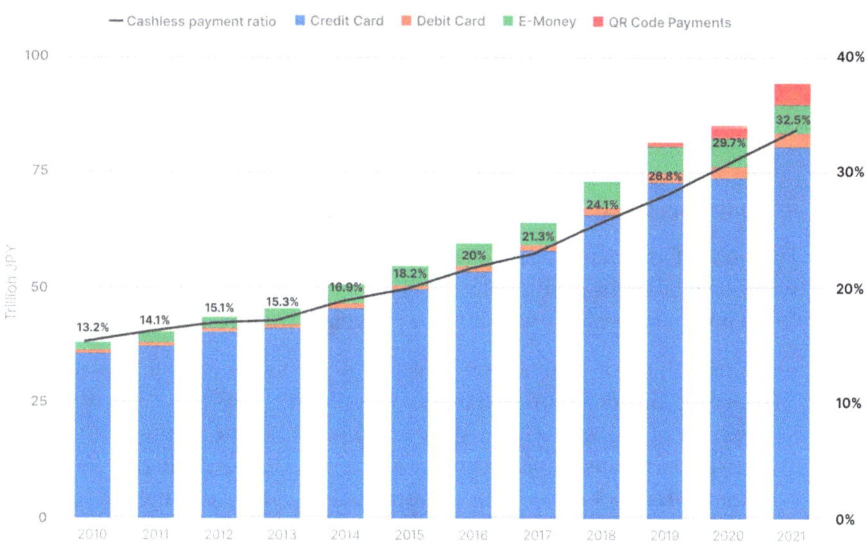

Fig. 3.8 Use of different payment instruments in Japan

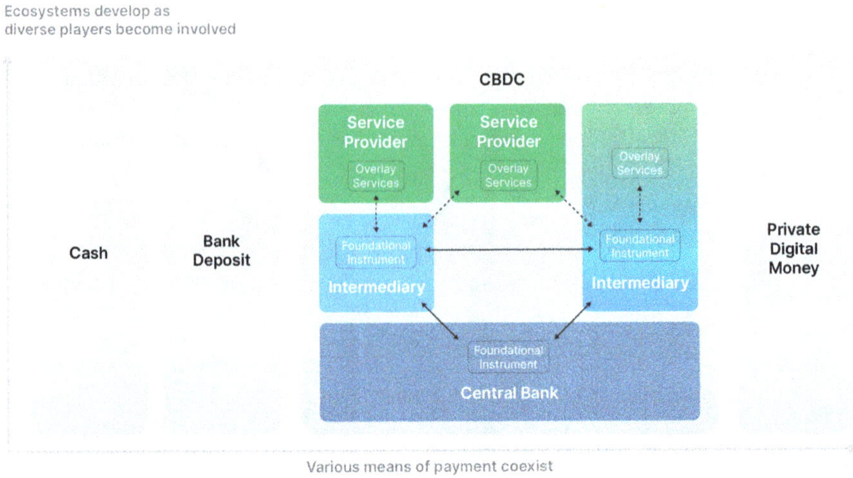

Fig. 3.9 Ecosystems and payment instruments

and other intermediaries. Overlay services are created by private third parties and offer customer-oriented services.

- For the next steps the following activities are planned:
  - Technologies.

    Proof of Concept Phase 2: User convenience, economic design (caps for holdings/transactions, remunerations, fees).
    Interoperability with other IT infrastructures.
    Considerations on possible field testing/pilot program.
    Research on technologies other than a "CBDC ledger".
    Follow-up on developments abroad.
  - Cost design for a sustainable CBDC system.
  - Legal design for certainty.
  - Communication.
- The goal of the current activities is to design "payment and settlement systems suitable for the digital society."
- Other important projects with a link to payments in Japan are:
  - A consortium of commercial banks with the aim to issue a stablecoin. However, this project is still in the pilot phase.
  - Creation of a post-payment system (named "Kotora") for small-value peer-to-peer transactions. This project is based on a debit card system from the Bank of Japan. This project shall be launched in the forthcoming months.

Source: Bank of Japan

Case Study: The Digital Dollar Project

- The Digital Dollar Project, a partnership between Accenture and the Digital Dollar Foundation, is a neutral, nonprofit, and non-partisan forum focused on exploring digital innovation in money and future-proofing the US dollar and its reserve currency status in a coming world of decentralized and centralized, digital currency networks. The Project does not call for ready deployment of a US CBDC. Yet, it does encourage the USA to assert principled leadership in CBDC consideration at home and digital currency standard setting abroad that is consistent with democratic norms, values, and rule of law.
- The Digital Dollar Project is devoted to real-world testing of the challenges and opportunities of sovereign digital money. The champion model of CBDC that the Project first published in 2020 is today the most common form of CBDC being examined by agencies of the world's democracies. In 2023, the Project published the results of a first-of-its-kind study on the retail use of a US digital dollar ("Retail Cross-Border Remittance Payments"). That study revealed the potential of a digital dollar to reduce counterparty risk, decrease settlement times, expand access, and provide greater visibility and transparency to individuals sending money to loved ones worldwide. This pilot followed on the Digital Dollar Project's earlier work exploring CBDC for securities settlement. The Digital Dollar, a technology-neutral project, is based on the concepts of tokenized fiat money, not account-based money, where the process of verification is different. Tokenized verification is primarily confirmed by the recipient who confirms that the token is authentic. This means that tokenized money can be transferred directly between peers without any third parties involved in the process. On the other hand, account-based money requires third-party authentication of the identity of both parties for a specific transaction.
- The Digital Dollar Project has initiated 9 pilot projects to test the application of the Digital Dollar which include the following stakeholders: (1) un- and underbanked consumers (rural, urban, and benefits distribution), (2) banked consumers (national usage), (3) SME and multinational users (small business, multinational business users), (4) financial market infrastructure players (international payments, domestic payment/transfers, domestic atomic settlement). The pilot programs are designed to explore how a US CBDC could serve important public policy goals while addressing specific challenges faced by different economic stakeholders, including consumers, businesses, financial institutions, and fintech startups.

Source: www.digitaldollarproject.org

Case Study: The People's Bank of China e-CNY

- The e-CNY pilots are now open to pilot regions and specified industries. By the end of 2022, e-CNY covered 17 provinces, with a total of 83 million wallets opened through e-CNY App.
- The e-CNY aims to create a digital version of the renminbi that meets the growing demand for money in the digital economy era. With this, the e-CNY can be defined as the digital version of fiat currency issued by the People's Bank of China (PBoC) and operated by authorized operators. E-CNY with physical RMB is a component of the fiat currency system. Meanwhile, e-CNY is a value-based, quasi-account-based, and account-based hybrid payment instrument, with legal tender status and loosely coupled account linkage, and supports managed anonymity.
- The e-CNY system is based on a two-tier architecture in which the PBoC is responsible for issuance and disposal. Additionally, it selects commercial banks as authorized operators to provide e-CNY exchange services. The e-CNY has three motivations:
  - *First*, the e-CNY aims to improve the efficiency of central bank money issuance and central bank payment systems. It has the objective of reducing costs and improving the efficiency of currency issuance, circulation, and statistical analysis, while also enhancing payment systems in terms of coverage, participants, capacity, efficiency, and operating hours.
  - *Second*, the e-CNY will provide a backup or redundancy to the retail payment system and upgrade the payment instrument. By offering e-CNY as a universal payment instrument, PBoC can ensure that the public always has access to central bank money in the digital economy. While bigtech companies have become very important for retail payments that might lead to systemic risks, the e-CNY will provide a backup or redundancy for the retail payment system to maintain the public access to payment services even when any malfunction happened to other electronic payment methods.
  - *Third*, the e-CNY aims to promote financial inclusion. The e-CNY enables underbanked people in the remote and poor areas to have access to more financial services. Besides, the e-CNY has developed accessibility payment products and services for physically challenged people and the elderly who may have digital gap in using smart devices or electronic payment instruments. The e-CNY also facilitates access for foreign visitors who may experience difficulties in making mobile payments in China.
- Currently, the system is based on four different wallet categories based on the different KYC levels. The fourth category can be opened with a mobile phone number. For the third and second category, which allows for higher

amounts of transactions, users must provide more information like their ID and bank account information. The first category requires the wallet account to be opened at a bank branch. This then allows transactions without any limits.

- Importantly, the e-CNY is not intended to substitute the cash system, but complement it for so long, as cash is demanded by the public for payments. In addition, the e-CNY system aims to provide anonymity for small-value transactions and the ability to trace high-value transactions in the case of illegal and criminal activities and to comply with AML/CFT requirements. Finally, the e-CNY aims to provide payment programmability (e.g., by deploying smart contracts, enabling conditional payments, guaranteed payments, etc.).
- Another important characteristic is the e-CNY interoperability. It today supports the major e-commerce platforms in China by providing a e-CNY payment by aligning with those platforms' payment settlement mechanisms (see Fig. 3.10). This can either be a jump-app payments method, where users jump from the e-commerce provider's app to the e-CNY app or a closed-loop payments method, where users pay within the merchant's wallet having the e-CNY checkout completely integrated in their own wallet (see Fig. 3.10). In addition, the e-CNY is also interoperable with traditional payment gateway integration mechanisms, such as payment terminals in shops, QR codes, etc.
- A new functionality of the e-CNY is the so-called "red packet" which allows users to make money presents to individuals and collect money from groups (see Fig. 3.11). This connects the e-CNY app also to other social media platforms.

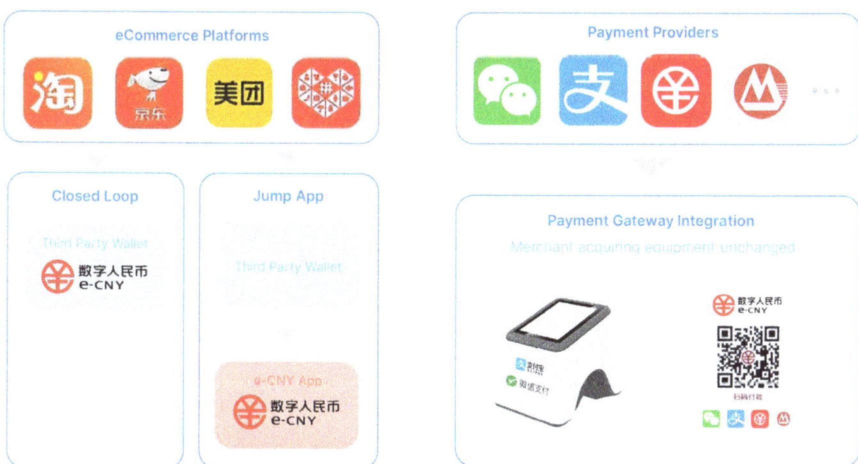

Fig. 3.10 e-CNY interoperability

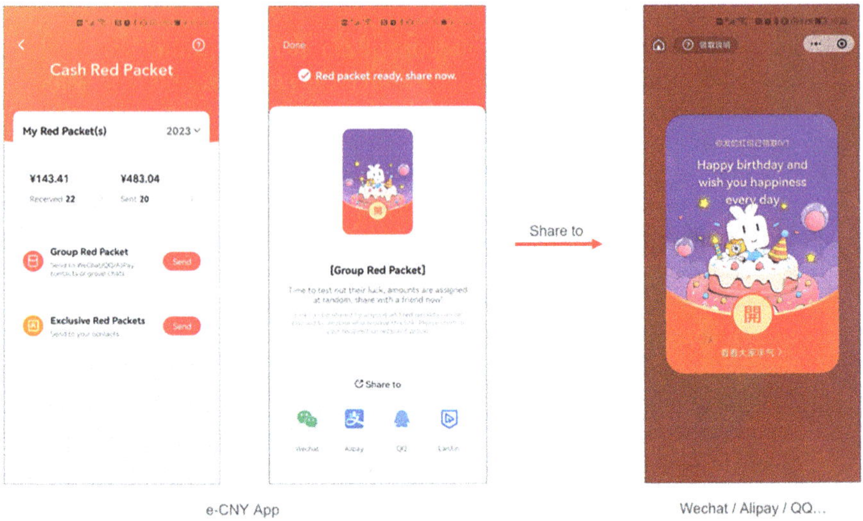

Fig. 3.11 Cash red packets

- Another dimension of interoperability is cross-border interoperability which is also part of the G20's initiative on using CBDCs as an instrument to solve the issue of slow and costly cross-border payments. This might follow three guiding principles:
  - *No disruption.* The issuance and use of different CBDCs and their use for cross-border payments should not disrupt the status quo of each involved jurisdiction.
  - *Compliance.* Cross-border arrangements with CBDC should comply with all involved jurisdictions.
  - *Interoperability.* Interoperability between different CBDCs of different jurisdictions could be processed though the conversion of different currencies at the virtual "border" of digital wallets using a blockchain platform for currency exchange. An example is the mBridge project which was explored by 20 central banks (see https://www.bis.org/about/bisih/topics/cbdc/mcbdc_bridge.htm). Exemplary use cases are international trade, supply chain financing, etc.

Source: People's Bank of China

Case Study: The Digital Euro

- The Digital Euro is discussed in the European Union as a complement to cash and central bank deposits. It is understood as a digital central bank liability for retail payments of citizens and businesses in the entire Euro area and shall have the following characteristics:
  - *Complementing,* not substituting, cash and wholesale central bank deposits.

- *Supervised intermediaries* (payment service providers (PSPs), such as banks) will facilitate the distribution of a digital euro.
- *Source of innovation and public good*, shall not crowd out banks nor hinder innovation in payments.

• The main reasons for the implementation of the Digital Euro are (1) to ensure access to public money and its role as monetary anchor and (2) to protect the European strategic autonomy and monetary sovereignty, while avoiding market dominance of private providers. This shall be insured by defining five core principles for the Digital Euro, namely:

- *Conversion*. Convertible at par with other forms of the Euro.
- *Trust*. Should be trusted like all other forms of the Euro.
- *Neutrality*. Shall not crowd out private initiatives and solutions.
- *Accessibility*. Widely accessible on equal terms throughout euro area.
- *Risk*. Should not create financial or other undue risks to the Eurosystem.

• Currently, the Digital Euro focuses on p2p, c2b, and X2G/G2X payment scenarios. It does not consider b2b and machine-initiated payments. The Eurosystem is considering a payment scheme approach which aims at developing a common rules-based framework for participants to develop their products. These scenarios will be implemented based on two releases (see Fig. 3.12). This covers first a p2p and e-commerce version and the second one physical stores. However, a full anonymity and full transparency to the central bank are not to be pursued. Instead, the baseline scenario is that limited data is transparent to the intermediaries for customer onboarding and AML/CFT purposes, as is the case for electronic payments today. The settlement of digital euros which are transferred between two parties could therefore be done by so-called hierarchical deterministic

Fig. 3.12 Planned digital Euro roll-out phases

(HD) wallets. In this case the infrastructure would only "see" payments between randomly created wallet addresses, as such a HD wallet creates randomly generates key that are backed up in the wallet. For cross-border payments, the digital euro is based on the same principle as the e-CNY, where a virtual border between two countries exists. This means that a digital euro can only be used domestically to reduce the risk of "euroization," etc.

- The Digital Euro will not be programmable, but it will allow for conditional or automated payments. Table 3.6 summarizes all the requirements of the Digital Euro.

Table 3.6 Requirements of a Digital Euro

Requirement	Description
Enhanced digital efficiency	The Digital Euro should always keep pace with state-of-the-art technology in order to best address the needs of the market as regards, among other attributes, usability, convenience, speed, cost-efficiency, and programmability. It should be made available through standard interoperable front-end solutions throughout the entire euro area and should be interoperable with private payment solutions
Cash-like features	To match the key distinctive features of cash, a digital euro aiming to tackle a decline in the acceptance of cash should permit offline payments. Moreover, a Digital Euro should be easy for vulnerable groups to use and free of charge for basic use by payers and should protect privacy. It should have a strong European branding
Competitive features	The Digital Euro should have features which are at the technological frontier. It should offer the basis for providing functionalities that are at least as attractive as those of the payment solutions available in foreign currencies or through unregulated entities
Monetary policy option	If considered to be a tool for improving the transmission of monetary policy, the digital euro should be remunerated at interest rate(s) that the central bank can modify over time
Backup system	If aiming to improve the overall resilience of the payment system, the Digital Euro should be widely available and transacted via resilient channels that are separate from those of other payment services and can withstand extreme events
International use	The Digital Euro should be potentially accessible outside the euro area in a way that is consistent with the objectives of the Eurosystem and convenient to non-euro area residents
Cost saving	If launched for cost-efficiency: The design of the Digital Euro should achieve a reduction in the cost of the current payment ecosystem
Environmentally friendly	The design of the Digital Euro should be based on technological solutions that minimize its ecological footprint and improve that of the current payment ecosystem
Ability to control the amount of digital euro in circulation	The Digital Euro should be an attractive means of payment but should be designed so as to avoid its use as a form of investment and the associated risk of large shifts from private money (e.g., bank deposits) to Digital Euro

Table 3.6 (continued)

Requirement	Description
Cooperation with market participants	A project to introduce a digital euro should be carried out in line with best practices in IT project management. The Digital Euro should then be made available on an equal basis in all euro countries through supervised intermediaries, which could leverage their existing customer facing services and avoid the costly duplication of processes
Compliance with the regulatory framework	Although central bank liabilities are not subject to regulation and oversight, in issuing the digital euro the Eurosystem should still aim at complying with regulatory standards, including in the area of payments
Safety and efficiency in the fulfillment of the Eurosystem's goals	The Digital Euro should be designed in a safe and efficient way. Its project and operating costs should be estimated and compared with the expected benefits, considering alternative solutions in any future scenario. The provision of non-core services should be left to supervised private entities
Easy accessibility throughout the euro area	The Digital Euro should be made available through standardized front-end solutions throughout the entire euro area and should be interoperable with private payment solutions. It should be easily accessible by anyone, including citizens who currently do not participate in the financial system (e.g., those who do not have an account at a commercial bank), and should be easy to use. The Digital Euro would need to coexist with cash
Conditional use by non-euro area residents	The design of the Digital Euro should include specific conditions for access and use by non-euro area residents, to ensure that it does not contribute to excessively volatile capital flows or exchange rates. Such conditions could take the form, for instance, of limits or adequate remuneration policies for holdings of Digital Euro of non-euro area residents
Cyber resilience	Digital Euro services will need to be highly resilient to cyber threats and capable of providing a high level of protection to the financial ecosystem from cyberattacks. In the event of successful attacks, the recovery time should be short and the integrity of the data protected

- The Digital Euro project was started in the fourth quarter of 2021 based on a governing council decision. After a prioritization of use cases, the project focused on the definition of privacy levels and offline/online availability, the discussion of design options and the distribution model as well as the settlement model, the role of intermediaries and the amount in circulation, the compensation model, the access to the Digital Euro ecosystem, value-added services, advanced functionalities, and prototyping results. This was followed by a governing council decision to launch the realization phase in autumn 2023.

Source: Public Material of the European Central Bank

Case Study: BIS Innovation Hub CBDC Projects

- The BIS Innovation Hub has a threefold mandate:
  - Identify, in a structured and systematic way, critical trends in technology affecting central banking in different locations and develop in-depth insights into these technologies that can be shared with the central banking community.
  - Develop public goods in the technology space geared toward improving the functioning of the global financial system.
  - Serve as the focal point for a network of central bank experts on innovation, with regular events to promote exchange of views and knowledge sharing. These efforts complement the well-established cooperation within the BIS-hosted committees.
- The BIS Innovation Hub has developed several projects which all address the development of wholesale or retail CBDCs. All of them are based on the concept of a single common platform.
- The People's Bank of China and the Central Bank of the United Arab Emirates joined the original members of ILR2 to create a third phase of the project under the umbrella of BISIH Hong Kong Centre, renamed Project mBridge. The work of the previous ILR2 proof of concept (PoC) was extended to explore multi-currency cross-border payment capabilities built on DLT. It envisages the development of a DLT platform through which multiple central banks can issue their own CBDC and distribute it to participants. These participants can in turn conduct peer-to-peer payments and redeem the CBDC for reserves at the issuing central bank.
- The BISIH Hong Kong Centre completed Project Inthanon-LionRock2 (ILR2) together with the Hong Kong Monetary Authority and the Bank of Thailand. The goal of the project mBridge was to explore the use of DLT for facilitating real-time cross-border funds transfers using an atomic payment versus payment mechanism for foreign exchange transactions between the two jurisdictions.
- The project Dunbar brought together the Reserve Bank of Australia, Bank Negara Malaysia, the Monetary Authority of Singapore, and the South African Reserve Bank with the BISIH to test the use of multiple wholesale CBDCs for international settlements. The project developed two prototypes, based on different DLTs, for a shared platform that could enable international settlements using digital currencies issued by multiple central banks. The platform was designed to facilitate direct cross-border transactions between financial institutions in different currencies, with the potential to cut costs and increase the speed of settlement.
- The project Jura explored the direct transfer of euro and Swiss franc wholesale CBDCs between French and Swiss commercial banks on a single DLT platform operated by a third party. Tokenized asset and FX trades were settled using PvP and delivery-versus-payment mechanisms. The Jura

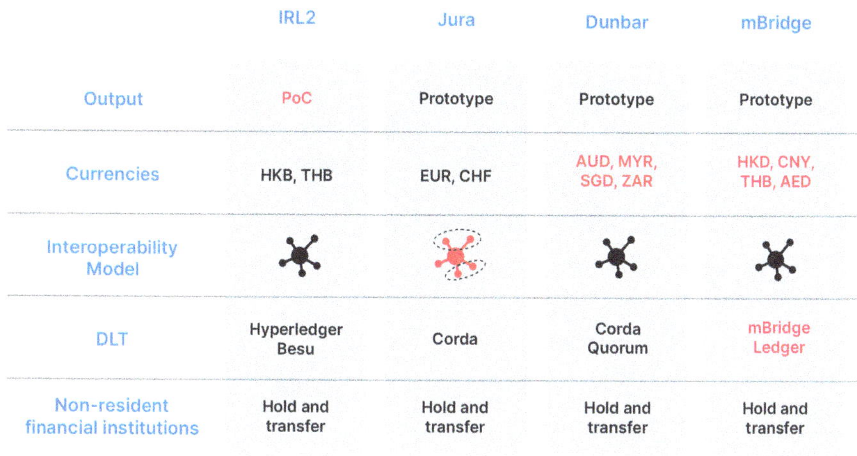

Fig. 3.13 Overview on selected BIS innovation hub projects

experiment was conducted in a near-real setting, using real-value transactions and complying with current regulatory requirements.

- The four projects differ in terms of their output, the currencies used, and the underlying technical infrastructure (see Fig. 3.13).

Source: Bank for International Settlements

The CBDC approaches in Table 3.7 reflect the countries' different motivations and purposes. Some of the characteristics are not yet specified, which also shows that many CBDC initiatives are still in an exploration or pilot phase rather than an implementation phase.

3.3.3 *Architectures of CBDCs*

Although blockchain technology has been discussed in the context of CBDCs as the major technology approach in recent years, a traditional approach using centralized database technology might also be an option in some cases. The main difference between the two architecture options is the way data is managed. A conventional database technology typically stores data distributed among multiple physical nodes which are controlled by a single central entity. Contrariwise, a blockchain is jointly managed by different entities. Updating data between them requires harmonization among the different nodes involving consensus mechanisms (see Sect. 2.4). Importantly, both architecture designs have strengths and weaknesses, yet different ones. While in a centralized system the central node is the most vulnerable part, the

Table 3.7 Comparison of CBDC initiatives

CBDC Initiatives Characteristics	EU (Digital Euro)	USA (Digital Dollar Project)	China (e-CNY)	Japan (Digital Yen)	Bhutan (Digital Ngultrum)
Type	Retail CBDC	Retail CBDC	Retail CBDC	Retail CBDC	Retail CBDC
Phase	Research	Research	Pilot	Research	Pilot
Focus	p2p, b2c, x2g/g2x	P2p, b2c	p2p, b2c	p2p, b2c	p2p, b2c
Purpose	(1) Efficiency (2) Protect the European strategic autonomy and monetary sovereignty	(1) Efficiency (2) Financial inclusion	(1) Financial inclusion (2) Interoperability	(1) Payment instrument alongside cash (2) Supporting private payment services	(1) Financial inclusion (2) Efficient and cost-effective cross-border transfers
Cross-border payments	Yes	Yes	Yes	Not specified yet	Yes
Programmability	No	No	Yes	Not specified yet	No
Interoperability	Yes	No	Yes	Yes	No
Offline functionality	Yes	No	Yes	Not specified yet	Yes
Architecture	Account-based (HD wallets)	Token-based	Account-based	Not specified yet	Account-based

consensus mechanism is the equivalent vulnerable element in a blockchain-based system. For example, benefits such as improved resilience and security may be more easily implemented through distributed systems. Some of the major barriers of blockchain-based CBDCs include (Welfare, 2019; BIS, 2020b):

- *Control vs. innovation.* Central banks need to balance currency management and stability with innovation.
- *Confirming identities.* Central banks need to confirm the identities of users to ensure appropriate behavior.
- *Connecting across borders.* Central banks need to create global frameworks and standards to facilitate cross-border payments.
- *Non-bank channels.* Central banks need to provide non-bank participants access to core payment systems.

Although a concept for the implementation of digital cash was already suggested early by Chaum (1983), the implementation did not catch up since then. But the introduction of Nakamoto's (2008) proposal for a p2p Bitcoin architecture has led to various novel concepts for digital money from both private institutions (e.g., Diem) and central banks (e.g., Bahamas Sand Dollar, e-CNY). But so far, the proposed digital money architectures differ regarding various dimensions, such as the stakeholders involved (e.g., wholesale and retail CBDC) and the applied network architecture (centralized vs. decentralized). For example, literature on CBDCs frequently distinguishes between wholesale CBDCs with limited access to financial institutions and retail CBDCs, which are accessible to the public (Bech and Garratt 2017). While wholesale CBDCs would only replace existing real-time gross settlement systems (RTGS) in payments with, e.g., blockchain-based systems, retail CBDCs could, depending on their design (direct access of consumers to central bank money or indirect access via commercial banks), have far more impact than wholesale CBDCs. While blockchain was often used in the context of consortia, a CBDC, which is issued by a central bank, could also benefit from a centralized architecture, where a trusted party, the central bank, provides the central node.

Another important distinction is between account-based CBDCs (e.g., analogous to central bank reserves) and token-based CBDCs (e.g., analogous to banknotes). While a token-based CBDC, which relies on cash, has proven transaction privacy (a banknote can be anonymously handed over from one person to another), this has not yet been the case for a digital token-based CBDC (Garratt et al. 2020). But such an architecture has recently been proposed by Chaum and Moser (2022). One important benefit of such a token-based CBDC architecture, compared to an account-based CBDC, is that token-based systems would also work offline (users could exchange the tokens peer-to-peer without involving any intermediaries) and would provide the same level of privacy as cash. The key components and benefits of this architecture are (Chaum and Moser, 2022):

- Free and *open-source software* implementation to provide wide adoption as well as improved integration and interoperability between all involved stakeholders (merchants, consumers, banks, etc.).
- All consumer and merchant *interactions are via commercial banks* (which are also responsible for authentication, etc.), while money creation and database management are provided by a central bank which ensures KYC and AML/CFT compliance.
- The CBDC is a *genuine digital bearer instrument* because when the user withdraws money in the form of a number, this number is "blinded" by the system's encryption.
- Digital signatures distinguish *private and public keys*, where the owner of a private key can solely sign a message and the public key can be used by anyone to verify a private key owner's signature.
- *Blind signatures* protect the privacy of payers and payees like the exchange of banknotes in a physical transaction.
- A *key-exchange protocol* provides a link between an original coin and the change returned without losing transparency and privacy (e.g., GNU Taler, www.gnu.org).

The technology around this concept called "eCash 2.0" is designed to be secure against counterfeiters with access to quantum computing. For this, the concept of mix networks can be applied, which makes it possible to send virtually untraceable communications. This approach is used in eCash 2.0 to preserve privacy while addressing the threat of a quantum computer being used in counterfeiting. Every coin formed uses a one-way function by any user's device which is forwarded through a mix network to be checked against a database of spent coins by the central bank. These one-way functions ensure that even quantum computing cannot be used to forge a coin already on the list. Additionally, the solution can be implemented on public blockchains and be extended to offline use. When a user spends CBDC, the process is analogous to paying a merchant for a good or a service in cash: the customer's phone transmits coins in the payment amount to the merchant. In the next step, the merchant's system validates the payment details and passes the coins (together with the merchant's account information) to the merchant's commercial bank. The merchant's commercial bank then validates that this is one of its merchant customers and forwards the digital coins to the central bank. Since a corrupted customer device might attempt to spend the same coins more than once, the central bank verifies the signature but also checks for double spending in its own database(s). If everything is in order, the central bank credits the commercial bank's account at the central bank and sends confirmation to the commercial bank. Next, the commercial bank credits the merchant's account and informs the merchant, so the merchant can release the product to the customer.

Figure 3.14 shows how the withdrawal process for a token-based CBDC would work from a user's point of view. This process is the same as withdrawing banknotes from an ATM; however, the transaction in the background involves the elements described earlier: First, a user authenticates itself to the commercial bank and the user's smartphone or computer obtains the public denomination key which is provided by the central bank. Second, the application installed on the user's phone or computer computes the key pair for a coin, for which the public key is then hashed and blinded. Third, the user sends the public key for the withdrawal of the coin and to debit the user's account to the commercial bank. Fourth, the bank debits the amount from the user's account and authorizes the request to the central bank. Fifth, the central bank authorizes the request. Sixth, the central bank deducts the amount from the commercial bank's balance and blindly signs the coin. Seventh, it returns the blind signature to the commercial bank which, eight, forwards it to the user's digital wallet, where, ninth, it can be used as an unblinded "minted" coin.

3.3.4 Banknote Design and CBDC

CBDC, and here specifically retail CBDC, is currently the only digital, user-accessible form of money that is a liability of the central bank. Because of these attributes, it might have the potential to expand financial inclusion. However, CBDC is not a payments instrument with common attributes across countries but reflects various approaches which differ significantly. That is why there must be further knowledge gathered about the design of a retail CBDC and how it will derive value from these different attributes that might make it eventually more accessible to all. For example, in Africa it used to be very popular to use payment cards to transfer money from one person to another by simply texting the code on the back of the

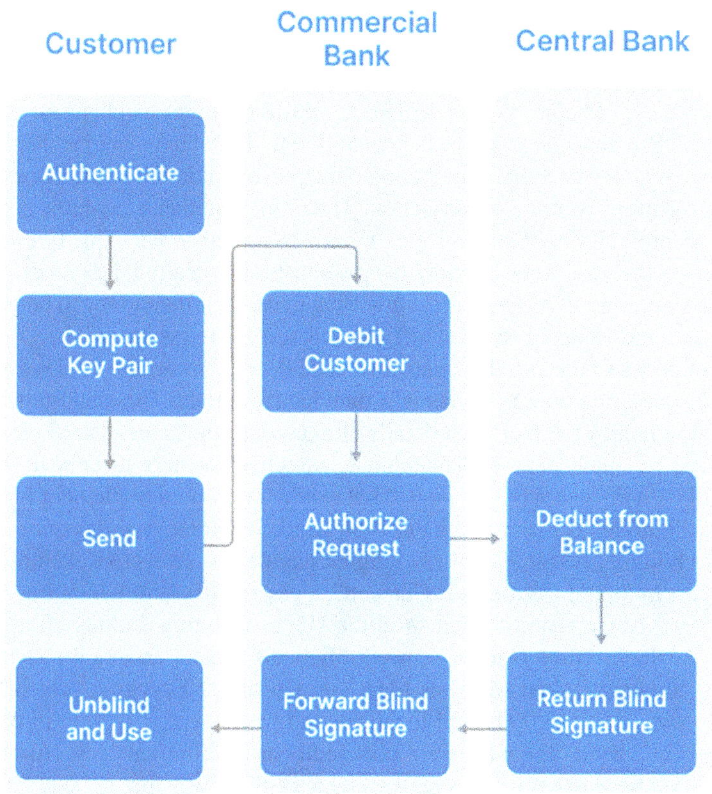

Fig. 3.14 CBDC withdrawal process (according to Chaum & Moser, 2022)

payment card which then automatically releases the amount for which the payment card is authorized. Later, other forms of mobile payment like M-PESA in Kenya or QR code payments like Bharat, etc. emerged. A good illustration of how people in Africa still today use money is a very traditional one. In Africa, people sometimes visit soothsayers who call their ancestors and usually pay a consultation fee for this. Very often, these soothsayers do only accept cash, as they want to touch and feel the money. In a broader study about existing digital and mobile payment systems in Nigeria, India, Mexico, and Indonesia, the following areas were explored as relevant (Narula et al., 2023):

- *Monetary ecology.* What are the sets of instruments that people use to pay? For example, people use all kinds of instruments like different banknotes, animals, etc.
- *Monetary repertoires.* What can one do with those instruments and how? For example, in many countries people use different repertoires to ultimately get US banknotes.

The key results from this analysis are that (1) social intermediaries matter, which means that there are always humans involved because, for example, there is only one person in a village who has a mobile phone, because of financial illiteracy, etc. (2) Another important takeaway is that digital networks are often unreliable so there needs to be a fallback (e.g., induced by natural catastrophes, etc.). And (3), trust is paramount (e.g., whether people will stick with a payment mechanism, including banknotes). But how can this trust be transferred to digital payment mechanisms? In an interview in North India, for example, one person claimed: "Sometimes money gets stuck while executing a transaction. The money neither goes back to the customer's account and neither can I give money to the customer. This has led many customers in the post office blaming the postmaster for stealing the money from the customer's account. Customers are not willing to wait for the money to be sent back to their account. Hence, I stopped offering this service to everyone."

One important aspect in this context is fraud. For example, the Paytm Spoof app is used by scanning the QR codes in a merchant's outlets. The fraudsters use this moment to identify the merchant details and then use the same data to create their customized payment page and manipulate merchant owners to believe that they have paid with the exact bill amount. That is why an important element for trust in the case of banknotes is the genuineness on which banknote designers have already spent much time. The same applies to digital payment systems. An example for the role of trust in digital payments is CurrentC, a payment system which was founded in 2011 by a consortium of retailers in the USA, including Walmart, Target, Best Buy, CVS, Shell, Olive Garden, Lowes, Michaels, Sears, and more. These firms started a company called MCX or Merchant Customer Exchange which by then covered more than 110,000 retail locations and processed $1 trillion in payments annually. The overall aim was to cut out credit cards with their fees. However, the project failed because of various reasons. One of them was that nobody knew who was standing behind this initiative (no branding of the founding companies). Another one was focusing on solving the retailers' problem instead of a customer problem, while knowing that credit cards are very popular in the USA. Instead, purchases made over CurrentC were debited directly from customers' bank accounts. Finally, the payment process was very complex for users, as it required a QR code instead of simply swiping a credit card. All these reasons show that there is a need to use banknote insights to ensure that the durability of that idea is transposable to other forms of currency. Table 3.8 summarizes the differences of cash and digital forms of money from which requirements for the future design of CBDCs can be derived. For example, CBDC designers might consider the benefits of self-custody instead of the currently favored intermediated custody and access

Table 3.8 Differences of cash and digital forms of money (according to Narula et al., 2023)

Differences	Cash design	Digital money design
Custody	Self-custody	Intermediated custody
Access	Anyone	Authenticated and authorized individuals
Finality	Instant settlement and reversibility	Delayed settlement and often complex dispute arbitration
Data	No data trails	Data trails which require privacy rules
Distance	Short distances	Long distances (e.g., remittances)

might be authenticated and for authorized individuals only instead of anyone in the case of cash.

The following case study shows with the example of the Central Reserve Bank of Peru how a CBDC might foster financial inclusion.

Case Study: Central Reserve Bank of Perú (BCRP)

- The Central Reserve Bank of Perú (BCRP) is currently evaluating the benefits and risks of issuing a CBDC.
- Since the comprehensive modernization of its payment infrastructure, which went live in 2000, digital payments have been growing, but at a significantly high rate since the pandemic, thanks to using digital wallets and immediate payments, which allow real-time payments. The number of digital payments per adult increased from 29 in 2015 to 152 in 2022 (see Fig. 3.15).
- However, Peru currently faces the following challenges for the introduction of digital payments:
  - *Low financial inclusion.* According to Global Findex around 56% of adults did not have access to bank accounts in 2021 for various reasons like income is not enough, banks charge fees for operating accounts, and, in some cases, people do not trust the financial system (Peru had a

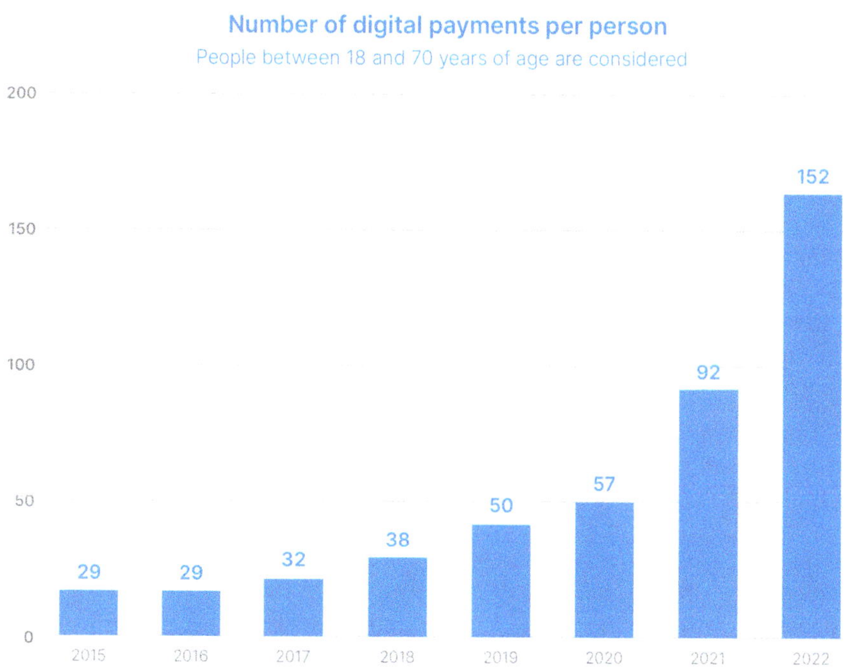

Fig. 3.15 Number of digital payments per person in Peru

financial crisis by the end of the 1990s). Peru sees a retail CBDC as a potential answer to foster financial inclusion. For this, the central bank analyzes different use cases like P2P and P2M, where today cash is still largely used. Other use cases are payments for informal workers (around 70% of the entire workforce), where today cash is used as well as government subsidies which could be transferred via a CBDC. In March 2023, BCRP published a white paper, CBDC: Promoting digital payments in Peru, which is the first in a series referring to the work being carried out by the BCRP on the possible implementation of a CBDC with the aim of promoting access and use of digital payments, as well as strengthening the monetary and financial stability, and the security and efficiency of payment systems.

- *Isolated systems.* Many financial services systems are not interconnected. For example, digital wallets mostly work as closed-loop systems. In 2022, Peru issued regulation that induced interoperability of digital wallets in March 2023 and immediate payments and QR codes in September 2023. Also, in 2023, access was granted to issuers of electronic money to the RTGS and ACH.

Source: Central Reserve Bank of Peru

3.4 Payment Infrastructures

Payment infrastructures are an important pillar of financial systems and of nation states as they provide basic functions for supporting an economy with basic services for the exchange of goods and services. In general, payment systems have three functions (Benons, 2020):

- *Exchange data.* Payment systems provide functions for data exchange regarding a payment transaction including the payment itself.
- *Record facts.* They record the data of the payer and the payee, the settlement transaction data, the time of a transaction, as well as KYC, AML, and other compliance data, etc.
- *Manage liquidity.* As the amount of cash in the financial system is limited, the payment system must ensure that this maximum amount is not exceeded at any time.

From a payment perspective, the financial system considers the (incumbent) institutions and their digital payment instruments. This comprises the sum of all systemic elements necessary for the organization of financial transactions in an economy and includes public and private actors, their organizational configurations, and the legal system. The latter sets the legal framework and includes national organizations (e.g., the Financial Conduct Authority (FCA) in the UK) as well as international supervisory authorities (e.g., the European Banking Authority (EBA) in the European Union). This is complemented by national and international central banks as well as the commercial banking system and most recently with fintech start-ups and biotech companies. Figure 3.16 gives an overview of the global payment revenues with regard to commercial and consumer payments and the comparison across different continents/regions. In 2022, the global payment revenues accounted for $750 billion globally with the largest part generated in the Asia-Pacific region.

Within the financial system, the payments sector was one of the first to provide innovations. For example, in 1872 Western Union launched the wire transfer over its telegraph network; in 1958 American Express launched the first credit card; in 1959 the first automated teller machine (ATM) was put up in Arlington, Ohio; in 1998 PayPal founded the first online payment platform; in 2004 Alibaba launched Alipay; and in 2008 Bitcoin emerged first as a payment instrument. Just as the financial sector more generally differentiates into more fine-grained services, this also applies to the payments industry with different application domains in the areas of "payment volume" and "payment value" (see Fig. 3.17). Regarding the payment volume, there is a growing trend toward micro, IoT, and streaming payments with billions of transactions every year. On the other hand, the payment value is constantly decreasing to micro payments smaller than one US dollar which especially become important in the case of machine-to-machine payments.

This area is especially covered by fintech startups and bigtechs. Examples of new entrants are startups like Square or TransferWise, but also the bigtech companies like Google with Google Pay or Alibaba with Alipay. Most of them are positioning themselves in the field of low to micro payment value and high payment volume. One example is Brave, a free and open-source web browser developed by Brave

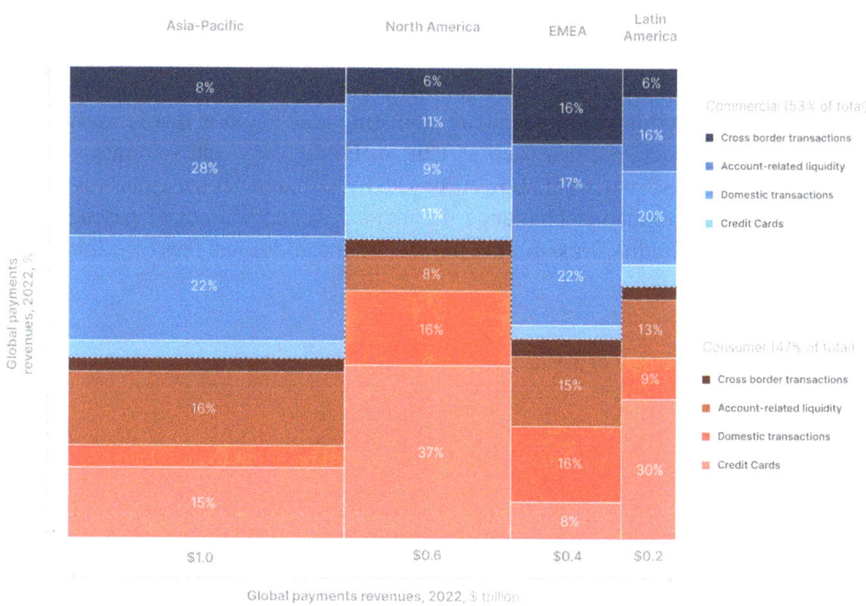

Fig. 3.16 Global payments revenues (McKinsey & Company, 2023)

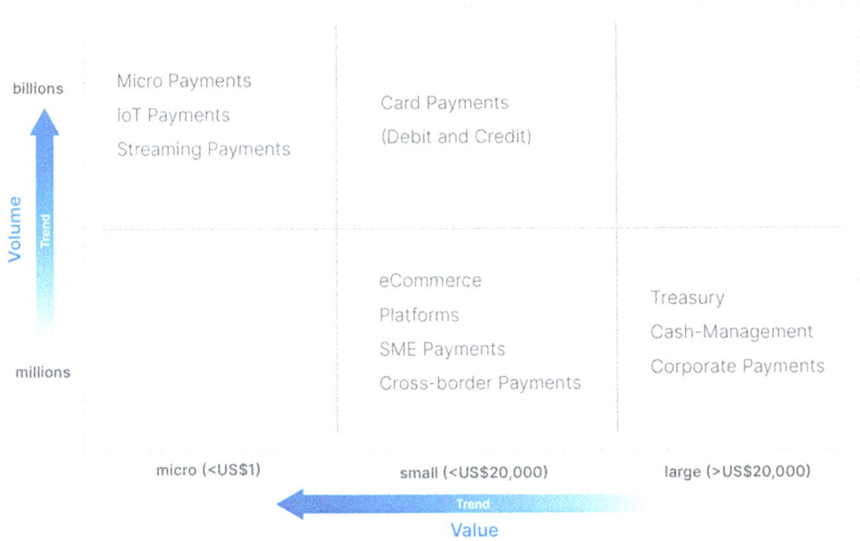

Fig. 3.17 Payment instruments (Ripple, 2019)

Software Inc. based on the Chromium web browser. Brave aims to pay content users and themselves 15% of the revenue and 70% to the publishers. The users would also be able to donate their revenue share to content publishers through micropayments. Another example is cross-border payments for which the total global market volume alone was $ 190.1 trillion in 2023 and is expected to increase to $ 290.2 until 2030 (Statista, 2024).

For the payment infrastructures more and more non-banks are entering the market and a new payment infrastructure is evolving aside from the incumbent financial institutions operated infrastructure. The payment value chain is increasingly being unbundled by fintech startups such as Chime, Digit, Varo, and Aspiration in the USA, Monzo and Revolut in the UK, Alipay and WeChat in China, as well as Nuank in Brazil. These companies challenge the major revenue sources of payments for interchange fees, credits, cross-border payments, and additional fees (see Table 3.9).

Table 3.9 Revenue sources of payments (according to McKinsey & Company, 2019b, 27)

Revenue sources of payments	Potential changes
Interchange fees	From interchange fees and reward programs to interchange fee caps
Credit	From credit revenues to customers looking for cheaper solutions like POS lending
Cross-border/FX payments	From high margins of cross-border payments to decreasing fees due to competition by platforms
Additional fees	From late payments penalty fees to increased customer awareness due to tracking tools

Table 3.10 Services in payments based on digital currencies according to Rauchs et al. (2018)

Payment services based on digital currencies	Description
Merchant services	Process payments of digital currencies on behalf of merchants
Personal remittances	Cross-border payments using digital currencies
B2b cross-border	B2b platforms for cross-border international funds transfer
Micropayments	Transfer of very small amounts of money
General-purpose platforms	Platforms that offer a variety of payment services
Consumer payments	Use of virtual currencies for consumer purchases
Bill payment services	Use of virtual currencies for the payment of bills
Machine-to-machine payments	Financial transactions between machines

For example, the cost of an international payment transaction today is approx. \$25–35 and could in the future decrease to \$1–2 (McKinsey & Company, 2019b).

In addition to this, in recent years a broad variety of new services based on digital currencies has evolved (see Table 3.10).

The following case studies show examples how incumbent payments infrastructures are being transformed to meet the future requirements of payment infrastructures.

Case Study: Transformation of the Indian Banking System by the Unified Payments Interface

- In 2016, India implemented the so-called "Unified Payments Interface" (UPI). The UPI is an overlay to the country's banking infrastructure that exposes an application programming interface (API) for third-party organizations that can conduct payments over this interface. The initiative was closely coupled with the introduction of a digital ID.
- Already back in 2010, India took the first steps to innovate its existing financial system with the launch of the Immediate Payment Service (IMPS) to get more people bank account access and increase cashless transactions. This was in combination with "Jan Dhan," the financial inclusion program of the Indian government.
- Today, more than 80% of all Indians have access to a bank account which is a sharp increase from approx. 53% in 2014.
- To drive consumer adoption, the Reserve Bank of India (RBI) decided that payments over the UPI are free of charge for the first few years.
- RBI invited all major banks to participate in the UPI and developed a common authentication system with all banks. It also provided support to merchants and technology providers for the design of the UPI. For example, Google Pay also provides a payment infrastructure.

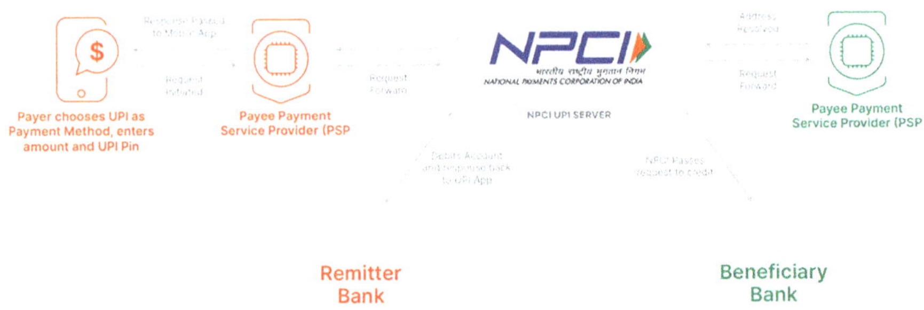

Fig. 3.18 The UPI architecture

- The UPI was used by 473 banks and covered 52% of all digital payments in 2022. This is equal to around 14.3 trillion transactions. Fig. 3.18 shows the UPI architecture.
- In 2022 India has signed a memorandum of understanding with 13 countries for adopting the UPI interface. Singapore, for example, has already successfully integrated with UPI.

Source: Google (2019) and Reserve Bank of India

Case Study: Digital Payment System and Securities Trading Platform in Cambodia

- From the ninth to the fifteenth century, Cambodia was a very big empire in the world and was Southeast Asia's largest empire during the twelfth century. During that time, Cambodia had no monetary system but a barter system. The lack of a monetary system was also one of the main reasons for the decline of the empire after the fifteenth century.
- Cambodia's central bank, the National Bank of Cambodia (NBC), was established in 1954, after Cambodia obtained its independence from France in 1953, taking over from the Institut d'Émission des États du Cambodge, du Laos et du Vietnam, a short-lived French quasi-central bank.
- Cambodia's economy is very "dollarized" with around 90% of payments in US dollar. This was one of the reasons why NBC initiated "Bakong," a retail and backbone payment system running on blockchain which was officially launched in October 2020. The main considerations for the project were:

  - *Financial inclusion*: NBC aims to respond to real demands for wider use of electronic means of payment and access to financial services for Cambodian people, especially those in the rural areas, where mobile phone penetration is greater than bank accounts ownership. In Cambodia, the mobile phone penetration is very high with around 17 million and around 20 million mobile subscriptions.
  - *Increased use of local currency*: As a heavy dollarized economy, Bakong will ease the use of KHR (Khmer Riel) for retail payments, as users don't have to deal with big numbers. (The KHR is exchanged at around 4000:1 against the US dollar.)
  - *Interoperability*: Even though the payment infrastructure has gradually developed in recent years, interconnectivity and interoperability between banks and payment service providers (PSPs) remains an issue.
  - *Lower regulatory compliance cost*: Finality of the payment is immediate using blockchain, reducing burden on liquidity management and regulatory compliance for payment service providers that are mere technology companies and are not directly linked to the settlement system provided by the NBC.
  - *Efficiency and safety*: The NBC is embracing modern technology (blockchain) to attain efficiency—better service at lower transaction costs.

- Before Bakong, the PSPs were not connected to the clearing house ACH (see Fig. 3.19). But this would be an important feature since people in rural areas are mostly using PSPs while people in the cities mostly use banks. To be able to transfer money from rural areas to the cities would thus require an easier connection than through a long chain of intermediaries.
- The associated Bakong smartphone app, which is based on a national digital wallet and is used by around 0.5 million users (around 8.5 million users already use the Bakong backbone for transferring money and other features outside of the wallet), can be used at stores and for transferring money. People do not need a bank account to register for Bakong, as long as they have a Cambodian mobile phone number. Users can send funds by scanning QR codes or specifying the recipient's phone number. Transactions can be performed in KHR or US$. In its extended version, Bakong also allows participants to use a desktop app for transactions in addition to the settlement account. The app also allows users to exchange their money from KHR in US$ and vice versa. Additionally, QR payments are accepted via Bakong as a backbone. Another important function of Bakong is cross-border payment which today is possible with Malaysia, Thailand, Laos, India, and China.

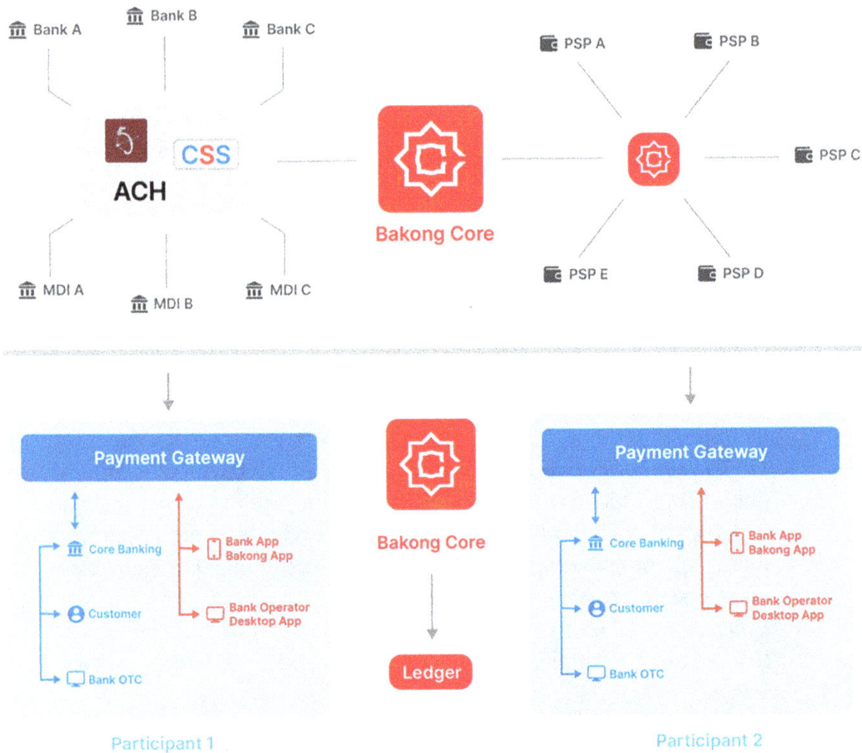

Fig. 3.19 The Cambodian Bakong architecture

- Another blockchain use case in Cambodia is the securities trading platform NBCP, a central security repository that allows the issue, trade, and repo of all kinds of securities including negotiable certificate of deposit (NCD) and T-Bond and ensures delivery versus payment (DVP) at all times based on atomic swaps of smart contracts. NBCP is built on top of Hyperledger Iroha, connected by financial institutions allowing them to trade securities with delivery vs. payment, no settlement risk, and the elimination of custodian accounts. The NBCP shall in the second step also be opened for individual buyers of government bonds starting with 10 US$ to raise funds cheaper than only the international financial markets (see Fig. 3.20).

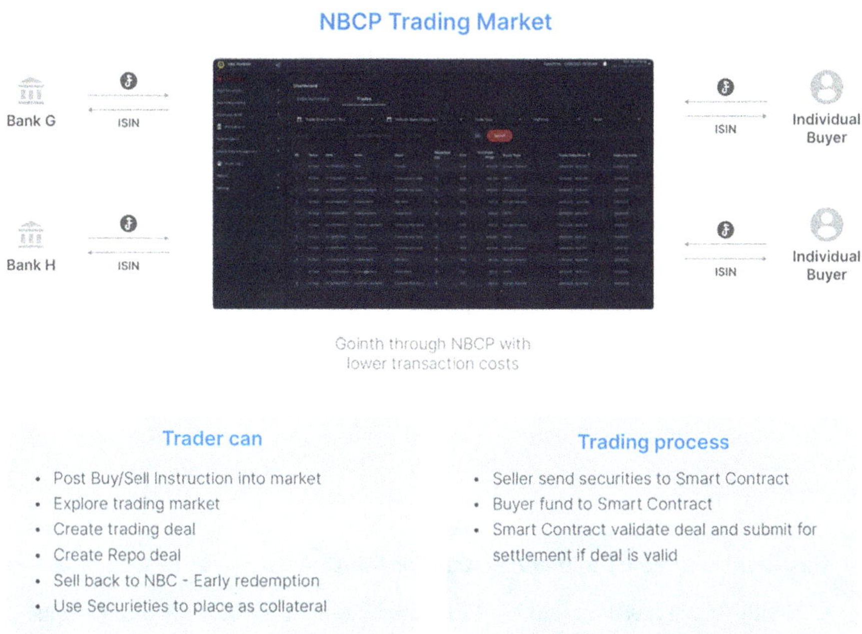

Fig. 3.20 The NBCP architecture

Source: National Bank of Cambodia

Case Study: A New Real-Time Payment System for the UK—"Faster Payments"

- The UK has one of the world's largest real-time payment systems by transaction volume (45.7 billion payments in 2022 (UK Finance, 2023)); the new system "Faster Payments" is operational since 2008.
- Cash remains the second most frequently used payment method in the UK, which was used for 15% of all payments in 2021.
- Most payments are through banks directly connected to Faster Payments, which are processed in real time, 24/7; payments through banks indirectly connected take up to 2 h.
- The UK banks only acted to build Faster Payments under pressure from the UK Government which objected to the slow speed of the existing system which took three business days to process a payment.
- However, the move to real-time payments happened by accident—the government only expected payments to be faster, either the same day or the

next day, but the UK banks decided to make the payments in real time to avoid future pressure to keep speeding up payments.

- The move to real-time payments has become a strong global trend over the past 2 years, and serendipitously the UK banks are in a leading position in real-time payments and in ancillary real-time capabilities (e.g., real-time fraud checking), and technology suppliers are strongly placed based on their experience in the UK market.
- However, the UK banks have never marketed Faster Payments and the benefits of real-time clearing, and even now most banks only guarantee delivery by the end of the next business day. However, UK consumers have come to expect their payments to be immediate, and any bank not directly connected to Faster Payments is at a disadvantage—this has led to a significant increase in directly connected banks.

Case study: A New Payment System for South Africa—

- South Africa has almost 60 million inhabitants. Approx. 75% of the population have a bank account; 15% of them only have a social card. 66% use smartphones for which a digital payment platform would be beneficial.
- In addition to South Africa, another 17 countries in southern Africa have a banking rate of approx. only 10%, while approx. every second person has a mobile phone—half of these are smartphones. Most of the countries are still cash-based economies with a very low degree of electronic payment system usage.
- BankServAfrica aims to develop an open payment platform for the entire South African continent. The solution shall be built on different layers (see Fig. 3.21). The transport layer (protocol layer) ensures the exchange of payment across different currencies, while the storage layer allows consumers and institutions to digitally store their money. The integration layer enables connectivity with different applications across different kinds of providers (banks and non-banks).
- The major challenge to develop this new payment system is to agree on standards for all layers with all involved actors. Without these standards not only interaction within one layer becomes impossible, but also across the different layers.

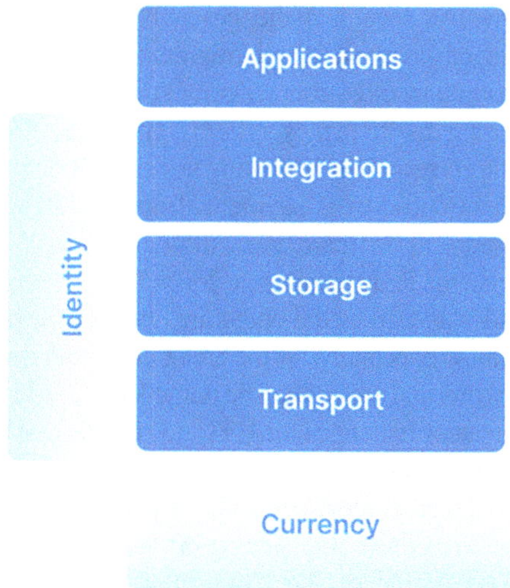

Fig. 3.21 Architecture of the BankServAfrica payment system

3.4.1 Cross-Border Payments

In some countries, remittances are greater than 30% of the GDP. From a provider perspective, the consumer and commercial cross-border payments market accounts for 11% (Asia-Pacific), 9% (North America), 18% (EMEA), and 7% (Latin America) (see Fig. 3.16). The UK, for example, is a cross-border payment hub. In 2019, the UK payment system CHAPS (Clearing House Automated Payment System) processed £34 trillion compared with £41 trillion in domestic payments. In fact, most cross-border payments are processed by a small number of US and European banks, even though, for example, SWIFT has more than 11,000 banks connected to its network, indicating how centralized cross-border payments are. A large proportion of these payments are made in US dollar, even between countries where the USA is not involved, where local currency is converted into US dollar and then converted from US dollar to the payment currency. This can also happen in-country; for example, it is common in Africa for payments to be made between banks in the same country through New York banks in US dollar. In addition, cross-border transactions are still very complex and time-consuming and often require many banks (so-called correspondent banks) in their own and other countries to transfer money.

Although the term "cross-border payments" suggests that payments are crossing real borders, they are "closed loops," which means that in fact they never really cross borders. Instead, a payment message goes either through a large bank that has a presence in both countries involved in a specific payment transaction or through one or even several correspondent banks that can make and receive payments in two jurisdictions. This involves several challenges and frictions, such as a low rate of straight-through processing of payments due to fragmented and truncated data formats, complexities in meeting compliance requirements for AML/CFT and data protection, a lack of real-time monitoring due to legacy systems, etc. (BIS, 2020a). One major challenge in the context of the correspondent banking system is long payment corridors. An example for long payment corridors is payments from the UK to Vietnam. The main corridor for such payments to Vietnam goes through Australia and involves different types of payment systems in different time zones. This means that the supplier of liquidity along this corridor as well as the operating hours of the banks and the central banks change multiple times. Especially for the area of remittances, further constraints must be considered: (1) Payers and payees can be unbanked, (2) a lack of presence in the formal financial system creates challenges for KYC, (3) the decreasing number of banks has led to a decrease of banks in high-risk remittance countries, and (4) remittances are very often low in value, so the costs represent a higher percentage of the total payment.

In a comprehensive report, the Financial Stability Board's Cross-border Payments Task Force of the Committee on Payments and Market Infrastructures (CPMI) defined a global roadmap for enhancing cross-border payments (see Fig. 3.22). In

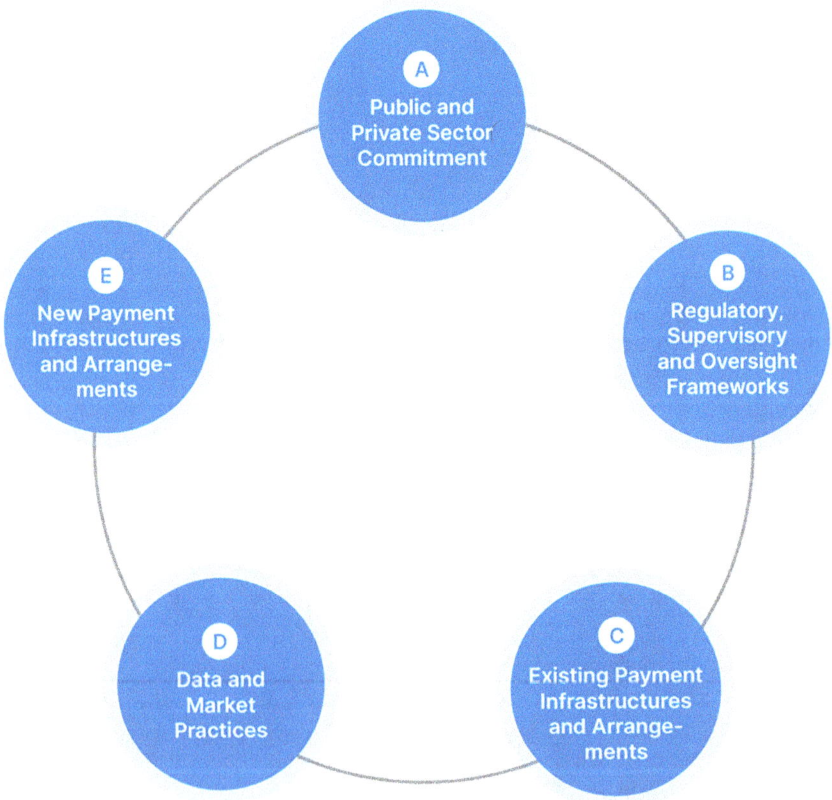

Fig. 3.22 Five focus areas and building blocks of cross-border payments (BIS, 2020a)

this roadmap, CBDCs play a major role in certain areas along these five focus building blocks. With the introduction of new (multilateral payment infrastructures and arrangements based on CBDC and stablecoins, also novel ways for AML/CFT design, novel data frameworks, and KYC and identity information sharing can be implemented in regulatory, supervisory, and oversight frameworks. This also allows increased adoption of PvP, reciprocal liquidity arrangements, the extension of operating hours, the improved interlinking of payment systems, the harmonization of API protocols, and the establishment of unique identifiers and proxy registers.

The following case studies demonstrate how these existing challenges can be overcome by introducing novel approaches.

Case Study: Cross-border Payments with Ripple

- Cross-border payments are of high complexity due to fragmented and truncated data formats, weak competition, complex processing and compliance checks, limited operating hours, legacy technology platforms, long transaction chains, and high funding costs (BIS, 2020a).
- This requires new common public and private sector commitments, regulatory frameworks, and improved existing/development of new payment infrastructures as well as data and market practices (e.g., ISO 20022 message format etc.).
- An example for a new payment infrastructure is from Ripple (see Fig. 3.23). The firm provides a multi-currency distributed financial technology with a native digital asset, XRP, which directly bridges any two currencies.
- With XRP, cross-border payments can be simplified and costs be reduced.

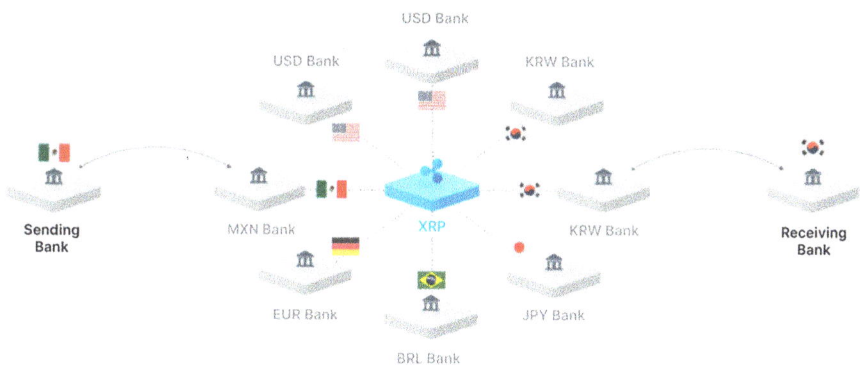

Fig.3.23 Ripple cross-border payment architecture

Source: Ripple

Case Study: Africa's Financial System Today and in the Future

- In 2007, the only mobile money solution in Africa was M-PESA in Kenya.
- In 2018, in most African countries already up to 10% of adults used a mobile phone for payments. However, countries like Algeria, Sudan, Somalia, Gabon, Congo, Angola, Uganda, and Kenya show even higher numbers ranging from 26% (Angola) up to 68% (Kenya) (see Fig. 3.24).
- Currently, a variety of new payment platforms emerge which not only focus on specific countries but cover whole regions (see Fig. 3.25).
- Among the relevant platforms is a real-time platform in Tanzania, Mowali's cross-border remittances system, the regional platform WAEMU (Benin, Burkina Faso, Côte D'Ivoire, Guinea-Bissau, Mali, Niger, Senegal, Togo), the Southern African Community Development (SADC) countries (Angola, Botswana, Comoros, Congo, Eswatini, Lesotho, Madagascar, Malawi, Mauritius, Mozambique, Namibia, Seychelles, South Africa, Tanzania, Zambia, Zimbabwe) which develop a retail payment system on top of their real-time gross settlement system (RTGS), the multi-currency payment platform from the 45 BUNA member countries which provides clearing and settlement and investment services for the trading partners of Arab countries in this region. Finally, an inter-regional platform is being developed from the East African Community (EAC, Burundi, Kenya, Rwanda, Uganda, Tanzania), the SADC, and the Common Market for Eastern and South Africa (COMESA, Burundi, Comoros, Congo, Djibouti, Egypt, Eritrea, Ethiopia, Kenya, Libya, Madagascar, Malawi, Mauritius, Rwanda, Seychelles, Sudan, Swaziland, Uganda, Zambia, Zimbabwe).

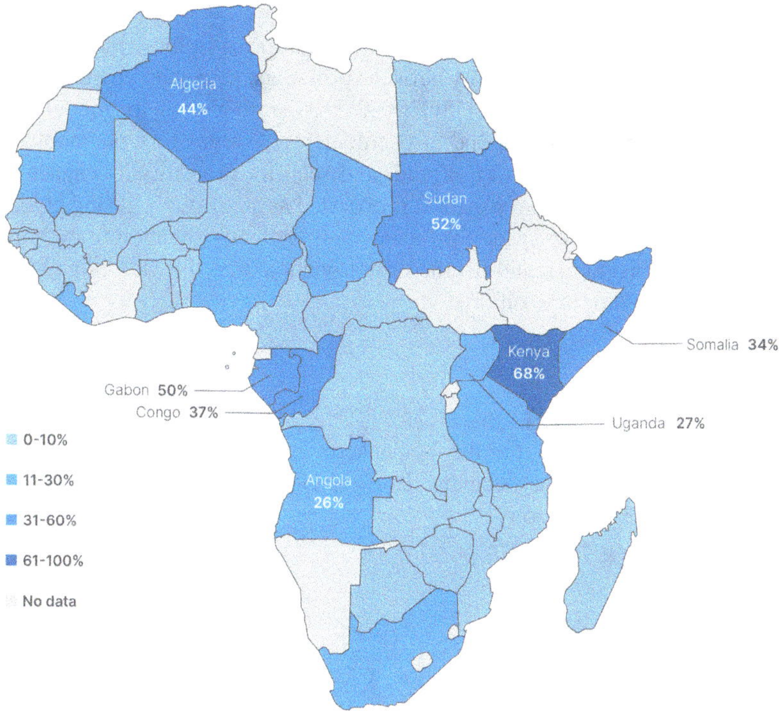

Fig. 3.24 Mobile payment in Africa

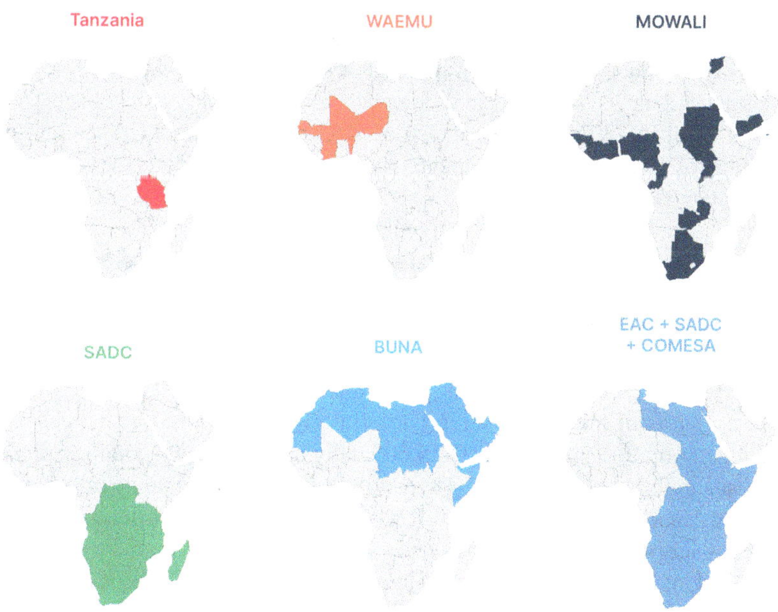

Fig. 3.25 Currently emerging payment systems across the African continent

- Important enablers of inclusive payment platforms in these countries are (1) open-loop interoperability between providers, (2) adherence to international payment standards (ISO20022), (3) push payments model with immediate funds transfer and fast settlement, (3) regulatory playbook and scheme templates for KYC, fraud, and security protection, 4) space for non-banks, (6) payment platform is operated as a utility, (7) strong guiding principles that leave space for localization and customization (e.g., http://leveloneproject.org), and (8) the use of open-source software (e.g., http://mojaloop.io, http://mosip.io).

Source: Mobile Money for the Unbanked: State of the Industry, GSMA, World Bank, MMU Deployment Tracker, GSMA, BCG analysis, Bill & Melinda Gates Foundation

Case Study: Singapore's and Thailand's Real-Time Payment Systems Integration

- Singapore in 2017 introduced the proxy payment system PayNow for small payments, which allows account holders to pay each other based on the mobile phone or national identity number. At the same time, Thailand developed a similar system called PromptPay.
- While in Singapore PayNow was designed as a centralized system, PromptPay is a distributed system, where different commercial banks are involved.
- On April 29, 2021, the Monetary Authority of Singapore (MAS) and the Bank of Thailand (BOT) launched the linkage of Singapore's PayNow and Thailand's PromptPay real-time retail payment systems.
- The aim was to get customers the same customer experience as with PayNow or PromptPay when transferring money from one country to the other. The project was implemented within 3 years. Around 2.5 years of this was spent on regulatory and legal issues, processes, different service level agreements, etc., while around 6 months were spent on the technical integration of the two systems.
- Customers of the participating banks in Singapore and Thailand can now transfer up to S$1000 or THB25,000 daily across the two countries, using just a mobile phone number. There will be no need to populate information fields such as the recipient's full name and bank account details, as with normal remittance solutions.
- The transfers are completed within minutes, which is an improvement over the average of 1–2 working days needed by most cross-border remittance solutions.

- In addition, the costs are only $3 per $100 transfer, although cross-border payments usually involve around $15 costs, if processed via the traditional banking system. Most of these costs are in the clearing process. Fintech startups offer this service for around $5. The effect of this was a drop from around $2000 to around $300 per transfer.
- It is planned to expand this bilateral linkage into a network of linked retail payment systems across ASEAN. It is already planned that PayNow will be connected to India's UPI payment system by June 2022 as well as to Indonesia, Malaysia, and the Philippines soon.
- The basis for this multi-country solution will be a novel gateway, which allows us to manage different rules for different jurisdictions.
- The solution is not only open for banks but also for fintech startups like TransferWise to connect to the new system. This is especially relevant as most of the startups concentrate on merchant integration and thus also use it for cross-border payments.

Source: https://www.mas.gov.sg/news/media-releases/2021/singapore-and-thailand-launch-worlds-first-linkage-of-real-time-payment-systems

Case Study: Partior

- Partior is an open industry platform, developed to transform and accelerate interbank value movements, for Payments, Trade, and Foreign Exchange settlement, which was founded in 2021 by DBS, JPMorgan, and Temasek and went live in October 2021.
- Traditional cross-border payments use a "hub and spoke" model, whereby funds travel through a network of correspondent banks, adding inefficiencies such as time and costs along the way.
- Partior developed a wholesale payments platform based on digitized M1 commercial bank money to enable instantaneous clearing and settlement for cross-border payments.
- For this, Partior provides a blockchain-based settlement network built on the Ethereum-based ConsenSys Quorum blockchain, which is shared among banks and where all relevant services for cross-border payments, such as AML and KYC, are developed as a utility service. On top of that, a smart contract-based system is used to define rules that are used to settle payment transactions.
- In another experiment with Banque de France, which simulated cross-border and cross-currency transactions for Singapore dollar (SGD) CBDC and Euro (EUR) CBDC, a permissioned, privacy-enabled blockchain based on Quorum technology was used (see Fig. 3.26).

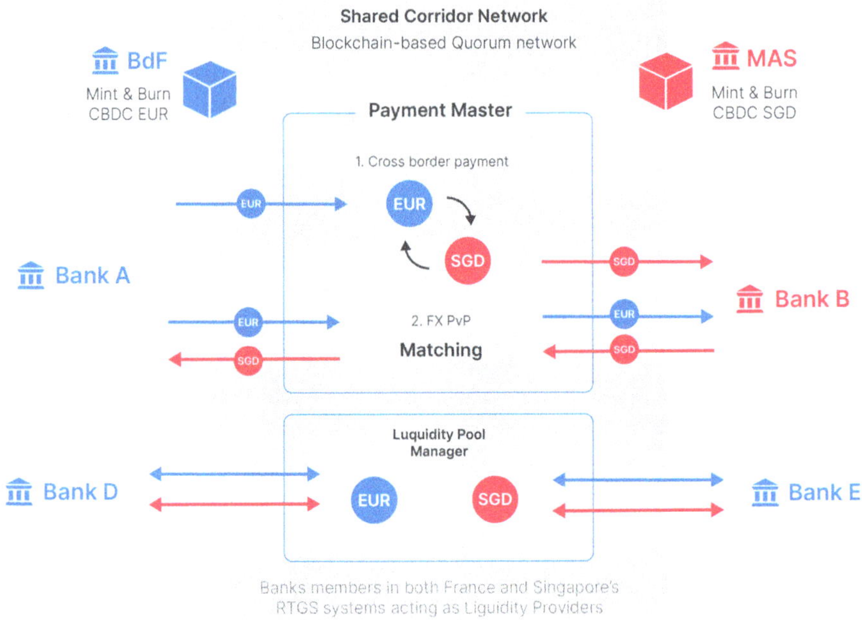

Fig. 3.26 mCBDC on single multi-currency system

- Four key outcomes could be overserved:
  - *Interoperability:* blockchain nodes were set up across private and public cloud infrastructures in both countries.
  - *Visibility:* the design of a common mCBDC network enabled the two central banks to have both visibility on cross-border payments and retaining independent control over the issuance and distribution of their own CBDC.
  - *Liquidity*: the setup of an experimental mCBDC network that incorporated an automated liquidity pool and market-making service for EUR/SGD currency pairs. The use of smart contracts automatically managed the EUR/SGD currency exchange rate in line with real-time market transactions and demands.
  - *Simulation*: the simulation of experimental mCBDC network that showed that the number of correspondent banking parties involved in the payment chain for cross-border transactions can be reduced. Consequently, the number of contractual arrangements, the KYC burden, as well as the associated costs could be cut down.

Source: Public Material of the Monetary Authority of Singapore

The redesign of cross-border payments, as suggested in the five focus areas and building blocks mentioned before, shows that many of today's problems can be solved by better coordinating harmonization of existing regulations and technologies. However, a real leap forward might be achieved with the introduction of CBDCs. The multilateral project Dunbar, for example, which involved the Reserve Bank of Australia, the Central Bank of Malaysia, the Monetary Authority of Singapore, the South African Reserve Bank, and the Bank for International Settlements Innovation Hub, explores the use of a multi-currency common settlement platform that enables transacting parties to pay each other in different currencies directly, without the need for correspondent banks (see Sect. 3.4).

3.5 The Web3 Economy

The currently evolving next iteration of the Internet, also called "web3" (see Sect. 2.7), proposes a new Internet architecture both from a technical perspective and from an organizational perspective. While the technical perspective focuses on the development of new protocols and software layers (basic service providers; see Fig. 3.27, Sect. 2.7), the organizational view concentrates on how the different stakeholders interact (users, business service providers, and regulatory institutions). Examples for basic services are custody (e.g., digital wallets) or distributed service marketplaces (e.g., Sharetribe) which allows the development of electronic marketplaces without intermediaries like Amazon.

In contrast to existing models like, for example, the bigtech platforms (see Sect. 5.2), the web3 model is characterized by p2p interaction like the ones from Lending Club, Kiva, or Prosper which focus on lending as one important area in financial services. However, this p2p phenomenon is emerging as a broader concept across all industries even beyond financial services. For example, Ethlance is a blockchain-based infrastructure which provides all kinds of services around "work." Ethlance runs on Ethereum and includes all relevant activities in this field like finding a job, invoicing existing work contracts, etc. Another example from the area of "leisure" is Mediachain. Mediachain is a p2p, decentralized database for sharing media content. With this, publishers and consumers of content can interact directly without central platforms. The financial industry acts as an enabler in these p2p models, as it provides services for payments, investments, and credits for all different sectors.

Such p2p infrastructures rely on basic services like access and channels, transaction management, etc., which are themselves developed on the p2p paradigm. An example is the custody solution Storj which is a decentralized storage system that provides unused storage of participating computers (nodes). For this, data is encrypted, split into smaller pieces, and, as soon as suitable nodes are identified, distributed. For downloading the

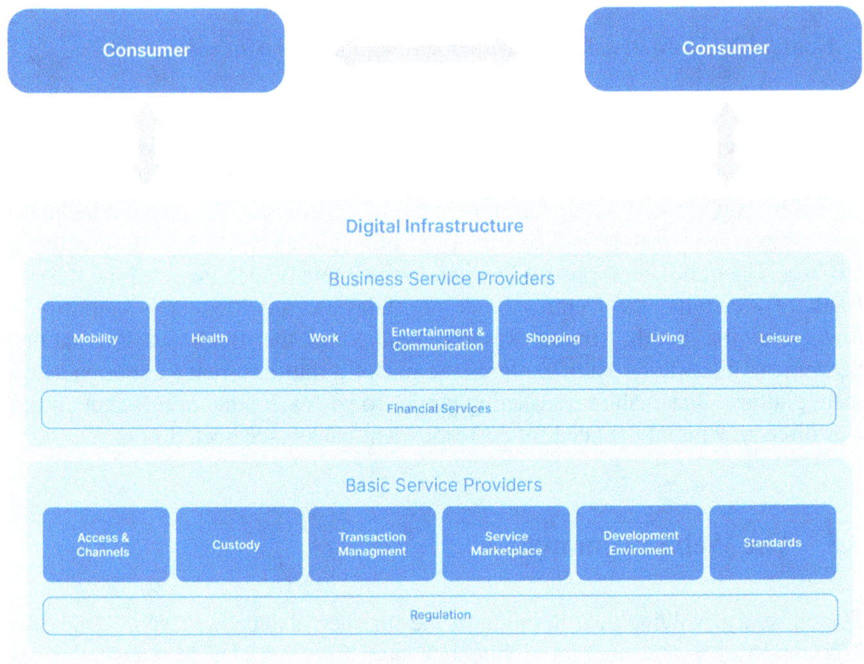

Fig. 3.27 Digital infrastructure for the p2p economy

data, the process is reversed: first, the nodes where the data is stored are identified; the different parts of the files are downloaded and assembled and then decrypted.

Another very important element as part of "access and channels" is digital identity. Identity management systems have evolved from centralized over federated to self-sovereign models. In the physical world, people manage their (physical) identity credentials from different organizations like governments, financial institutions, businesses, etc. Online identity, however, cannot rely on physical authentication mechanisms (e.g., a passport), and in most cases, each provider has built its own identity system which is not interoperable with other providers' systems. A novel concept is so-called "decentralized identifiers" (DIDs) which represent a new type of identifiers that provide a verifiable, decentralized digital identity (W3C Credentials Community Group, 2019). DIDs are URLs that connect a DID subject (i.e., a human person) to a DID document (i.e., a set of data like biometric data for authentication) which enable trustable interactions with a certain subject. In the model shown in Fig. 3.28, an issuer (e.g., a government) provides verifiable claims to people and organizations which are stored in a repository (e.g., Bill & Melinda Gates Foundation). An inspector (e.g., a financial institution) checks verifiable claims from people and organizations and provides them access to (digital) data, whereas a holder (e.g., a citizen) stores verifiable claims in repositories and provides them to inspectors to get access to protected resources. A public ledger stores verifiable claims (e.g., a proof of existence), and a decentralized identifier DHT

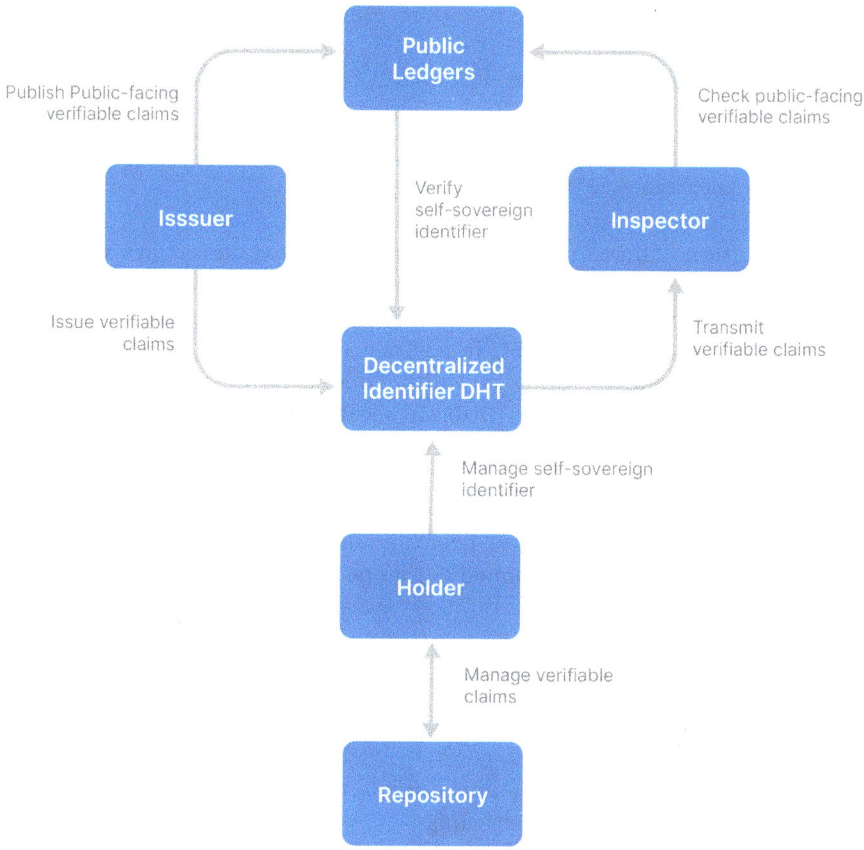

Fig. 3.28 Components of a verifiable claims ecosystem (Sporny and Longley 2016)

stores and updates self-sovereign documents and verifies the cryptographic authenticity of information associated with a self-sovereign identifier.

In July 2022, the World Wide Web Consortium (W3C) announced that DIDs are now an official web standard. This new type of verifiable identifiers, which do not require a centralized registry, will enable both individuals and organizations to take greater control of their online information and relationships while also providing greater security and privacy (W3C 2022). As Fig. 3.29 shows, these DIDs are separated in methods (e.g., send data) and method-specifier identifiers (e.g., personal data). DIDs are an important component for managing personal and organizational data.

Digital IDs are enablers of the future p2p economy. A digital ID enables access to any kind of digital services that a consumer wants to access over his or her interface on a service marketplace. Implementations of such a solution are from organizations like uPort, etc. APIs, on the other hand, are the prerequisite for enabling digital ecosystems as they standardize interfaces between organizations and thus allow consumers to use services across different providers in

Fig. 3.29 Decentralized identifiers (W3C 2022)

bundling custom-tailored solutions. A study calculated the savings from standardizing and digitizing applications for onboarding customers and regulatory compliance to approx. $2.5–4.0 billion and fraud to approx. $7.0–9.0 billion (McKinsey & Company, 2019b). In addition to cost savings, data, and especially customer data, are often said to provide additional value. Should this value also be reflected in banks' balance sheets, and if so, how could this be achieved? And should customers receive paybacks for sharing their data with companies? This is especially relevant as data approaches and cultures across different jurisdictions vary. For example, Chinese firms use customer data very intensively to analyze customer behavior and offer personalized services, whereas such approaches are limited in Europe.

Case Study: The "Verifiable Organizations Network" (VON)

- The Verifiable Organizations Network (VON) is a community of different organizations including the governments of British Columbia, Ontario, and Canada to establish an infrastructure to find, issue, store, and share trustworthy data about organizations.
- VON is based on an open-source approach and the cryptographic foundations of DIDs and verifiable credentials (VCs).
- The focus of VON is on (1) applying for credentials faster and less error-prone, (2) issuing (and reissuing) credentials simpler and more secure, and (3) verifying credentials more standard, trustworthy, and transparent, anywhere in the world.
- For example, Ontario's Verifiable Businesses allows us to search for registrations, certificates, licenses, or permits that an Ontario business may have, and verify the authenticity of each using blockchain.
- Figure 3.30 shows the involved actors and processes in more detail. If for example, someone wants to open a new restaurant, this person needs different licenses that are issued by different organizations. With VON, one can register a company on a public verifiable data registry (OrgBook), where all credentials are saved, and processes become more efficient and less redundant.

Source: https://vonx.io

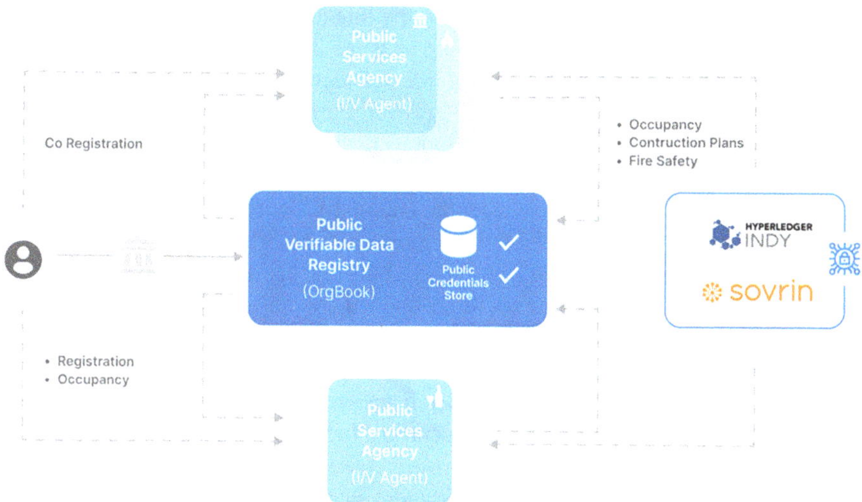

Fig. 3.30 Architecture of VON

3.6 Digital Communities

Over millions of years, life of humans was primarily influenced by local communities in which people lived together. Later, with cheaper and more convenient mobility available people started to move from one geographical area to another, by ship, later by trains and cars, and finally by planes. However, the geographic anchor of an individual remained her or his country of origin, either the one where she was born or the one where the ancestors were from and where the citizenship originated from. Now digitalization might lead to digital communities which emerge as a new dimension across geographic boundaries. For example, during COVID-19 companies started to hire employees from all around the world and, in contrast to former ways of employment, these workers stayed in their countries and started to work remotely (and still do). On a government level, countries then started to issue digital citizenships, digital work visa and develop toward "digital nations," where urban and rural citizens, government, and businesses live in a digital society and only interact digitally with each other (Kar et al., 2019). But such a development has consequences. Estonia, for example, provides a digital citizenship, the so-called "E-Resident." As an E-Resident, entrepreneurs can now very easily open a post mail account and a bank account, register a company, etc. online, and become part of the Estonian society. With these digital communities, geographical ones are overlayed and exist complementary to geographical country boundaries. However, this creates additional complexity and raises questions about citizenship, taxation, etc. and thus has an enormous impact not only on society and on businesses but also on the financial system.

An important question is therefore how the financial system in general and central bank money specifically will develop in these digital communities. While for now, privately issued digital currencies like stablecoins or Bitcoin are often used, CBDCs might be a logical next step. However, currently, the developments point into the direction of a "splinter net," a (digital) financial system based on an Internet which is divided along geopolitical lines. If life follows art, it is not hard to imagine a splintered world and political economy akin to George Orwell's dystopia in 1984—a world divided into at least three global networks belonging to the states of Oceania, Eurasia, and East Asia (see Fig. 3.31).

These three global networks could be divided by major CBDCs—a digital US dollar, a digital euro, and an e-CNY—with Bitcoin perhaps serving as the currency for "disputed territories." However, there are also positive signs. For example, at the G20 in 2022 in Bali the central banks from Indonesia, Malaysia, Philippines, Singapore, and Thailand sealed a cooperation for regional payment connectivity based on the BIS-moderated mBridge project (see Sect. 3.4). But it remains unclear how the development of cross-border payment systems and CBDC integration will continue, given the geopolitical tensions.

As a result of this development, this might also ultimately lead to several financial systems instead of a single one. Is the peak globalization then also the peak Internet? Will the financial system lead to a societal change through the separation of money and state, just as this happened to the church and state during secularism? Or will there be another way of separating monetary and fiscal policy? What if the financial system might increase Internet surveillance in the name of tax purposes? All these questions will be raised in the future and answers need to be provided.

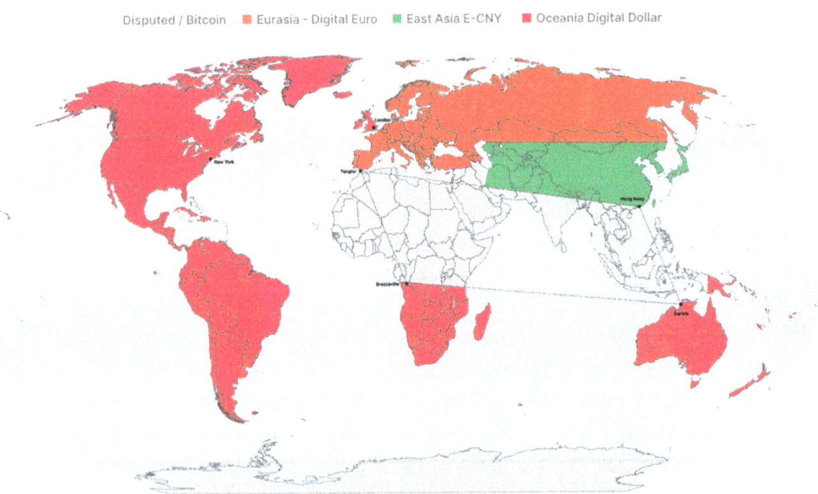

Fig. 3.31 Depicting the three superstates of nineteen eighty-four (according to Orwell, 1984)

Chapter 4
(De-)Regulation

"I have a dream. It is futuristic, but realistic. It involves a Star Trek chair and a bank of monitors. It would involve tracking the global flow of funds in close to real time (from a Star Trek chair using a bank of monitors), in much the same way as happens with global weather systems and global internet traffic. Its centerpiece would be a global map of financial flows, charting spill-overs and correlations" (Andy Haldane, Chief Economist, Bank of England, Speech at the Maxwell Fry Annual Global Finance Lecture: Managing Global Finance as a System, Birmingham University 10 (October 29, 2014) (transcript available online on the Bank of England's website). This approach reflects the regulators' and supervisors' point of view, which, in the aftermath of the 2008 financial crisis, has led to an increased regulatory regime in many countries with bank fines having exceeded $200 billion, and the ongoing cost of regulation and compliance, which has become a primary concern industry-wide. Approximately 10–15% of all employees in the financial services industry already work in regulation- or compliance-related areas (English & Hammond, 2016). On the other hand, many countries started to introduce new regulatory schemes that apply lower barriers for startup companies (deregulation). Examples are Singapore, the UK, and Switzerland with the introduction of regulatory "sandboxes" to explore new approaches in a safe environment. How does the right balance between regulation and innovation look like?

T. Puschmann, H. S. H. P. M. of Liechtenstein, *Financial System 2030*, Financial Innovation and Technology,
https://doi.org/10.1007/978-3-031-55700-2_4

4.1 IT and Financial Regulation

4.1.1 Fintech Regulation

Financial regulation has been challenged through technology innovations by the "innovation trilemma" which forces regulators to provide clear rules, maintain market integrity, and encourage financial innovation, but, at best, only two out of these three goals very often can be achieved (see Fig. 4.1; Brummer & Yadav, 2017).

For example, if a regulator aims to encourage innovation and provides clear rules, this results in a simpler, low-intensity regulatory framework which increases the risks of market integrity. Among the examples are certain deregulations for fintech startups (light licenses) as well as sandboxes for experimentation. While this triangle was applicable to former regulations like the Dodd-Frank Act (which already showed the trade-offs of this trilemma), technology innovations differ in at least three areas and exacerbate the challenges:

- *Data.* The availability and (re-)combination of vast quantities of conventional as well as novel types of data.
- *Technology.* Novel technologies like AI and blockchain lead to entirely new concepts and thus require new rules.
- *Non-banks.* The emergence of non-banks whose business models aim to disintermediate incumbent financial institutions and intend to become monopolies in certain areas.

An example of how this trilemma may be intensified by IT innovations is the use and analysis of data which can lead to disparate results for customers like disadvantaged minority communities. Combined with the use of AI systems that automatically analyze these datasets and determine which customers receive credits and which don't, the probability that certain customer groups are completely excluded from financial services might increase. The correctness of data and their analysis is also a risk for financial markets who rely on correct and trustworthy datasets. An answer to these challenges might be domestic agency cooperation, international standard setting, and better private self-governance of emerging technologies.

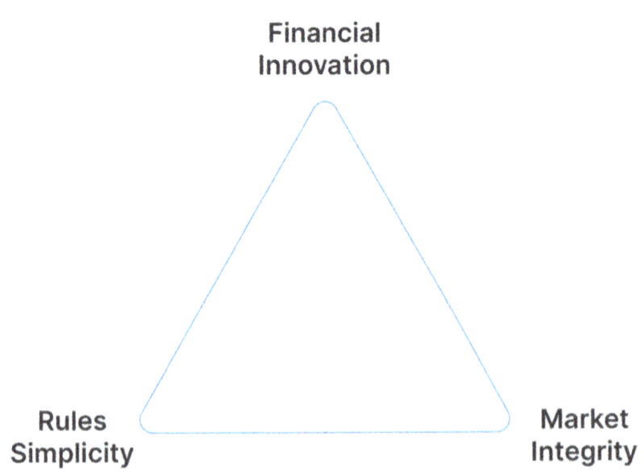

Fig. 4.1 Innovation trilemma (Brummer & Yadav, 2017)

Regulation has had until now been oriented toward financial institutions and is mostly limited to single countries with different rules. This means that, for example, an organization must apply for a specific license in one country (e.g., a payment or a banking license) to provide financial services in this country. In addition, regulation today often focuses on technology-neutral regulation approaches which primarily adapt changes induced by novel IT like blockchain and AI for existing legal rules and regulations. An example is the Swiss adaptation to blockchain, which was approved in 2022 or the Liechtenstein Blockchain Act. However, one of the core principles of financial regulation to apply the same rules for the same risks requires a different approach when novel approaches are developed that, in its most extreme case, don't even require any institutions anymore. For example, if DeFi concepts (see Sect. 5.4) that disintermediate banks are developed, new rules must be developed too. Another example is the use of data instead of collateral which has been used in China as a novel approach from bigtech firms like Ant Financial (Gambacorta et al., 2020). This might have even macroeconomic implications as the provision of credits is detached from the movement of asset prices. These examples show that not the technology itself is regulated but the activities which the technology automates and supports (e.g., credit rating, etc.) are regulated in these cases. Prominent examples of this approach are digital identities, data hubs, and novel payment infrastructures for digital currencies.

Although IT provides novel services and models and might lead to a trilemma in many cases, there is no legal vacuum. This means that any new developments in blockchain and smart contracts or AI, for example, must be aligned with the legal and regulatory environment in or across jurisdictions. At least four major areas must be considered as relevant when designing regulation for a future financial system:

- *Comprehensive regulation.* Many fintech-related regulations have been incrementally developed based on their emergence. While early approaches focused on mobile payments and robo-advisors, many discussions today concentrate on AI, blockchain, etc. But as fintech moves toward a complete digitization of money to even embrace the monetization of data, the regulatory framework will need to be entirely reanalyzed. The emergence of a completely new financial system complementary to the existing one raises questions across all areas and not only single banking activities like PSD2 for payments. Although a comprehensive framework requires a holistic approach, a more fine- grained exploration and regulation is needed. An example was the discussion about "too small to care" and "too big to fail" after the financial crisis. Such a multi-layered, modular approach is also needed for fintech, as the different novel technologies, actors, banking processes, and business models often require different ways and fields of regulation (e.g., DeFi).
- *Appropriate (de-)regulation.* Countries have followed different approaches in regulation. While some followed a "laissez-faire approach" (e.g., China in the early days of p2p lending) others tried to regulate every single element of the new evolving financial system (e.g., EU). But appropriate regulation will only be

possible if risk and innovation are balanced. This requires a more in-depth understanding by regulators of technical developments and a more in-depth understanding of regulatory objectives by technology entrepreneurs. In general, regulation follows the maxim that similar activities should be regulated in similar ways without including technological discussions and to avoid regulatory arbitrage. However, the move of financial services activities to unregulated areas in combination with the credulity that financial institutions' risk management systems would signal eventual problems were two of the major reasons of the 2008 financial crisis.

- *Harmonized regulation.* The harmonization of global regulation has a long history. As the economy and the financial system became global, first institutions and regulations were introduced on a global level. But in many areas, regulations are still stuck on a national level and integration challenges remain. For example, organizations are faced with a lot of regulatory requirements across various jurisdictions. Thus, the integration of financial monitoring systems on a global scale could be very beneficial. Novel financial market infrastructures based on new technologies like blockchain might even increase the need for a harmonized approach. This harmonization also applies for new digital platforms which provide financial services like the biotech firms Amazon, Google, Alibaba or Tencent. Current regulatory approaches primarily focus on financial institutions, the incumbent players. But digital platforms follow an entirely different approach, although they became dominant financial services providers like in the case of China. For example, traditional regulation focuses on those institutions that hold the client balance, which is not the case with digital platforms in many cases.
- *Digitized regulation.* The IT-driven innovations require novel ways of regulation that can dynamically adapt to new technologies and changing environments and to move from an "ex post facto" regulatory approach to "ex ante" outcomes-based regime. But today's legal structures and regulations were written decades or even centuries ago and they were written on paper. To meet future requirements, regulation must follow a "digital by default" approach. With each new page of paper, complexity and implementation efforts increase. Just in the same way as companies started to develop open APIs and new infrastructures, regulators should also rethink their existing (analogue) regulation approaches (e.g., FCA's approach to increase regulatory reporting). For sure, the term "Code is Law" should not be interpreted literally, but instead new rights standards could in the future be implemented as algorithms for many (but not for all) areas. Those algorithms, on the other hand, require a new field of (technical) expertise by the regulators. For example, pricing algorithms often automatically coordinate prices among different companies and thus can lead to market manipulation and price rigging.

Despite all the dynamic IT developments, the regulation of fintech is still in its early stages both from a national and from an international perspective. Therefore, the process of identifying the right balance between innovation and precautionary principles is still ongoing. From a country-level perspective, a generic framework which distinguishes three alternative regulation methods can be differentiated (see Fig. 4.2; Amstad, 2019):

- *Ignore ("keep it unregulated").* Many regulators chose this method in the early days of the fintech development. A prominent example is China that gave room to the evolving p2p lending platforms and then regulated them when the risks were increasing. Regulation of this type can be applied, if no information asymmetry, no moral hazard, and no monopoly power are affecting investor protection, financial stability, and market integrity. An example in this category is payment providers which simply provide another form of access to already existing payment channels (e.g., Apple Pay).
- *Duck-type ("same risk, same rules").* A second method is to apply the same rules for the same kind of instrument, institution, or platform. This means that digitalizing an existing instrument (which formerly may only have an analogue representation) does not justify a different regulation compared with its analogue sister. This type of regulation applies principle-based regulation and technology-neutral regulation as the two major foundations. An example is ICOs for tokens that fall into the category of security tokens and can, therefore, be treated in the same way as traditional securities.
- *Code ("new functionality, new rules").* If fintech leads to novel instruments, institutions, or platforms, regulation needs to provide new ways of regulation due to new combinations of the market, credit, liquidity, and operational risks or changes in these risk categories. This, for example, applies to new features enabled by blockchain or the novel combination of business models enabled by fintech. A prominent example is a "fork" which splits one existing blockchain into two separated parts and thus creates a new platform, new instruments, and eventually even new institutions.

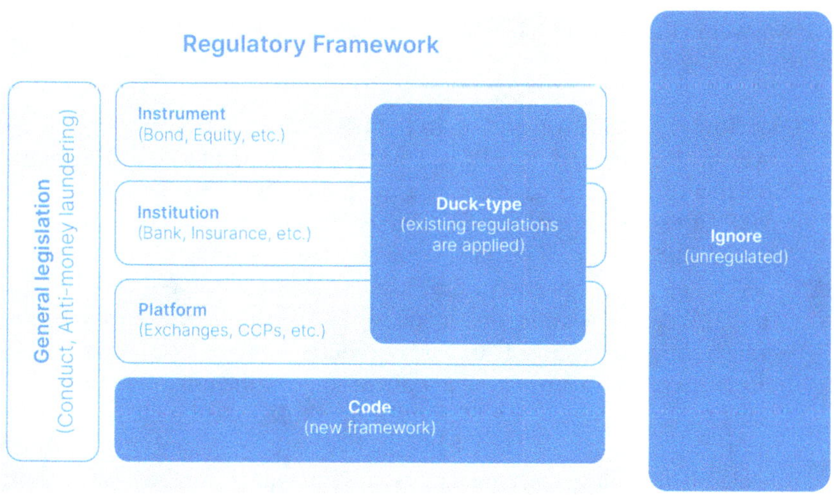

Fig. 4.2 Framework for fintech regulation (Amstad, 2019)

This generic perspective can be complemented by future developments in the areas of market access (sandboxes), data access (open banking), and market structures (non-banks requiring banking licenses). In the first field of market access, great efforts were undertaken in recent years to lower market entry hurdles for fintech startups by introducing sandboxes like in the UK, Singapore, or Switzerland. The approaches of the various countries differ regarding financial volumes and support by the regulator. The Australian Securities and Investments Commission (ASIC), for example, has limited its sandbox to AUD 10,000, while the one in Switzerland allows startups to experiment up to CHF one million. In 2018, the FCA introduced the so-called "Global Financial Innovation Network" (GFIN), an initiative to connect regulators around the world (see case study). The second field of data access is apparent in many countries like Australia, New Zealand, UK, Singapore, and the European Union and touches the topic of "open banking." Finally, the field of market structures holds implications especially for non-financial institutions which are connected to financial services or provide services for financial institutions. An example is cloud service providers for banks which might become regulated in the future.

But as many new applications, which will be developed in the future, cannot be foreseen, yet a comprehensive approach is required. An example for such a comprehensive regulatory approach is the European Commission's "Digital Finance Package" (https://ec.europa.eu/info/publications/200924-digital-finance-proposals_en). The strategy focuses on four main priorities: (1) removing fragmentation in the EU market, (2) adapt the EU regulatory framework to facilitate digital innovation, (3) promote a data-driven finance and addressing the challenges and risks with the digital transformation, and (4) enhancing the digital operational resilience of the financial system. Part of this framework is a digital finance strategy, a framework for crypto assets, a framework for digital operational resilience to prevent and mitigate cyber threats, and a renewed strategy for modern and safe retail payments. Another early mover in the field of fintech regulation was the UK.

Case Study: Fintech Regulation in the UK

- Already back in 2005, the UK laid the foundation for fintech with the introduction of real-time payments via the Faster Payments network. And in 2007, it became one of the first markets in the world to issue contactless cards. Later, as part of its fintech strategy, the "Department of Innovation" was set up in 2014 as part of the Financial Conduct Authority (FCA).
- In 2016, the UK was the first in the world to create a regulatory sandbox, which allows innovators to trial new products, services, and business models in a real-world environment without some of the usual rules applying. This was an answer of the FCA of being a rules-based regulator (in contrast, for example, the USA has principle-based regulators) which often makes it difficult to react to innovations. The sandbox in the meantime has switched to a digital environment, where startups can access simulated

data based on real customers (e.g., from Barclays or Lloyds). Another activity of the Department of Innovation is so-called "Innovation Pathways," which started as "office hours" for supporting startups in their various activities. For example, the FCA now allows for self-certification for private equity investments. After some self-learning one must pass an exam and is then allowed to invest in private equity. Another element that the department operates is the "Emerging Technologies Research Hub," which analyzes novel technologies according to their impact for banking and finance. Finally, the FCA has launched a digital assets sandbox for tokenized securities. Finally, the FCA created the "Innovation Advisory Group" which includes other players that are important for the design of the financial system, including the tax authority and the Bank of England (which is also one of the advantages in the UK, where all relevant stakeholders in London are just a footstep away from each other). Other activities in fintech are:

- The FCA provides digital banks like Starling and Monzo a special banking license "with restrictions" which is designed for startup companies that do not have the required capital.
- Fintech companies (e.g., Wise, Modulr, and Form3) can open accounts with the Bank of England and gain access to the payment system.
- The FCA created an Open Banking Implementation Entity which is a company that designed a model for data sharing and the definition of open banking API standards.
- In June 2023, the UK introduced the Financial Services and Markets Act, which defines crypto assets as regulated financial assets. This includes also capital requirements for stablecoin issuers and consumer rights.
- Recently, the FCA also announced an AI sandbox, which will define how AI algorithms are going to be regulated.

• From an international perspective, in 2018, the FCA introduced the so-called "Global Financial Innovation Network" (GFIN), an initiative to connect regulators around the world and which is chaired by the FCA.

Source: Financial Conduct Authority

4.1.2 Regulatory Sandboxes

To achieve a better balance toward financial innovation in the innovation trilemma, a regulatory sandbox was introduced by the British regulator FCA in 2016 as the first worldwide. Already in 2012, following the financial crisis, the UK government created the Financial Conduct Authority (FCA), to replace the former Financial

Services Authority (FSA). With this, the new regulator also became the new pacemaker to encourage innovation in the financial industry. In 2016 the FCA's Innovate Department launched the world's first regulatory sandbox which "allows innovators to trial new products, services and business models in a real-world environment without some of the usual rules applying" (Ofgem, 2018). Since then, around 200 companies (from a total of around 8000 fintech companies in the UK) have gone through this sandbox. Already by 2021, 73 sandboxes in 57 countries were launched. Currently, most regulators provide the sandbox as a service to prove that the firms who apply are compliant with existing rules. However, a specific learning environment for the regulators has not yet been established. For example, the FCA's sandbox model comprises four steps (Deloitte, 2018):

- The *first step* for a company is to submit an application which includes a company's business plan and describes how it meets the sandbox's eligibility criteria. As part of this process, the FCA may contact other organizations to obtain clarification or further information before deciding on the application. Once accepted, firms normally stay between 3 and 6 months in the sandbox.
- The *second step* is to complete all required paperwork and set up the capabilities to obtain the necessary authorizations, typically with restrictions such as the number of customers and/or the volume of transactions.
- The *third step* is testing. In many cases, it might take some weeks to months to receive all necessary authorizations. But even after a company is authorized, setting up all capabilities for testing can be very time-consuming, especially for customer acquisition and opening a business bank account.
- The *fourth step* is the exit. After the end of the testing period, companies need to transition out of the sandbox. As part of this process, companies have clearly defined exit plans regarding customer transition, etc. In addition, firms need to submit a final report to the FCA.

After a company has exited the sandbox, it must decide on how to continue its business. Most apply for a "variation of permission" to lift the restrictions imposed during the test. Most companies choose this option, while only a few reconsider their business model and regulatory position to become unregulated.

In general, the major benefit of the regulatory sandbox is that it reduces the costs of entering the financial services industry, as regulatory costs are in most cases the biggest part of launching a new business in this industry. However, it is not clear who benefits most from this sandbox approach: On the one hand, policy makers emphasize the benefits to the economy and the public, and on the other hand, entrepreneurs and investors see it as an instrument for more investment opportunities and high growth. These results are confirmed by two studies which note that the likelihood of being accepted into the sandbox increases the credibility of firms with both investors and customers alike (Deloitte 2018), and an entry into the sandbox is associated with a higher probability of raising funding and an increase of about 15% in the average amount of funding raised (Cornelli et al., 2022). In another study. Hellmann et al. (2022) found evidence of positive externalities even at the industry level. Participation in the sandbox by one startup is followed by increased entry and more money being raised by other startups in the same industry. In addition, there is some evidence that the sandbox screens out better companies, but there is no evidence that companies' momentum significantly increases after their participation in the sandbox. This means that the positive effect on a single company is lower than on the industry overall. Another effect of the industry-level increase of market entry and money being raised might be companies that try to avoid regulation by observing the sandbox outcomes very closely.

The following case study of the Global Financial Innovation Network (GFIN) shows how regulators aim to cooperate internationally to reduce cross-jurisdictional frictions and foster innovation across boundaries.

Case Study: Global Financial Innovation Network (GFIN)
In collaboration with 11 financial regulators and related organizations, the Financial Conduct Authority (FCA) in 2018 proposed the creation of the Global Financial Innovation Network (GFIN) to create a global sandbox and foster collaboration in four main areas:

- *Regulatory cooperation:* Collaborate on common challenges and policy questions in different jurisdictions.
- *Speed to market:* Reducing the time it takes to bring ideas to new international markets.
- *Governance:* Supporting firms in cross-border testing of novel business models.
- *Emerging technologies/business models:* Support cross-border focused concepts like artificial intelligence, distributed ledger technology, data protection, regulation of securities and initial coin offerings (ICOs), know your customer (KYC), and anti-money laundering (AML).

Source: GFIN (2018)

4.2 Non-bank Regulation

While regulators across the globe have heavily regulated the incumbents after the financial crisis in 2008, recent developments opened the regulatory landscape for non-banks to foster innovation. Among the examples are PSD2 in Europe, open banking in the UK, or the sandbox initiatives in various countries. While innovation holds a lot of potential, it also poses some risks which are associated with this potential (see Table 4.1). For example, the Financial Stability Board explores whether non-banks, with a special focus on the bigtechs, should be enforced to share data with other companies like banks. More generally, this raises the question of whether it might make sense "(…) to promote the mobility of data between the various actors that are involved in the provision of financial services" (Financial Stability Board, 2019).

Table 4.1 Potential areas of regulatory risks by non-banks

Potential areas of risks	Examples for regulatory risks by non-banks
Systemic risks	• Digital ecosystems which include new players like the GAFA companies may evolve to big players with critical market infrastructures (e.g., Apple Pay, Google Pay, etc.) • Non-banks may become providers of financial services outside the regulated financial infrastructure (e.g., Libra, Amazon Lending, etc.)
Credit risks	• The credit quality of banks could decrease if non-banks increase their lending business and improve their risk management capabilities due to access to more and better customer data. • Non-banks may take more risk than the incumbent banks if they follow models like the new originate-to-distribute model from WeBank in China, etc.
Liquidity risks	• Non-banks could nudge herding behavior of customers and lead to monopolies in deposit-taking as this is the case with Ant Financial in China which already manages the world's largest fund. • If a non-bank has reached a critical mass as a provider outside the existing financial infrastructure, deposits could flow from the incumbent banking system to a reduced number of custodians (e.g., Libra).
Profitability risks	• When non-banks have partnerships with incumbents or develop new digital layers on top of the existing financial market infrastructure, the incumbents might have to pay a premium to them. • An increased competition of the incumbents with non-banks might reduce the margins for banks.
Operational risks	• With non-banks emerging as relevant players, they may face operational risks. For example, the Diem Reserve would have been required to be calculated several times daily accurately. • Non-banks also face risks in the field of cybersecurity as they provide services that are networked with other consumer-related services in digital ecosystems. In contrast to banks, non-banks don't have to comply with special regulations yet.

These risks have a close connection to technologies like open banking APIs and digital IDs (see Sect. 5.6). However, now, the emerging financial system and the existing one coexist side by side with non-sovereign (e.g., stablecoins) and sovereign money (e.g., fiat currencies and first examples of CBDCs). But there are several connections between the two, such as the exchange of fiat currencies into privately issued digital currencies and in reverse, stablecoins backed by fiat currencies, custody of crypto assets, CBDCs, and securities settlement. This connection poses new risks, as existing AML and KYC requirements have to be met, since the same rules apply for both worlds. But different regulatory frameworks for different jurisdictions might additionally apply, and also depending on whether, for example, a stablecoin relies on one currency or multiple ones. Therefore, solutions like privately issued digital currencies might not lead to a single unified regulatory framework, but eventually to a more coordinated approach for fintech regulation between the different jurisdictions. In addition, financial privacy where the government is not monitoring every individual's financial transactions is a value, which reflects individual freedom and privacy. For example, CBDCs can lead to a loss of privacy in this respect, as transactions can be monitored. So, the best solution might come from the existing cash world, where transactions between two individuals and their (physical) wallets can be anonymous. A token-based digital money solution, where an individual can transfer a digital token to another individual, might therefore be a good alternative to an account-based approach (see Sect. 3.3.3). An example of how both worlds currently coexist is El Salvador, which approved Bitcoin as a legal tender on September 7, 2021.

Case Study: Bitcoin as a Legal Tender in El Salvador

- The US dollar has been the official currency in El Salvador, which has now been supplemented with Bitcoin. For this, the country acquired $200 Mio. of Bitcoin reserves.
- Bitcoin is freely convertible over the ATM network and an app, which subsidizes transactions. For this, users must download the Chivo digital wallet and register with their national identity number.
- Citizens can pay for items from global companies such as Pizza Hut and Starbucks that operate in El Salvador as well as pay for bills for those involved with Claro, a mobile phone company. Grocery shopping and trips to the hairdresser are also payable by Bitcoin with El Salvador ramping up the number of businesses that can accept Bitcoin with the country fully embracing the digital economy for now and the future.
- However, according to surveys, less than 5% of Salvadorans even know what a Bitcoin is. 70% of the population do not want to use it.
- One obvious reason for the introduction is to increase financial inclusion as approximately 70% of El Salvador does not have access to traditional financial services. In addition, Bitcoin is of particular interest to El Salvador for remittances. Around two million Salvadorans live in the USA. That's almost a third of the population. They transfer between $ 4 billion and $ 6 billion a year to their homeland, which corresponds to about a fifth of the GDP. On the other hand, there is the fear that illegal transactions could be transacted over Bitcoin, as El Salvador is considered a drug corridor for cocaine shipments from South America to the USA. The drug cartels increasingly used cryptocurrencies in their money laundering transactions.

Source: https://finance.yahoo.com/news/people-buy-bitcoin-el-salvador-150054767.html

A very prominent example of an entirely new fintech-based infrastructure, which also has connections to the incumbent financial system, is stablecoins. Stablecoins rely on an ecosystem of multiple interdependent entities with different roles, technologies, and governance structures. Appropriate regulation and accountability therefore require an understanding of the ecosystem as a whole and how all the different stakeholders interact. Table 4.2 shows fields of legal and regulatory relevance, potential challenges for the use of stablecoins, and potential solution approaches to these challenges.

Table 4.2 Legal and regulatory challenges of stablecoins and potential solution approaches

Legal and regulatory fields of relevance	Legal and regulatory challenges	Potential solution approaches
Jurisdictions	Potential conflicts of law if stablecoin payments are cross-jurisdictional (e.g., tax, etc.)	Cross-jurisdictional standardization
Governance	Interconnected stakeholders with some not necessarily falling under regulatory oversight (e.g., for recovery)	Using principles of activity-based regulation instead of institution-centric regulation
Compliance	Stablecoins pose risks for money laundering and other illicit activities	The frameworks of the Financial Action Task Force (FATF) could be applied and extended to stablecoins
Safety	Prevent liquidity dislocation and credit loss	Application, extension, and certification of the principles for financial market infrastructures (PFMI) defined by IOSCO
Cybersecurity	Prevent fraud, theft, and other cyber incidents	Application, extension, and certification of ISO, IEC NIST, etc. standards
Integrity	Stablecoins might be affected by price manipulations (e.g., if linked to an asset portfolio)	Clear separation of certain activities and roles in the ecosystem (e.g., portfolio manager, trading platform, etc.)
Data	Cross-jurisdictional data policies may cause conflicting scenarios	International standards for the exchange of cross-jurisdictional data
Protection	Consumer and investor protection might be affected	Application and extension of investor protection laws and capital market laws (e.g., if the stablecoin is defined as a security)
Competition	Increase market competition due to novel players and stablecoins	Cross-jurisdictional coordination of competition authorities as well as development and application of competition frameworks
Stability	Stablecoins may impact credit risks, liquidity mismatches, etc. and transmission to the real economy and monetary policy	International coordination of financial stability based on new frameworks as well as SupTech and RegTech

Despite their potential, stablecoins also hold some serious risks, such as cross-border spillover effects through the dislocation of currencies from their local issuance (e.g., "dollarization" effect in some countries), how to manage bank runs in case users want to exchange their stablecoins in fiat currencies all at once, or what would it mean for the credit function of banks if investors would deposit their funds in stablecoins instead of using banks? These risks call for regulation. For example, the Financial Stability Board proposes recommendations for stablecoin regulation, including (1) authorities' readiness to regulate and supervise, (2) comprehensive oversight, (3) cross-border cooperation, (4) governance structures, (5) appropriate risk management, (6) data storage and access to data, (7) recovery and resolution,

(8) disclosures of providers, (9) redemption rights, stabilization, and prudential requirements, and (10) conformance with regulatory, supervisory, and oversight requirements before commencing operations (Financial Stability Board, 2023a).

In general, there are two potential ways to regulate stablecoins, considering that regulation shall be used globally, the costs of regulation should be minimized, and whether transactions are enforceable under law:

- *Classic treaty or convention agreed to by various nations.* A classic treaty or convention typically needs to be agreed to by various jurisdictions. This process of adoption can take a very long time, and is a very slow process, considering the very dynamic development of stablecoins.
- *Model or uniform law.* A law that is proposed in a certain form with the aim of adopting it in different jurisdictions in a uniform version is called a model or uniform law. A model law is applicable for innovations, as they require much flexibility. Often, model laws are adopted by slightly different versions of the text to suit different jurisdictions' requirements. Given the enormous speed of market development, a model law could be a better solution than a classic treaty or convention. If implemented as a model law, the following aspects must be considered as relevant:

  - *Involved parties.* A stablecoin would involve a supervisory agency that holds administrative tasks and the issuer of the stablecoin. Such a supervisory agency would be needed in each country, where the stablecoin can be used. In addition, international coordination like the FATF would be required for best practices and standards for global stablecoins. The issuers would be limited to only approved organizations, which demonstrate reliability, integrity, and stability. This could involve only government insured banks, but also to other entities if they are approved by the supervisory agency.
  - *Consumer protection.* The model law must provide consumer protection function, such as the right to correct erroneous transactions, the protection of privacy and from excessive fees, etc.
  - *Monetary integrity.* The model law must provide elements for money laundering and terrorist financing according to worldwide standards of the G7's Financial Action Task Force (FATF), breaches of cybersecurity, where counterfeiting could be minimized by using a central clearing house and using blockchain technology, as well as failures of operational resilience.
  - *Financial stability.* Financial stability for global stablecoins is another major element for a model law This can be achieved by different elements, such as a redemption obligation of the stablecoin issuer (e.g., by governments through public–private partnerships; in Japan, for example, the stablecoin issuers are already limited to banks or licensed financial institutions), by collateralizing the redemption obligation (this could be very costly), derivatives (might not be large enough), or central banks that could extend their liquidity facilities in the same way a commercial bank already does this today.

Such a model law could cover the same regulation whether it's for retail or wholesale use.

4.3 Digital Finance Platforms

In the industrial era, most companies relied on supply-side economies of scale, whereas in the Internet era most companies rely on demand-side economies of scale. The traditional system employed by most businesses in the industrial era can be described as a pipeline in which a firm organizes a step-by-step process to create and transfer value, with producers at one end and consumers at the other. On the other hand, companies such as Amazon, Alibaba, or Airbnb are not valuable because of their cost structures, i.e., their capital, their machinery, or human resources. Instead, they are valuable because of the communities that participate in them. This phenomenon is called "network effect." In general, two types of network effects can be distinguished (Parker et al., 2016, 29ff): (1) Same-side network effects are created by the impact of users from the same side of the market (e.g., customers or providers). (2) Cross-side effects are created by the other side of the market. Both categories can come with different characteristics as either positive or negative ones. For example, positive same-side effects mean the positive benefits received by users when the number of users of the same kind increases. Conversely, negative cross-side effects can lead to a high complexity. An example is a digital media sharing platform, where too many varying digital rights management forms lead to such a high complexity for consumers that they reduce their usage of the platform. As digital platforms are fueled by massive amounts of data, they enable their operators to make faster and better decisions.

One of the first fintech platforms in finance that used this network effect was Blackrock's Aladdin (Asset Liability and Debt and Derivatives Investment Network). Aladdin was first provided externally in the mid-1990s and is now found at more than 80 asset managers and institutional investors with around 25,000 professionals who manage about $20 trillion in assets. The system carries out 250,000 trades and billions of financial calculations every day and aims to achieve data control. In contrast to this example, robo-advisors like Schwab/TD Ameritrade with around 26 million users and around $4.7 trillion assets under management, Vanguard with around 30 million clients and $6.7 trillion assets under management, and Fidelity with around 20 million customers and $5.2 trillion assets under management are still smaller but are steadily growing due to a zero-fee trend for achieving liquidity control. All these digital platforms have in common that they provide their own services and often link services from other third-party providers (linked services). Another very big provider of platform-based financial services is Ant Financial which provides a highly integrated business model.

Case Study: Ant Financial

- Ant Financial was officially founded in 2014. However, it originally dates to Alipay which was founded in 2004. Alipay was developed for facilitating payments on Alibaba's e-commerce platform. However, in 2010 the People's Bank of China (PBoC) announced that non-bank payment providers would need to obtain a license to operate in China. But Alibaba was registered as an offshore entity in the Cayman Islands for which the PBoC had not issued any application guidelines for foreign controlled payment entities. Alibaba Group therefore spun off Alipay to a legally separate entity that in 2014 developed into Ant Financial.

- Ant Financial focuses on providing equal access to financial services for individuals and businesses in need which is defined as "inclusive finance." The name "Ant" indicates the deliberate focus on previously underserved segments for financial products in China.
- Ant Financial has brought multiple digital finance innovations to the Chinese market. The company (and as part of its former structure within Alibaba) introduced at least six innovations to the Chinese market:
  - In 2002, Alibaba established Chengxintong as a credit rating system for small and medium-sized enterprises (SMEs). Until today the system has successfully certified the credit status of more than one million SMEs with more than 30 million SMEs using the system to facilitate their business.
  - In 2004, Alibaba introduced Alipay which is one of the world's largest third-party mobile and online payment platform with approximately 520 million active monthly users.
  - In 2007, the firm launched AliLoan and in 2015 MYbank. While AliLoan focuses on providing loans for SMEs, MYbank provides loans with reduced rates or, in some instances, even interest-free loans to SMEs. By the end of 2017, MYbank provided more than seven million loans with more than 400 billion RMB with an average loan size of 8000 RMB.
  - In 2013, Ant Financial established ZhongAn Insurance in partnership with Tencent and Ping An Insurance. ZhongAn Insurance was the first online insurance company in China and was granted a license by the China Insurance Regulatory Commission. By 2020, the insurer had served more than 520 million customers and received more than RMB 55 billion in premiums.
  - In 2013, the company also launched Yu'e bao. Yu'e bao, until 2020, was the largest money market fund in the world with a volume of around $250 billion. Yu'e bao is not used in a traditional way or solving the same "business issue" as other similar funds. The fund is used as an instrument for consumers to save money on Taobao, Alibaba's online marketplace, while receiving interest. Thus, it works as a kind of micro saving tool which gives rural and unbanked Chinese consumers a saving product, as most Chinese consumers had no other savings products before.
  - In 2015, Ant Financial created Zhima Credit which provides individual Chinese consumers a credit rating and access to credit-based services such as microloans. For this, Ant Financial developed a credit rating

system with scores ranging from 350 to 950 determined from five factors based on big data collected from reliable sources. The five factors are (1) credit history to reflect the user's past payment history, where sources, for instance, counted the Alibaba e-commerce ecosystem, (2) behavior and preferences to illustrate the user's online behavior for segmentation purposes, (3) fulfillment capacity to reflect the user's ability of adhering to contracts such as financial products and loans, with sources counting other services in the Ant Financial ecosystem, (4) identity characteristics which rate the extent and accuracy of user's personal information, and (5) social relationships which reveal the user's influence within his/her network, his/her influence to the network, and his/her friends' credit scores.

Source: Ant Financial; Bonde and Pedersen (2018)

In addition to bigtech companies like Ant Financial, various large financial ecosystems are also emerging around State Street, JPMorgan, and Goldman Sachs, all with a focus on front side liquidity control and back side data control. A focus on digital finance platforms is primarily concentrated in the USA and China, while in Europe, language barriers, lower market integration, and higher fragmentation have not yet supported the emergence of dominant digital finance platforms.

Although digital finance platforms provide benefits for their users (e.g., reduced transaction costs and higher service levels), they also pose various risks like reduced client protection due to uncovered technology risks and platform complexity, lower innovation and restricted access of third-party developers, impact on national security as these platforms provide a single point of failure, technology risks of systemic dimension, as many financial institutions rely on the same technology, oligopolization of the financial system and platforms can escape regulation because of jurisdictional and sectoral conflicts. For regulation, four potential approaches might be used (see Table 4.3; Zetsche et al., 2020): no regulation, stimulate competition, moderate interventions, and regulation as public utility.

Table 4.3 Regulation approaches for digital finance platforms

Approach	No regulation	Stimulate competition	Moderate interventions	Regulation as public utility
Characteristics	• Test and learn. • Might lead to concentration.	• For example, by open data requirement for dominant platforms. • Unbundling of services and prices.	• Command and control regulation. • For example, by financial data gathering and analytics, code review.	• Nationalization/ co-ownership of large digital financial platforms. • Unbundling and separation of digital financial platforms functions, e.g., investment funds.

A major effect of digital finance platforms is a change in the regulation approach, which now deals with the regulation of systems instead of institutions. However, also for digital finance platforms it is not yet clear how these systems can be regulated effectively.

The following case study shows the impact of Switzerland's new DLT Act on the issuance of a wholesale CBDC and its impact on the new financial market infrastructure, which has been developed by SIX SDX.

Case Study: Switzerland's new DLT Legislation

- On February 1, 2021, the parts of the Swiss DLT act that amend the Swiss Code of Obligations, the Federal Intermediated Securities Act and the Federal Act on International Private Law, have entered into force. With this law, entries in electronic registers entail the same protection as negotiable securities and a wholesale CBDC token can be issued in the form of a so-called ledger-based security which means that (a) the token embodies the holder's claim against the Swiss National Bank, (b) the underlying right passes to the beneficiary simultaneously with the ownership of the token without further ado, and (c) the token transaction can be executed peer-to-peer, i.e., without the involvement of an intermediary.
- The new SIX Digital Exchange (SDX) infrastructure qualifies as a financial market infrastructure as per the Swiss Financial Market Infrastructure Act.
- Under the new Swiss DLT act, it is now possible to issue, transfer, and redeem wholesale CBDC. Under the applicable civil law, legal irrevocability in the context of cashless payment systems occurs with the update of the payor's account by the system (see Fig. 4.3).

Source: Swiss Federal Department of Finance and Swiss National Bank

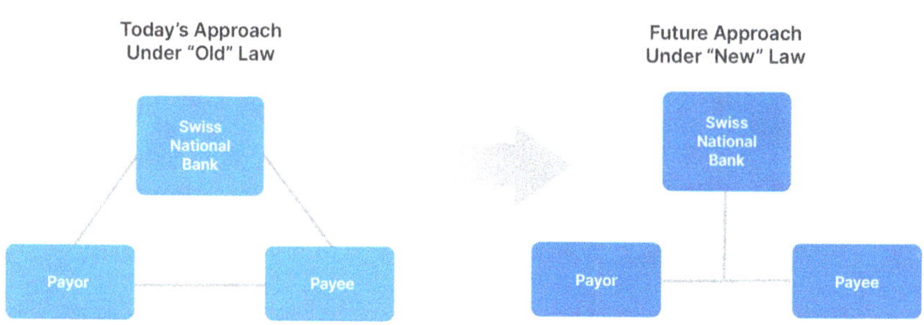

Fig. 4.3 Wholesale CBDC architectures under "old" and "new law

4.4 Crypto Asset Regulation

In an analysis of different jurisdictions worldwide, 32% have created classification frameworks for crypto assets (Blandin et al., 2021). These jurisdictions use three main categories of crypto assets:

- *Payment tokens.* A digital means of payment or exchange.
- *Utility tokens.* Access and use of a digital resource (e.g., a specific application).
- *Security tokens.* An investment similar in nature to traditional securities.

The regulatory response to crypto asset is for now best described as ad hoc, rhetorical, or driven by enforcement in some instances. This means that these regulations are in most countries still work in progress. A country-specific view shows that most parts of North and South America, Europe, and Australia have defined crypto assets as mostly legal, while countries like Russia, India, and Mexico have raised some significant concerns, and countries like China, Algeria, Colombia, Bolivia, Morocco, and Turkey see them as illegal (see Fig. 4.4).

Over the past few years, the regulatory message has flipped from being crypto friendly to being more crypto critical. Although regulation is not just about being restrictive recently the industry observed hardening pronouncements made by the IMF (2023), Financial Stability Board (2022), and European Union (2022) as well as the USA's Lummis-Gillibrand Act and the UK's HMT consultation paper which are an outcome of some of market failures like FTX. For example, on January 3, 2023, the Board of Governors of the Federal Reserve System (Federal Reserve), the Federal Deposit Insurance Corporation (FDIC), and the Office of the Comptroller of the Currency (OCC) collectively were issuing a statement on crypto asset risks to banking organizations and came to the conclusion that "(…) issuing or holding as principal crypto assets that are issued, stored, or transferred on an open, public, and/

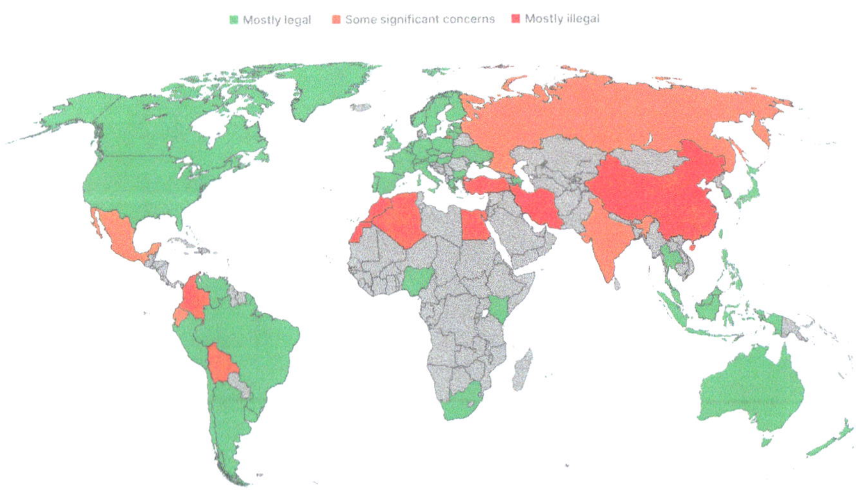

Fig. 4.4 Crypto asset regulation by country (Thomson Reuters, 2022, 2)

or decentralized network, or similar system is highly likely to be inconsistent with safe and sound banking practices" (Federal Reserve, 2023). This can be interpreted as an answer to the many fraud-like activities that happened over the past few years within the crypto sector. Examples are artificially inflated crypto trading volumes, no KYC, and no AML in the name of financial inclusion or lies about deposit protection (FDIC). These events demonstrate that some form of regulation is required.

The Financial Stability Board has also issued some general recommendations for the regulation, supervision, and oversight of crypto assets which include (1) authorities should have and utilize the appropriate powers and tools, (2) a general regulatory framework, (3) cross-border cooperation, coordination, and information sharing, (4) governance, (5) risk management, (6) data collection, recording, and reporting, (7) disclosures of crypto asset issuers, and (8) addressing financial stability risks arising from interconnections and interdependencies (Financial Stability Board, 2023b).

The following case studies outline some first concepts on crypto asset regulation from the EU and the USA.

Case Study: EU "Markets in Crypto assets" (MiCA) Regulation

- The European Union "Markets in Crypto assets" (MiCA) regulation introduced in 2020 provides a sound legal framework for crypto asset markets to develop within the EU by clearly defining the regulatory treatment of crypto assets that are not covered by existing financial services legislation. MiCA will enact a single licensing regime across the European Union for crypto assets that are not currently caught by existing financial regulation. The European Parliament adopted the draft on Monday March 14, 2022, and the entered into force on June 29th, 2023.
- MiCA has four broad objectives:
  - Instill appropriate levels of consumer and investor protection and market integrity.
  - Provide legal certainty for crypto assets not covered by existing EU financial services legislation.
  - Support innovation by promoting the development of crypto assets and the wider use of DLT (distributed ledger technology).
  - Ensure financial stability with specific rules for so-called "stablecoins," including when these are e-money.
- Under MiCa, the definition of crypto asset services is such that a business providing at least one of the following activities may be classed as a crypto asset service provider (CASP):
  - Exchanging crypto assets and fiat currency (e.g., using Euro to buy Bitcoin).

- Exchanging one class of crypto assets for another (e.g., using Bitcoin to buy Ethereum).
- The custody and administration of crypto assets on behalf of third parties.
- The operation of a trading platform for crypto assets.
- The execution of orders for crypto assets on behalf of third parties.
- The placing of crypto assets.
- The reception and transmission of orders for crypto assets on behalf of third parties.
- Providing advice on crypto assets.

- CASPs are defined in MiCA as "any person whose occupation or business is the provision of one or more crypto-asset services to third parties on a professional basis."

Source: https://www.esma.europa.eu/esmas-activities/digital-finance-and-innovation/markets-crypto-assets-regulation-mica

Case Study: US Executive Order on Ensuring Responsible Development of Digital Assets

- The US Executive Order lays out a national policy for digital assets across six key priorities:
- "*Protect U.S. Consumers, Investors, and Businesses* by directing the Department of the Treasury and other agency partners to assess and develop policy recommendations to address the implications of the growing digital asset sector and changes in financial markets for consumers, investors, businesses, and equitable economic growth. The Order also encourages regulators to ensure sufficient oversight and safeguard against any systemic financial risks posed by digital assets.
- *Protect U.S. and Global Financial Stability and Mitigate Systemic Risk* by encouraging the Financial Stability Oversight Council to identify and mitigate economy-wide (i.e., systemic) financial risks posed by digital assets and to develop appropriate policy recommendations to address any regulatory gaps.
- *Mitigate the Illicit Finance and National Security Risks* Posed by the Illicit Use of Digital Assets by directing an unprecedented focus of coordinated action across all relevant U.S. Government agencies to mitigate these risks. It also directs agencies to work with our allies and partners to ensure international frameworks, capabilities, and partnerships are aligned and responsive to risks.
- *Promote U.S. Leadership in Technology and Economic Competitiveness* to Reinforce U.S. Leadership in the Global Financial System by directing the

Department of Commerce to work across the U.S. Government in establishing a framework to drive U.S. competitiveness and leadership in and leveraging of digital asset technologies. This framework will serve as a foundation for agencies and integrate this as a priority into their policy, research and development, and operational approaches to digital assets.

- *Promote Equitable Access to Safe and Affordable Financial Services* by affirming the critical need for safe, affordable, and accessible financial services as a U.S. national interest that must inform our approach to digital asset innovation, including disparate impact risk. Such safe access is especially important for communities that have long had insufficient access to financial services. The Secretary of the Treasury, working with all relevant agencies, will produce a report on the future of money and payment systems, to include implications for economic growth, financial growth and inclusion, national security, and the extent to which technological innovation may influence that future.
- *Support Technological Advances and Ensure Responsible Development* and Use of Digital Assets by directing the U.S. Government to take concrete steps to study and support technological advances in the responsible development, design, and implementation of digital asset systems while prioritizing privacy, security, combating illicit exploitation, and reducing negative climate impacts.
- *Explore a U.S. Central Bank Digital Currency (CBDC)* by placing urgency on research and development of a potential United States CBDC, should issuance be deemed in the national interest. The Order directs the U.S. Government to assess the technological infrastructure and capacity needs for a potential U.S. CBDC in a manner that protects Americans' interests. The Order also encourages the Federal Reserve to continue its research, development, and assessment efforts for a U.S. CBDC, including development of a plan for broader U.S. Government action in support of their work. This effort prioritizes U.S. participation in multi-country experimentation and ensures U.S. leadership internationally to promote CBDC development that is consistent with U.S. priorities and democratic values."

Source: The White House (2022)

For the first time in history, the U.S. Federal Reserve is also included in broader activities of the U.S. Executive Order to analyze the issuance of a U.S. CBDC. One of the reasons is that, from an international perspective, CBDCs might lead to increased competition among nation states (see Sect. 3.5). Several factors have increased its international reach without adjusting existing capital controls. These factors are the increasing relevance of the Cross-Border Interbank Payment System (CIPS) and other alternatives to the SWIFT system, the global reach of payment platforms like Alipay and WeChat Pay, the developing role of the e-CNY in multi-CBDC cross-border payment corridors, and the use of the e-CNY in offshore instant payment systems.

While significant policy attention is placed on digital assets created in the crypto economy, there is only little attention what the economic innovation potential of web3 could entail (see Sect. 2.7; Chiu, 2021). Is there a broader commercial sphere that can be both enabled and governed by regulation, and not just a financial sphere? This means that financial regulation should be designed in a way that it considers broader implications of the crypto economy on the entire digital economy. One possible approach is to consider enterprise law for many of these models instead of focusing only on financial regulation. Among the examples are digital tokens which are used by entrepreneurs as an incentive to partner with other firms or security token offerings (STOs) which are often being referred to as an alternative approach to initial public offerings (IPOs) for smaller companies which could foster innovation for SMEs. These STOs are the followers of the former initial coin offerings (ICOs) which have been banned in many countries. But at least those crypto economic models have proven beneficial for funding the development of technology startups (see Sect. 2.7). For this, the European MiCAR regime, for example, demands a mandatory disclosure via white papers which have been sent to authorities and can then be published and marketed 20 days after the notification. MiCA also includes other requirements for this. However, given the early stage of such initiatives in the development, there might be different approaches for this as well, such as disclosures for pre-development projects may be tentative and more skeletal but relevant disclosures might be useful (e.g., team qualifications and expertise, description of the project concept, etc.), staged financing models which require funds to be held in escrow and can only be released according to certain milestones (which would also allow the refund of unspent balances), etc. Other examples for novel web3 approaches are p2p services in gaming, file storage (e.g., Filecoin), direct sales of digital goods (e.g., art, music, collectibles), etc. (see Sect. 3.4). All these examples are the result of the new possibilities to directly exchange values of all kinds on the Internet. Another important element of the p2p economy is payments. For this, most recently stablecoins have emerged. However, today, MiCA, for example, argues that only authorized entities can issue stablecoins.

For regulation, there is a conflict since centralized systems and decentralized systems both have their benefits and challenges (see Sect. 5.4). While centralized systems can be points of cybersecurity attacks and fraud, decentralized systems today do not have any processes in place for withdrawing transactions or any other issues related to centralized auditing. A major difference of all decentralized models is the absence of intermediaries. For example, are protocol providers intermediaries and with what responsibilities (e.g., whitelists of participating organizations) and how can KYC be performed? So, the question is if there are gaps in today's enterprise laws which would call for action to establish a new enterprise law for decentralized systems and a new DAO law? For example, many decentralized businesses are formed as companies. Also, this might make sense for a DAO, where a separate legal personality for the community of the DAO is beneficial. For example, this is the case for DAOs like PleasrDAO as the owner of the Doge meme NFT, where the lack of personality can raise queries with regard to the ownership of the NFT as fractionalized token holding is not the same as the ownership of the whole NFT. As such, DAOs may have different governance and especially exit protocols for token holders which are unlikely to be created under existing organizational law. This explains why DAOs cannot be companies. Companies have clearly separated governance bodies, while DAOs do not have any division of responsibility. In addition, enterprise laws do not cater for specifics of p2p and automated technologies and DAOs at scale could become platforms which would then require to be treated as such (see Sect. 4.3). So, one path forward could be to establish a DAO law which allows more flexibility for certain innovative businesses which can then be more agile and is not restricted by constraints of existing enterprise laws. However, the characteristics of decentralized finance show that an enterprise law could be a key element while financial regulation might be too specific. In other words, it might be more beneficial to internalize governance standards via enterprise law instead of externalizing standards via regulation.

4.5 RegTech

One major field of exploration in the field of regulation has been the use of technology, often termed as regulatory technology or for short "RegTech" (Buckley et al., 2020, 28). It focuses on the use of IT for regulation, monitoring, reporting, and compliance. Among the examples of RegTech are solutions for electronic know-your-customer (KYC) systems facilitating client onboarding by financial institutions and identifying patterns in payments in the context of Anti-Money Laundering (AML). While fintech is mostly related to the financial sector, RegTech is also applicable in other regulated sectors, such as healthcare. A comprehensive definition subsumes compliance controls ("ComplianceTech"), financial supervision ("OversightTech" or "SupTech"), and influencing the legislature ("PolicyTech") under the term (Buckley et al., 2020, 28). Concrete examples in the European Union are (1) digital regulatory reporting obligations, such as AIFMD and MIFIDII; (2) data protection with GDPR; (3) open banking with PSD2; and (4) digital identity solutions like eIDAS.

RegTech has evolved by demand- and supply-side drivers (see Fig. 4.5). While the demand drivers primarily view RegTech from the perspective of the regulating and regulated entities, the supply drivers take the perspective of the new opportunities provided by IT and novel data sources. For example, driven by COVID-19, regulatory support for e-KYC has increased by 33% across all surveyed fintech startups (Ziegler et al., 2021, 33).

RegTech involves at least three institutional domains (see Table 4.4). First, financial institutions are major drivers of RegTech development because they demand new tools to meet the new, increasingly more extensive regulatory requirements.

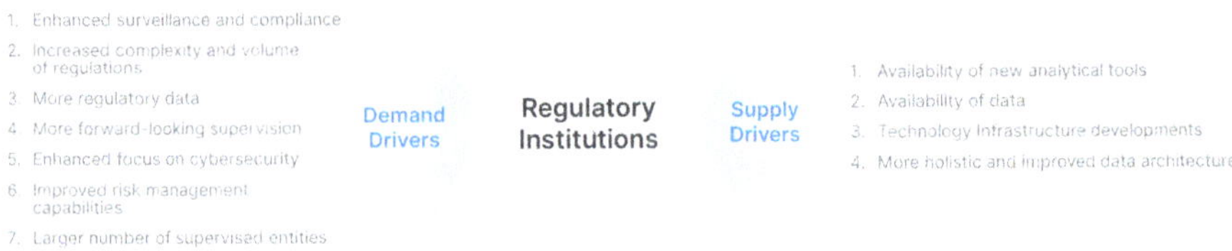

Fig. 4.5 Demand- and supply-side drivers of RegTech (according to Financial Stability Board 2020)

Table 4.4 RegTech focus and characteristics across different stakeholders

Institutions Characteristics	Financial institutions	Regulators	Startups
Focus	• Major drivers of RegTech development	• Lag in regulator adoption relative to private sector	• Incentives to trade off data for faster market entry
Systems requirements	• Demand efficient tools to deal with regulatory and compliance demands	• Yet need to develop systems to deal with rivers of new data and cybersecurity	• Automation of reporting and compliance more aligned with lean business model
Benefits	• Enhanced capabilities • Real-time monitoring • Cost reduction	• Improved data collection and visualization • Real-time monitoring • Cost reduction	• Novel business models enabled by IT
Risks	• Data standardization and data quality • Third-party dependencies • Improved resource requirements (e.g., rare specialists)	• Cyber risk and data security • Improved resource requirements (e.g., rare specialists) • Data localization (e.g., data storage across countries) • Regulatory arbitrage of regulated institutions (e.g., pre-warning systems of regulated institutions) • Reputational risks due to the lack of transparency of some RegTech tools	• Competition barriers for startups due to complexity and resource requirements compared to regulated institutions

Second, regulators need to develop new systems as well, but today lag in their adoption compared to the private sector. For example, in an analysis, only 29% of the regulators reported adequate resources for fintech regulation in their country during COVID-19 (Ziegler et al., 2021). Finally, startups develop novel approaches and systems based on innovative technologies for improved automation of reporting and compliance, often based on new business models.

Chapter 5
Financial System

IT, nation states, and (de-)regulation are strong drivers of change for the financial system for both the macro and the micro perspectives. From the macro perspective they redefine the transfer of resources from savers to those who need funds, from payors to payees, and from creditors to creditees. For this, the financial system today provides intermediaries (intermediary perspective) and holds five key functions (functional perspective): (1) produce information ex ante about possible investments and allocate capital, (2) monitor investments and exert corporate governance after providing finance, (3) facilitate the trading, diversification, and management of risk, (4) mobilize and pool savings, and (5) ease the exchange of goods and services (Levine, 2005). These functions are provided by financial institutions like central banks, commercial banks, non-bank financial institutions, and financial utilities, such as clearinghouses, credit rating agencies, central securities depositories, payment processors, credit card processors data providers, as well as regulatory and supervisory institutions (institutional perspective) (Law, 2018) who are complementary to each other (systemic perspective). The following sections outline how these different perspectives might change in the forthcoming years through the impact of digitalization, regulation, and nation states.

5.1 Banks

Banks, as part of the financial system, are an enabler for the real economy of physical goods and services (e.g., real estate, manufacturing plants, etc.) by providing services like payments, investments, and financing. As such, they play an important role in providing payment and lending services and allocating capital. Banks generate their revenues mostly by interest differential business, trading, and fees and commissions. For example, in 2017, the global financial intermediation system had

T. Puschmann, H. S. H. P. M. of Liechtenstein, *Financial System 2030*, Financial Innovation and Technology,
https://doi.org/10.1007/978-3-031-55700-2_5

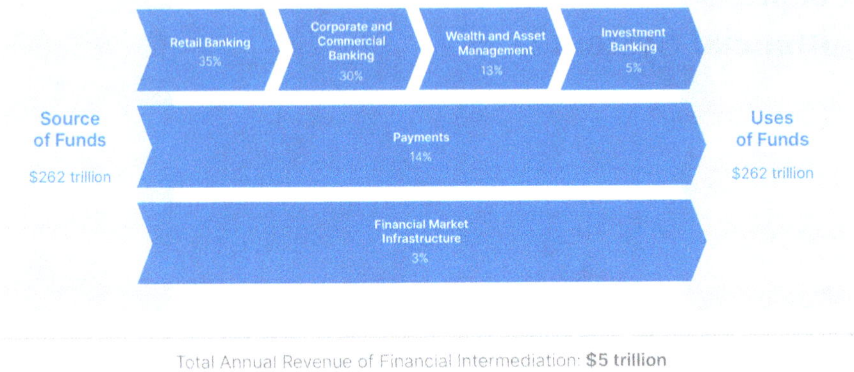

Fig. 5.1 The global financial intermediation system (modified according to McKinsey & Company, 2018)

a total volume of $262 trillion and the revenues associated with financial intermediation were $5 trillion (see Fig. 5.1). While retail and corporate/commercial banking together generated around 65% of this revenue, payments, wealth and asset management, investment banking, and market infrastructure accounted for around 35%. However, banks' position as financial intermediaries is currently challenged by fintech startups and other non-banks from outside the banking sector due to the following developments which are mainly driven by IT advancements:

- *In sales and advisory,* the use of digital channels for expert advice (e.g., video advice, AI chat bots) and digital self-advisory (e.g., robo-advisors like Betterment) are becoming more important (see Sect. 2.3).
- *In payments,* digital currencies of all kinds are penetrating the market. These include privately issued digital currencies like Bitcoin, stablecoins like USDC, or CBDCs which are currently explored in many countries (see Sect. 3.2).
- *In investments,* new business models in the field of digital assets are emerging (e.g., digitalization of non-bankable assets, NFTs, etc.) (see Sect. 2.7).
- *In financing,* blockchains allows us to tokenize physical goods like real estate and allows financing of property with smaller amounts (see Sect. 2.4).
- *In cross-processes,* novel applications in the field of knowledge transfer (financial education/literacy) and self-services emerge (e.g., self-IPOs with STOs).

Many of these services have first emerged in the non-banking sector rather than being implemented by banks (see Sect. 2.3). The reasons are in many cases heterogeneous and legacy IT systems and the fact that still most of the IT budget in banks is spent on maintenance of existing IT systems rather than on IT innovations (see Sect. 2.3). This has led to a sharp competition in various fields of the financial intermediation system. For example, the Americas is the region with the most fintech startups globally, accounting for 11,651 in total, which is an increase from 5686 in 2018. In contrast, the EMEA region accounts for 9681 fintech startups, an increase from 3581 in 2018, followed by the Asia Pacific region with 5061 startups with an increase from 2864 in 2018 (Statista, 2023). In addition, the non-bank financial

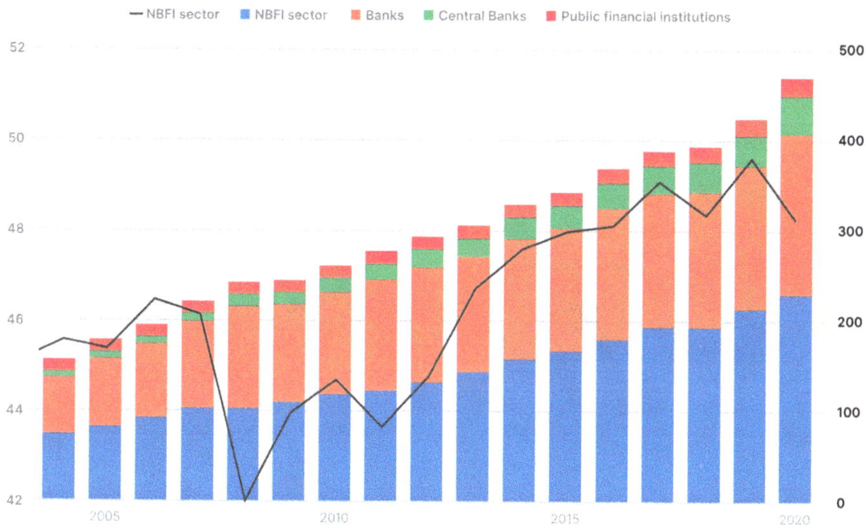

Fig. 5.2 Share of global financial assets (Financial Stability Board, 2021)

intermediation sector's relative share, which includes hedge funds, insurers, etc. of total global financial assets, has been continuously increasing to 48.3% in 2020, up from more than 43% in 2004 (see Fig. 5.2; Financial Stability Board, 2021).

These trends have led to a situation where banks are challenged from various sides. For example, by the middle of 2023 banks only make up 75% of the entire payment landscape's market capitalization, while fintech startups grew to 25%, up from around 10% in 2017 (Economist, 2023). These developments could lead to a reorganization of the banking sector and the financial system as a whole. The resulting potential future business models can be structured along the innovation degree (incremental vs. disruptive) and the banking process areas (back office vs. front office) and may result in four major patterns (see Fig. 5.3):

- *First,* banks provide secure custody and transaction services as one of their core competencies since their evolution as financial institutions. Currently, many examples in cyber risk demonstrate that the custodian function could be of increasing relevance for societies in the future. Examples are the storage of health or governmental data, etc. Banks could develop their competencies in this field and incrementally optimize their custody (e.g., digital wallets and assets) and transaction capabilities as well as develop new services for this area and to position themselves as a "Digital Custody and Transaction Bank."
- *Second,* although banks already operate complex IT infrastructures, the emergence of new blockchain-based environments could challenge the status quo soon. Over the past few decades, banks have heavily invested in their back-office infrastructures to meet increasing regulatory requirements and automate their internal processes. Currently, new initiatives based on blockchain infrastructures may lead to new infrastructures making those investments obsolete and requiring collaboration between incumbents, startups, and regulators to define standards

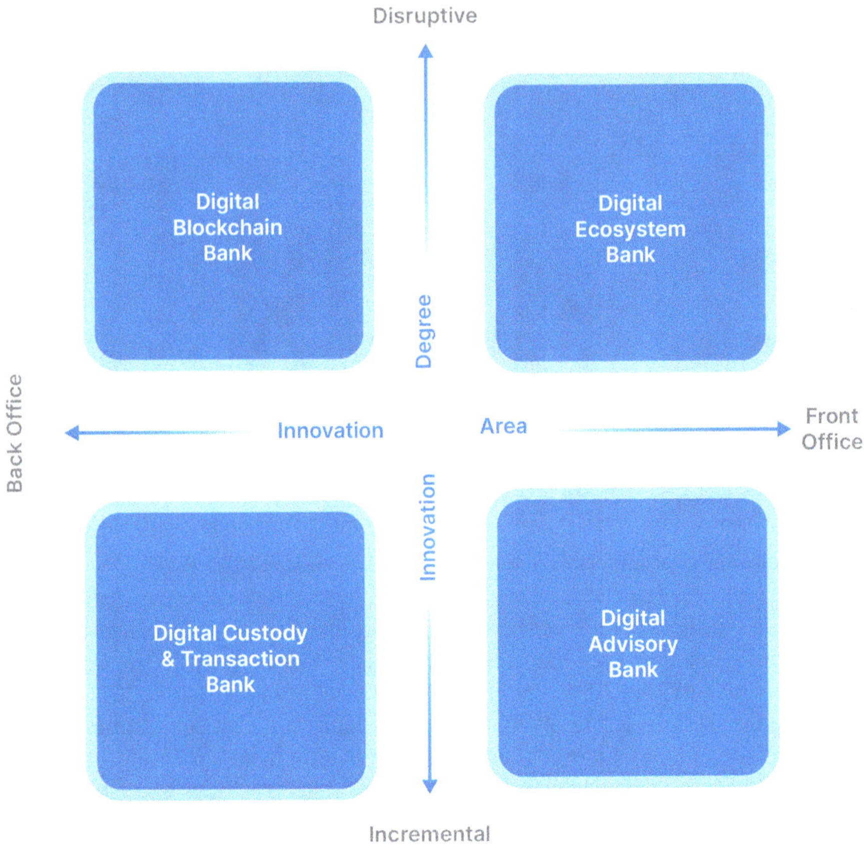

Fig. 5.3 Future digital banking models (Gasser et al., 2018)

and regulation governance. For this, new roles such as a "Digital Blockchain Bank" may evolve.

- *Third,* many banks currently increase their digital banking capabilities based on their existing IT infrastructures. As described in this book, the adoption rate of digital banking services is still low. In contrast to fintech startups, banks could use their existing client base and thus leverage their services to them. The emergence of core services like digital identity combined with digital advisory services will soon allow clients to conduct their financial services wholly online and support the development of a "Digital Advisory Bank."
- *Fourth,* banks have deep knowledge in complex banking products and processes that are implemented in existing IT infrastructures. Although the fintech startup companies provide innovative solutions for many areas, most of them still require transaction and custody processes that banks have provided as core competencies for centuries. Thus, future ecosystems could evolve as the cooperation of fintech startups and banks and lead to an entirely new "Digital Ecosystem Bank."

5.2 Financial Utilities and Market Infrastructures

In addition to banks and other financial institutions, financial utilities, which include central securities depositories, clearinghouses, credit rating agencies, information and data providers, payment processors, credit card processors, and exchanges, are other important elements of the financial system (Hubbard & O'Brien, 2018). Some of them are often bundled in financial market infrastructures (FMIs), for example, when capital markets substitute lending and savings functions offered by banks. But as banks realized that cost-efficiency dominates differentiation in these interbank processes, cooperation between banks has led to electronic infrastructures for multiple banks and increasingly also non-banks. FMIs are multilateral systems that connect various stakeholders and typically encompass institutions for business-to-business (b2b) payment and securities processing among banks as well as between banks and stock exchanges. Today's FMIs consist of three major elements (Gisiger & Weber, 2005): the stock exchange, the clearing and settlement provider (clearing organization), and the gross settlement payment system (payment organization). For example, the "Swiss Value Chain" is a joint venture of Swiss banks for the centralized processing of payment and securities transactions. The Swiss Value Chain enables integrated real-time processes from a market sales order to the completion of a securities transaction. Parts of this Swiss Value Chain are audited by the Swiss regulator FINMA, and all three FMI elements are bundled in one company called SIX. Consumers can only use these services via commercial banks. The architecture of the Swiss Value Chain is currently being transformed, which the following case study "Project Helvetia" shows. Just recently SIX introduced a new, blockchain-based FMI called SIX SDX which focuses on the instant (or "atomic") settlement of digital assets.

Case Study: Project Helvetia

- Project Helvetia is a project in the context of a wholesale CBDC which the Swiss National Bank (SNB) has developed together with the Bank for International Settlement (BIS) Innovation Hub and SIX Group.
- Today's Swiss Value Chain follows a sequential path along different processes from trading, clearing, securities settlement, and cash settlement which are all based on different IT systems (SIX Swiss Exchange, SIX x-clear, SIX SIS (SECOM), Swiss Interbank Clearing (SIC)) (see Fig. 5.4). Each of these processes includes a time delay of two days (T + 2), until its completion.
- SIX Group launched a new DLT platform for the issuance, settlement, asset servicing, and custody of tokenized assets (SDX Value Chain; see Fig. 5.4). The platform is a private permissioned peer-to-peer network and supports two trading mechanisms: (1) on-exchange on-book trading with multilateral settlement and (2) off-book and off-exchange over-the-counter

(OTC) trading with bilateral settlement. For this, SDX issues a Swiss franc-based stablecoin which ensures the settlement of tokenized assets on the SDX platform. This "SDX coin" will be funded one-to-one by participants' balances but will be a liability of SDX.

- To eliminate potential counterparty risks in the case of SDX issuing the SDX coin, Project Helvetia was launched. In this case, a Swiss franc-based stablecoin is backed by SNB. Project Helvetia involved two proofs of concepts (PoC). PoC 1 aimed at integrating a Swiss franc-based stablecoin backed by SNB into the novel SDX platform (wholesale CBDC) for issuance and redemption. PoC 2, on the other hand, aimed at linking the existing real-time gross settlement system (RTGS) with the SDX infrastructure for cash settlement.
- For PoC 1, an SNB technical account was introduced at SIC which tokenizes the amount and allows the issuance and redemption of the wholesale CBDC to an SNB node on the DLT platform by the commercial banks. For PoC 2, the SDX and SIC systems are synchronized by electronic messages between these two to ensure that the involved banks' node on the DLT platform and the SIC accounts on the SIC system rely on the same data. For this, the business hours of the RTGS and the SDX would have to be synchronized. Both PoCs were finalized successfully. The main advantage of this new architecture is the reduction in overall systemic risk for the settlement of securities. The other benefits are primarily on the banks' side as all process steps including clearing, securities settlement, and cash settlement are fully integrated without time delay (atomic swaps). However, one design question remained open at this time: who would be the provider of the notary node that oversees double spending and other central functions, and the architecture would have to ensure processing resilience as this node could be a single point of failure.
- The next phases of the project focused on (1) end-to-end connectivity between the systems involved and (2) cross-currency/cross-border scenarios.

Source: According to BIS (2020c)

As the example of the Swiss Value Chain shows, central bank money is, among other cases, used for the settlement of securities. In the traditional financial system with traditional assets, reserve balances (e.g., Fedwire and Depository Trust and Clearing Corporation (DTCC)) are used for this (see Table 5.1). However, in a fully digitized world, stablecoins and wholesale CBDCs might be used. For example, in Switzerland SDX deposits money in their account at the SNB and then issues a token on the platform that can be used by the institutions linked to the new digital exchange platform SDX. Helvetia I was a project for settling tokenized assets in central bank money, whereas Helvetia II focused on the issuance of a wholesale

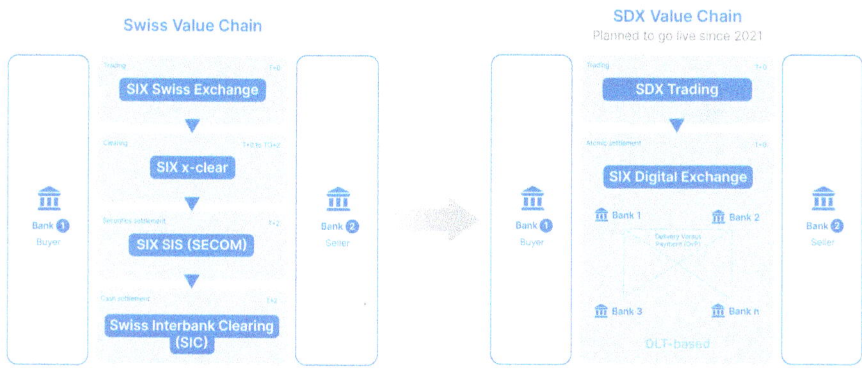

Fig. 5.4 As-is and to-be financial market infrastructure in Switzerland

Table 5.1 The future of settlement

		Cash leg payment in central bank money		
		Reserve balances	Stablecoin	Wholesale CBDC
Delivery (securities) leg	Traditional asset	Fedwire + DTCC	?	Unlikely
	Tokenized security	Helvetia I	SDX	Helvetia II, Jura

CBDC by the SNB. The project Jura extended this approach for cross-border settlement with Banque de France. All these projects focused on settling tokenized securities with central bank money.

The benefits and risks of stablecoins have already been explored in the previous section (see Sect. 5.5). In the context of FMIs, CBDC's role can be twofold:

- *CBDC for wholesale settlement within an FMI.* A security settlement platform operator uses central bank money to settle securities. Digitalization in wholesale settlement has emerged around financial markets that weren't always digital. For example, the orders were collected on the telephone or via fax machines and would then be transferred to the clearing house that would organize the payments on a ledger in pen. This process is still the same today but on digital ledgers and by using digital messages. One example for changing this process is Project Helvetia from BIS, SIX, and the Swiss National Bank. Clearly, token-based assets, which, for example, SIX SDX is built on, requires token-based money. Token-based money is also currently explored in the context of multi-currency settlement.
- *CBDC for retail payments.* Consumers use FMI services only via their banks, which assemble many other services for their customers. In this context, a CBDC is understood as a digital banknote and the (new) system around it. Consumers' needs and the design of a CBDC would vary from jurisdiction to jurisdiction, reflecting different economic and political structures as well as diverse payment landscapes. Therefore, the design of CBDC may vary in El Salvador, Syria, etc.

Three factors could be of relevance for the design of a retail CBDC (BIS, 2021): (1) it fulfills requirements, which are not yet met by the existing payment landscape (e.g., settlement finality), (2) it achieves network effects (e.g., by peer-to-peer functionality), and (3) it does not require consumers to buy new devices (e.g., new smartphones or additional hardware).

5.3 Bigtech

In recent years, large technology firms, the so-called bigtech companies in the USA (Facebook, Google, Amazon, Facebook, Apple) as well as their Chinese counterparts (Baidu, Alibaba, Tencent, Xiaomi) have undertaken major steps to enter the financial services industry. Among the examples was Facebook's project "Diem" to create its own digital currency or Alibaba's Ant Financial that offers its own core banking system to financial institutions and non-banks (see Sect. 4.3). The market capitalization of these companies combined with the huge number of billions of customers demonstrates the enormous power compared to the incumbent financial institutions. It is estimated that especially these large technology companies may have a profound impact on the existing financial system. However, as of today, financial services only make up 11.3% of the bigtech companies' revenues, while IT (46.2%) and consumer goods (21.6%) provide the largest part (Cornelli et al., 2020). Since most of the revenues are in payments and financing, the bigtech firms concentrate on these areas and do not favor investment services except Apple Savings and Yu'e Bao (see Table 5.2).

While the payment, investment, and financing activities of banks are well documented, data on the startup and the bigtech sector are still rare, although there have been efforts to improve these data (e.g., Serena, 2019; Cornelli et al., 2020; Financial Stability Board, 2020). A recent data collection in the financing domain (see Fig. 5.5) shows that credit volumes of fintech startups reached $297 billion and bigtech credit volumes increased to $397 billion in 2018 (which is a total of $694 billion for both sectors), up from $9.9 billion and $10.6 billion in 2013 (Cornelli

Table 5.2 Bigtech financial services (examples, not comprehensive)

Financial services Bigtech company	Payments	Investments	Financing
Google	Google Pay, Google Wallet	–	Google Store Financing
Amazon	Amazon Pay, Amazon Cash	–	Amazon Lending
Facebook	WhatsApp Pay	–	–
Apple	Apple Pay, Apple Pay Later	Apple Savings	Apple Card
Ant Financial	Alipay	Yu'e Bao	Chengxintong (for SMEs), Zhima Credit (for consumers)

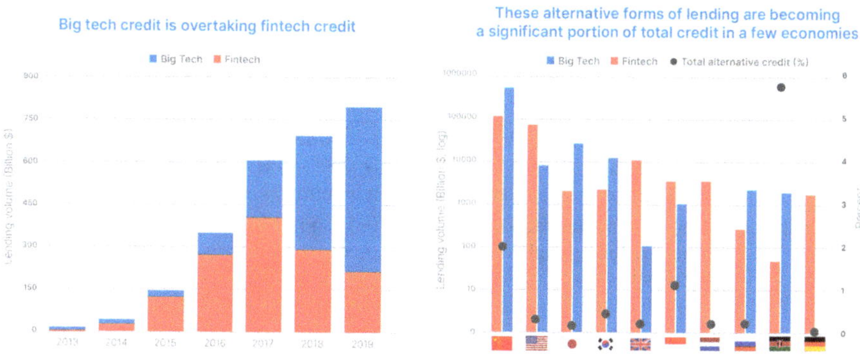

Fig. 5.5 Global bigtech and fintech financing (Cornelli et al., 2020)

et al., 2020). In 2019, bigtech credit volumes were estimated to reach $572 billion and fintech $223 billion, amounting to a total of $795 billion, an increase of 14.55% compared to 2018.

In contrast to banks that provide lending services to all customer segments, the bigtech companies primarily focus on micro-, small, and medium-sized enterprises (MSMEs). For example, the credit gap of these MSMEs in developing economies amounts to almost $8.1 trillion or about 40% of the GDP (Pazarbasioglu et al., 2020). The largest market for MSMEs is China, and the biggest companies therein are Ant Financial, WeBank, Baidu, and JD.com that in total provided a credit volume of $363 billion in 2018 and $516 billion in 2019. One pattern which can be identified from the data is that fintech startup lending is predominantly in Europe, while bigtechs are stronger in Asia. According to the same study, the credit volumes of fintech and bigtech are more developed with higher GDP per capita. In addition, fintech credit is more prevalent where there are fewer bank branches per capita. Total alternative credit is higher where ease of doing business is higher, with greater investor protection and judicial system quality where bank capital, provisions, and deposit funding are higher and where financial markets are more developed. Overall, alternative forms of credit seem to complement more traditional credit markets, not to substitute them.

Although the credit volumes increased over the past few years, they are still relatively small compared to the total numbers of credits provided globally. But from a strategic perspective, bigtech companies and banks are in competition and each provider type has its advantages and disadvantages (see Table 5.3). Banks already provide a high number of financial services and have personal interaction channels and verified and reliable customer data. On the other hand, bigtechs often have (until now) less regulatory requirements, modern IT systems, and a large amount of data for a large number of customers also from outside the financial services domain.

Despite the bigtech's efficiency advantages in modern IT systems and large amounts of data, bigtechs also pose risks and can lead to monopolies in certain areas. Regulation of bigtechs therefore means both simplifications (e.g., the Indian Unified Payments License, UPL) and tightening (e.g., the Indian E-Commerce

Table 5.3 Comparison of banks and bigtechs

Provider type Areas of competition	Banks	Bigtechs
Strategy	(+) High number of financial services (−) Strict regulatory requirements	(−) Still small number of financial services (+) (So far) less strict regulatory requirements
Organization	(+) Personal interaction and thereby selling higher margin products (−) Often old IT systems are a major hurdle to building new services	(−) (So far) limited sale of higher margin products like mortgages, etc. (+) Modern IT systems that enable cost-efficient product sales
Technology	(+) Verified and reliable customer data with personal interaction data (−) Small number of customers and no data from non-financial transactions	(−) Mixture of verified and less reliable data (+) Large amount of data for a large number of customers for financial and non-financial transactions

Law) at the same time. In addition, the regulation of bigtechs requires not only financial regulation but also the involvement of other regulators (competition authorities, data protection authorities, etc.) which makes bigtech regulation a very complex field.

5.4 Decentralized Finance

In a centralized financial system, financial institutions (and more recently also fintech startups and bigtech companies) act as intermediaries for financial transactions. These intermediaries reduce transaction costs and establish trust among the involved stakeholders of financial transactions (Benston & Smith, 1976). This also holds advantages for customers, as they don't have to bundle services from various providers (e.g., a fintech startup for different services in payments, investments, and financing) themselves; instead the intermediary integrates them in a regulatory compliant way. However, the same financial institutions can over time become too dominating. For example, a financial institution like a bank (but also a non-bank like a bigtech company) might accumulate too much market power in its role as an intermediary. Contrarily, in a decentralized finance (DeFi) system, financial transactions are facilitated in p2p networks (see Sect. 3.4) without intermediaries but by direct interactions of peers. This can lead to reduced transaction costs by reducing monopoly costs, while at the same time creating network effects from which all participants can benefit (Catalini & Gans, 2019). DeFi can therefore be defined as "(...) the elimination—or reduction in the role—of one or more intermediaries or centralized processes that have traditionally been involved in the provision of financial services" (Financial Stability Board, 2019).

The concept of DeFi is believed to have been first introduced in 2014 when Vitalik Buterin published the Ethereum White Paper presenting the future generation of smart contracts and DAOs. Ethereum allows financial services to depend on the execution of Turing-complete programs, so-called smart contracts (Buterin, 2014). A proliferation of traditionally centralized financial instruments and services are subsequently being replicated and operated on blockchain systems using smart contracts (Amler et al., 2021). While DeFi only recently gained broader interest, its roots date back to technological developments of cryptography in the 1980s as well as the early fintech movement in the 2000s. One example for this is the foreign currency (FX) market, where a fintech startup in 2001 introduced the concept of matching buyers and sellers of FX from different countries to match their currency exchange requests (Euromoney, 2021). Later, the cryptocurrency movement with the Bitcoin white paper from 2008 as well as concepts like Facebook's Diem continued the discussion around DeFi with novel approaches. Today, Ethereum is the major backbone of most DeFi approaches and most of the growth was driven by projects from mid-2020 until now. The total value locked (TVL), which is a metric used to measure the total value of digital assets that are locked or staked on a particular DeFi platform, increased from zero in 2018 to around $250 billion by December 2021 and decreased thereafter to currently around $43 billion as of November 2023 and more than doubled again to around $93 billion as of April 2024 (https://defillama.com).

As a recent analysis of DeFi solutions shows, most of the applications are built on Ethereum (58.7%), followed by Tron and Binance (8.8% each) as well as Avalanche (3.4%) (see Fig. 5.6).

DeFi applications exist in all areas in payments, investments, and financing (see Table 5.4). While fintechs like Venmo, Robinhood, and Lending Club are all examples for centralized finance approaches including incumbent intermediaries, Bitcoin, Yearn, and Aave are examples for DeFi applications which do not require any intermediaries to function.

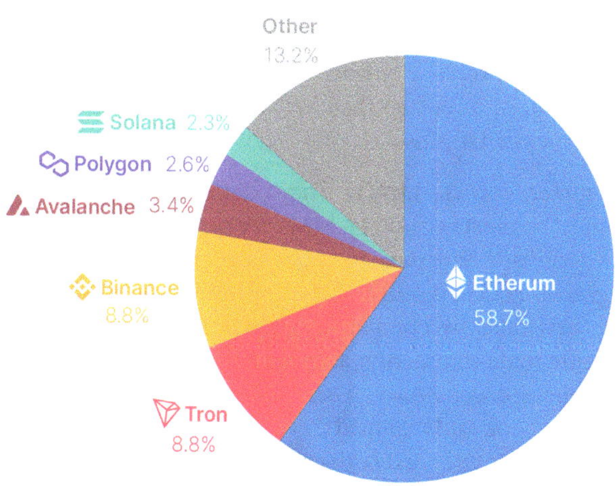

Fig. 5.6 TVL by protocol as of August 2022 (Puschmann & Huang, 2024)

Table 5.4 Examples for CeFi and DeFi

Financial processes Models of finance	Payments	Investments	Financing
Centralized finance	• Venmo	• Robinhood	• LendingClub
Decentralized finance	• Bitcoin	• Yearn	• AAve

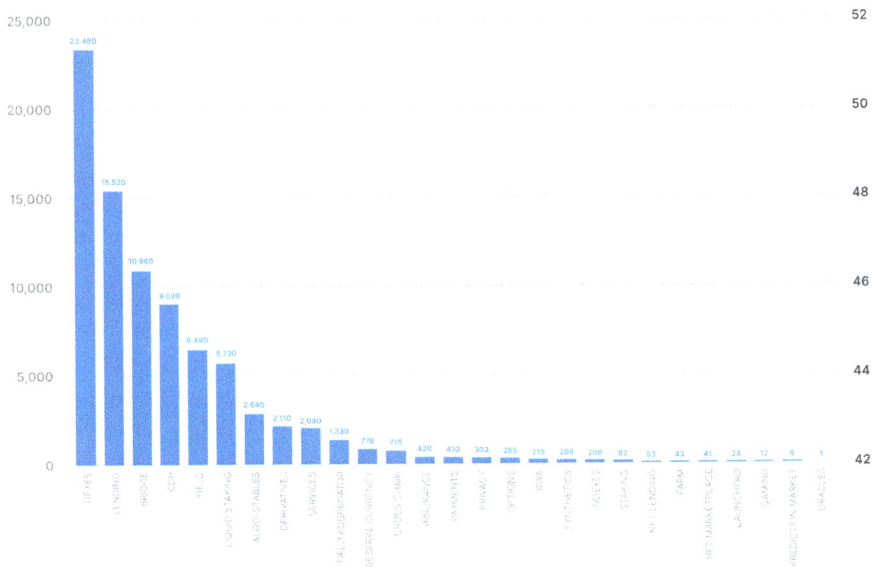

Fig. 5.7 DeFi applications (Puschmann & Huang, 2024)

The same study mentioned before revealed that most applications can be found in decentralized exchanges (DEXEs) (28% of use cases) and lending (9% of uses cases; see Fig. 5.7).

DEXEs are marketplaces built as distributed applications. They can connect buyers and sellers in a permissionless way, removing any central authority to oversee and authorize trades and relying on smart contracts instead. Users retain control of their funds, as they need to ensure their self-custody of crypto assets. There are at least four major types of DEXEs:

- *Automated market makers (AMMs).* They control exchange rates thanks to a certain algorithm. The most common AMMs are based on a liquidity pool consisting of at least two assets, where the combined asset reserves must remain unchanged.
- *Reserve aggregators.* They source liquidity from various liquidity pools and try to return the best rates by comparing all prices from these liquidity pools and splitting a single trade transaction across multiple DEXEs.
- *On-chain/off-chain order books.* There, users can issue orders that are aggregated in an order book and matched through a matching algorithm.
- *Over-the-counter (otc)/p2p exchanges.* They allow users to swap tokens with counterparties by negotiating the exchange rate bilaterally and, in case of an agreement, to execute the trade on-chain.

Some major players of DEXEs are Uniswap, Curve, and Bancor. These liquidity pools are used for crypto asset or stablecoin exchange transactions where an AMM approach is used. For this, a liquidity provider adds a pair of tokens to a smart contract and receives liquidity pool tokens that represent their stake. Traders can add one type of token and withdraw the other as long as the token in the pool remains the same. The trader pays a fee for the exchange trade. There are also secondary markets for tokens. In theory, such liquidity pools open access to FX at scale by establishing a user-to-contract model.

In addition to exchanges, lending DeFi applications allow users to borrow and lend assets in a decentralized and permissionless way. To ensure that the borrower pays back the borrowed funds, platforms usually require collateral tokens to be locked when minting new liquid assets, with algorithmic mechanisms to manage the cases of shrinking collateral value. Popular lending protocols include AAve, Compound, MakerDAO, and KAVA. At these DeFi applications lenders place available funds in a liquidity pool from which borrowers can then borrow. The borrowing can be fixed or work on a variable rate and the interest rate is usually calculated on Ethereum block time. Like in the traditional financial system, loans are collateralized and if a borrower defaults, then the collateral is immediately liquidated, which is an entirely different process compared to the traditional legal process in centralized finance models. In addition, lenders can withdraw their funds and interest earnings at any time and there is also a secondary market for the pledge tokens.

One of the questions that financial institutions and regulators are currently confronted with is the question whether these concepts can also be transferred to a regulated environment? One major challenge today is the difference between legal contracts and smart contracts, as smart contracts today cannot be enforced by courts because they operate outside of the established legal and regulatory system. However, there might be many use cases in the future if these constraints are resolved. But this would require adapting the existing legal system. For example, the enforcement of contracts might be extended from private persons and firms to software code (see Sect. 4.4).

The following case study about MakerDAO shows how the DeFi concept is applied in the case of lending.

Case Study: MakerDAO

- MakerDAO is the DeFi application behind the stablecoin DAI—a crypto asset that has a 1:1 peg to the USD (1 DAI = 1$).
- Initiated in 2015, MakerDAO did not conduct an initial coin offering (ICO) but sold MKR tokens privately to fund development.
- Users deposit/send ether to the MakerDAO smart contract, creating a collateralized debt position (CDP). Assuming a user has deposited 1 Ether (worth $100), they can borrow up to 40 DAI (assuming a 150% collateralization rate of $100/$1.50) against the $100. However, if the price of Ether

falls below $100, the CDP will be forced to close. To prevent this, the user must use more Ether or absorb less DAI. This is to ensure that there is always enough capital locked up for the amount of money withdrawn. If the user wants their Ether back, they must pay back the amount they took out plus a small fee.

- Example: A user decides to deposit 1 Ether at a price of $150. He chooses to take 100 DAI, which means his CDP is 150% collateralized. Now, however, Ethereum's price falls to $100, which means its CDP is undercollateralized by $50. A third party will determine that you do not have sufficient collateral and will liquidate the CDP on your behalf. This results in the position being liquidated by third parties with a penalty. These third parties have various opportunities to benefit from the liquidation of the position.
- System control: Within the MakerDAO ecosystem, the MKR token allows token holders to influence certain aspects such as the following: How much should the annual lending fee (stability fee) be? How much collateral should be behind each CDP (collateralization ratio)? For this, the MKR token owners receive a fee of 0.5%.
- MakerDAO currently holds about 2% of all Ether in its smart contracts and has issued $6.7 billion in DAI (i.e., debt) as loans, with collateral of $8.52 billion (as of June 2022; see Fig. 5.8).

Source: MakerDAO, Statista.com

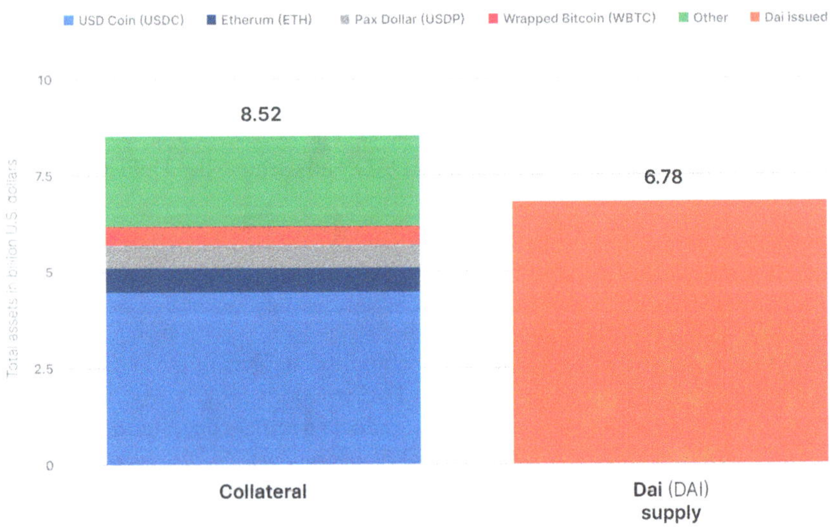

Fig. 5.8 MakerDAO collaterals

Table 5.5 Potentials and risks of DeFi

Potentials	Risks
• **Costs:** Reduction of transaction costs due to network effects and decreased monopoly costs. • **Quality:** Combinatorial innovation and permissionless innovation by empowering developers; enhance transparency in the financial system. • **Time:** Borderless and (near) real-time availability due to standardization (e.g., improved financial inclusion). • **Flexibility:** Improved interoperability due to open technologies.	• **Operational risks:** Especially in permissionless systems that involve large networks of anonymous users; new recovery mechanisms due to potentially anonymous identity and location; cyber risks. • **Financial system risks:** Novel forms of concentration of risks might emerge; increased procyclicality (e.g., for credits); diffused or unclear responsibility and accountability; solvency risks. • **Legal/regulatory risks:** Today's frameworks focus on institutions instead of activities.

Table 5.6 Comparison of centralized and decentralized approaches

Benefits of CeFi	Benefits of DeFi
• Security and integrity • Costs (freemium model) • User-friendliness • Economies of scale	• Unbundling of layers • Data portability and interoperability • Verifiable data and transactions • Incentives for open protocols • Diversification of risk

DeFi may lead to different levels of decentralization depending on the number of actors eliminated and/or reduced (partially, fully). Depending on the degree of disintermediation, DeFi impacts at least three areas (Financial Stability Board, 2019):

- *Governance.* The shift from the central institutions to a broad set of users deciding about financial transactions has implications on auditing, reversing transactions, etc.
- *Risk-taking.* The shift from risks on financial intermediaries' balance sheets to a direct matching of peers has implications on regulation and individual risks.
- *Record-keeping.* The shift from centrally held data and records to decentralized data storage, access, and verification has implications on data privacy, accessibility, etc.

The impact of DeFi in these three areas holds both potential and risks (see Table 5.5).

In general, both approaches, centralized and decentralized, have their benefits (see Table 5.6). Thus, a general recommendation, whether a service must be centralized or decentralized, cannot be given, but instead the benefits and risks must be weighed depending on the service. There is no "one-size-fits-all" approach for all applications and many questions are not yet solved such as the question of governance: the trust in delegating to a centralized entity is not given in the context of DeFi structures; instead, computed consensus algorithms shall solve this problem.

While existing DeFi approaches have primarily been discussed as an isolated field without any touchpoints to the existing financial system, recent approaches focus on a more comprehensive view which tries to integrate DeFi aspects into centralized finance and use for certain application areas where the benefits are stronger than the risks that they hold. Examples are FX trading blockchains for banks in permissioned environment. Another example of a financial services provider which aims at connecting centralized and decentralized finance concepts is Mastercard.

Case Study: Mastercard Multi-Token Network

- Mastercard has been connecting financial institutions and their customers for card-based payments for more than 50 years.
- The company aims at enabling digital asset payments through its Multi-Token Network (MTN). Though still in the early phase of its development, the MTN provides a set of foundational capabilities designed to make transactions within digital asset and blockchain ecosystems more secure, scalable, and interoperable.
- Unlocking the full potential of public blockchains will require an alignment of regulated actors around new scheme rules, as well as the technology to tokenize commercial bank deposits around two key elements:
  - Storing bank deposits or central bank money on a blockchain to create regulated tokens that can enable programmability in commercial bank money, support interoperability between traditional and crypto ecosystems, provide a scalable and regulated form of "money" for crypto ecosystems, and support integration to new and legacy settlement infrastructures.
  - Establishing a shared governance framework that binds participants to a set of shared standards for onboarding and monitoring of clients and funds (e.g., KYC, AML, CFT), stable and regulated payment tokens anchored in central bank money, cross-chain interoperability, and operational security as well as governance of errors, disputes, and chargebacks.
- This MTN consists of five layers. The user layer contains the users of the services, the wallet layer allows users to hold a variety of assets in a custodial wallet, the institution layer includes supervised intermediaries, the MTN governance practices, commercial agreements, and transaction standards, while the settlement layer would be responsible for the settlement of transactions, including public and private blockchains as well as legacy infrastructure. But how would these layers work together to provide a trusted environment (see Fig. 5.9)?
- In the first step, Alice could provide her ID and source of fund details, allowing a virtual asset service provider (VASP) A to complete an onboarding process that meets regulated MTN standards. In the second step, VASP

A provisions an MTN wallet to Alice and facilitates the transfer of assets into the wallet. In the third step, Bob provides his ID and source of funds details, allowing Bank B to complete an onboarding process that also meets regulated MTN standards. In step 4, Bank B provisions an MTN wallet to Bob and facilitates the transfer of assets into the wallet. Alice initiates in step 5 a transfer of $50 to Bob, using a stablecoin on the Ethereum blockchain. The transaction is governed by MTN network rules and subject to appropriate compliance checks (step 6). The settlement of the transfer of funds is executed via the public Ethereum blockchain (in the same was as any non-MTN transaction) in step 7 and Bob receives $50 in his MTN wallet in step 8.

- Another important function is cross-chain interoperability. In that case the VASP A and Bank B execute transfers via the MTN, ensuring the exchange is subject to compliance check and clear governance rules regarding cross-chain transactions. The MTN network would direct all updates to the Ethereum and Solana blockchains in order to execute the transfer of ownership for which an update to the Ethereum chain is executed, transferring ownership of Alice's NFT from an address controlled by her MTN wallet to an address controlled by Bob's wallet and an update to the Solana chain is executed, transferring ownership of $100 of Bob's stablecoin from an address controlled by his MTN wallet to an address controlled by Alice's MTN wallet. Alice and Bob's MTN wallets would reflect their updated holdings.
- A third important element of the MTN is error handling. In the case of the previous described example, the update to the Ethereum blockchain is executed successfully, transferring Alice's NFT to an address controlled by Bob's MTN wallet. Unfortunately, the update to the Solana chain fails, and the update in ownership to Bob's stablecoin is not recorded. As a result, the $100 in Bob's stablecoin remains at an address controlled by his MTN wallet. In that case, the MTN would recognize that the cross-chain transaction has not been conducted successfully and automatically initiates an error resolution process and the MTN notifies Alice's VASP and instructs Bob's bank not to allow transactions involving Alice's NFT while the error is addressed. An updated transaction is initiated on the Ethereum blockchain, effectively reversing the transfer of Alice's NFT to Bob. This unwinds Alice and Bob's positions to be the same as at before the transaction, with Alice in control of her NFT and Bob in control of his $100 in stablecoin. Both Alice and Bob are notified that their transaction has not been successful and offered an opportunity to try again.

Source: Mastercard (2023)

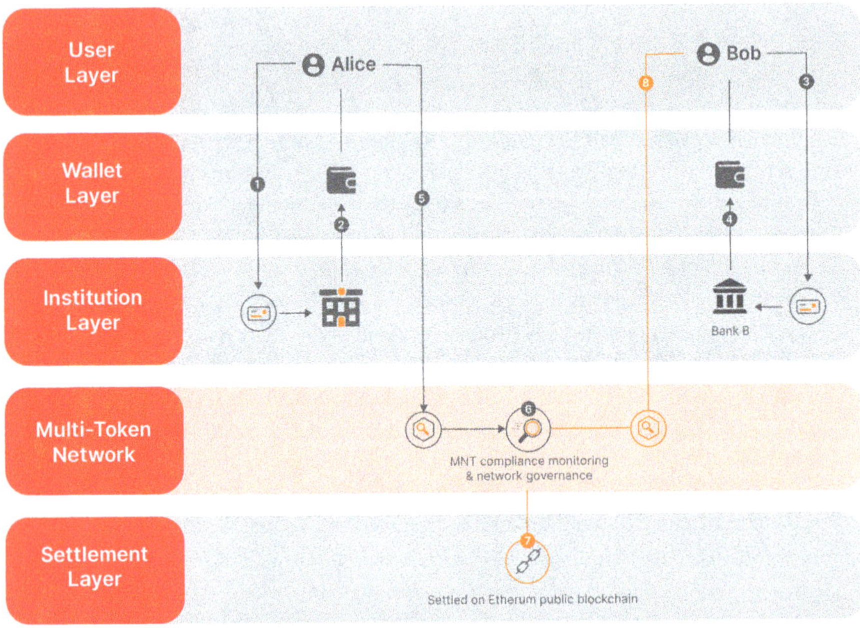

Fig. 5.9 Mastercard multi-token network

5.5 Stablecoins

As has been shown in the example of MakerDAO (see Sect. 5.4), stablecoins play a central role for DeFi since privately issued digital currencies' major challenge is their high volatility and hold various legal and regulatory fields of relevance (see Sect. 4.2). Stablecoins can be defined as non-government, i.e. privately issued, digital currencies that are backed by an asset that has intrinsic value. Stablecoins are digital tokens purportedly backed one-for-one with safe assets. Examples are USD Coin or Tether. However, there is no universally agreed legal or regulatory definition of stablecoins yet. In a recent report, the Financial Stability Board defined three characteristics of stablecoins (Financial Stability Board, 2022, 1): (1) the existence of a stabilization mechanism, (2) the usability as a means of payment and/or store of value, and (3) the potential reach and adoption across multiple jurisdictions. The first two characteristics and the unique risks that these characteristics pose distinguish stablecoins from other crypto assets. The third, the potential reach and adoption across multiple jurisdictions, differentiates global stablecoins from other stablecoins. Importantly, a stablecoin fulfills the functions as a means of exchange for payments and a store of value, but not as a unit of account and a legal tender (see Sect. 3.2). From a market perspective, stablecoins have increased from almost zero in 2019 to $124.2 billion on November 5, 2023 (https://www.coingecko.com/en/categories/stablecoins). Over the past few years, different types of stablecoins have emerged:

- *Fiat-collateralized:* These stablecoins are backed by fiat currencies, such as the US dollar.
- *Commodity-collateralized:* This type is backed by interchangeable assets, such as precious metals. An example is Digix Gold (DGX).
- *Crypto-collateralized:* These stablecoins are backed by other digital currencies, such as ETH, BAT, or USDC.
- *Non-collateralized:* These types of stablecoins use an algorithmically governed approach to control the stablecoin supply. An example is Ampleforth.

Stablecoins are beneficial for all kinds of applications, such as remittances; however, as of today, they are primarily used as settlement instruments for crypto assets. As such, stablecoins currently face some limitations to be used as a broader financial instrument. For example, stablecoins must undergo regular audits from third parties to ensure transparency. In addition, fiat-backed stablecoins are constrained by all regulations which apply to fiat currencies in general. Table 5.7 summarizes the potential benefits and risks of stablecoins.

Since they are issued by private organizations, stablecoins belong to the category of privately issued money which faces two major challenges (see Sect. 3.2):

- *Stable value.* Privately produced money mostly hasn't a stable value: "In the use of money, everyone is a trader; those whose habits and pursuits are little suited to explore the mechanism of trade are obliged to make use of money, and are now way qualified to ascertain the solidity of different banks whose paper is in circulation; accordingly, we find that individuals living on limited incomes, women, laborers, and mechanics of all descriptions, are often severe sufferers by the failure of country banks" (Ricardo, 1816, 409).
- *Bank runs.* Privately produced money is often subject to bank runs. If the price does not adjust (because no one knows what it should be if not $1), then quantities adjust. An adjustment to zero is a bank run.

Stablecoins provide liquidity and collateral in the crypto space because there is currently no other alternative to them, as Bitcoin and other crypto assets are too volatile. This means stablecoin issuers are acting as banks. But this faces some challenges Tether, for example, was in 2022 subject to a bank run (see Fig. 5.10) which demonstrated the volatility of stablecoins although it was not too extreme.

While the whole field of stablecoins is still small compared to the incumbent financial system, yet stablecoins already had an impact on the fiat financial system. For example, Tether and USD Coin used commercial paper to back their stablecoins. If their issuance went up, there was an immediate impact on the commercial paper market. For example, Sung (2022) identified that "a one standard deviation ($320 million) increase in the issuance of major stablecoins (Tether and USD Coin) on a given day resulted in a 10.7% increase in the commercial paper issuance quantity, a 20-basis point decrease in the commercial paper yield, and a 15-basis point decrease in the Treasury yield the following day."

Although the connection between the incumbent financial system and the private money-based financial system by stablecoins is still moderate, it might grow

Table 5.7 Benefits and risks of stablecoins (extended according to BIS, 2019b)

Benefits	**Description**
Access	Easier access to digital payments
Borderlessness	Stablecoins might decrease the complexity of cross-border payments if it is designed interoperable
Inclusion	Stablecoins might serve as a gateway to all kinds of financial services and thus improving financial inclusion
Competition	Stablecoins can increase competition by challenging the market dominance of incumbent financial institutions (depending on the interoperability)
Risks	**Description**
Legislation	Stablecoins must depend on clear legal and regulatory rules nationally and internationally which holds potential conflicts in case of conflicting laws—a circumstance which is not solved yet
Governance	Stablecoins have to include precisely defined governance architectures including lines of responsibility and accountability as well as recovery procedures which are still not yet defined precisely
Integrity	Stablecoins may create new risks for money laundering, terrorist financing, and other illicit financing activities
Safety	Stablecoins may cause financial shocks such as liquidity dislocation which affect the stability of the financial system as a whole
Security	Stablecoins may, like digital wallets and trading platforms, lead to fraud, theft, or other cyberattacks
Pricing	Stablecoins may pose some risks regarding pricing due to unclear pricing mechanisms (e.g., changing underlying asset portfolio), conflict of interest, and wrong incentives
Data	Stablecoins users may not have full information about how their personal data will be used by the ecosystem
Protection	Stablecoins may pose risks regarding investor protection due to unclear information when purchasing such coins
Compliance	Stablecoins may have an unclear legal status regarding taxes in foreign countries (e.g., sales tax for payments or taxes for securities)
Competition	Stablecoins may lead to market concentration and thus undermine market competition in certain market conditions
Stability	Stablecoins may have very complex systemic arrangements and thus lead to unpredictable crises (e.g., when reference assets include bank deposits they can lead to credit and liquidity risks of the involved financial institutions)

significantly soon. One reason is that many digital transactions are transferred from account-based systems, where transaction are recorded on bank accounts, to blockchains which are often based on private-issued money like stablecoins. An example is global supply chains (e.g., in the logistics sector) where payments can be made directly and instantaneously on blockchains as soon as goods are delivered from the place of origin to the place of destination (trade finance applications). The central banks' answer to this increasingly growing trend of privately produced money is CBDCs (see Sect. 3.2). Solution other than CBDC might be the tokenization of commercial bank deposits, which could be underpinned by a wholesale CBDC for transactions between banks (see Sect. 5.2). However, one important application of

Fig. 5.10 Tether exchange rate fluctuation (Sung, 2022)

stablecoins is cross-border payments (see Sect. 3.3), which requires novel infrastructures when the same field of application shall be applied to central bank money or cross-border payments in the incumbent financial system.

5.6 Digital Ecosystems and Embedded Finance

"The battle of devices has now become a war of ecosystems, where ecosystems include not only the hardware and software of the device, but developers, applications, eCommerce, advertising, search, social applications, location-based services, unified communications, and many other things. Our competitors aren't taking our market share with devices; they are taking our market share with an entire ecosystem. This means we're going to have to decide how we either build, catalyze or join an ecosystem" (Stephen Elop, Nokia CEO, email, 2011).

With the emergence of ecosystems, a convergence across industries can be observed. In such digital ecosystems, organizations from different industries work together to achieve a common goal. However, expanding into new business segments is found not to be beneficial in all cases and has a performance impact that is an order of magnitude greater than creating a new subsidiary in an existing segment (Cetorelli et al., 2021). An example is the US banking sector. During the 1990s and 2000s, financial intermediation changed dramatically in the USA. In the past, banking firms operated with a very narrow scope, focusing on deposit-taking and loan-making. But 20 years later, the industry showed a much more decentralized system, in which matching deposit supply and loan demand increasingly took place through much longer credit intermediation chains. Between 1990 and 2006, more than 230

US banks incorporated securities-dealer or broker subsidiaries; about 500 took control of insurance agencies, and over 1000 added special-purpose vehicle legal entities to their organizations. While these instances of change in banks' scope are certainly significant, they represent just the tip of the iceberg in what has been the largest and deepest process of scope transformation in the history of US banking. Indeed, throughout the 1990s and early 2000s, more than half of the banks either created or took control of tens of thousands of subsidiaries, spanning virtually every business segment within the financial services sector and beyond. This created new opportunities for potential synergies across a variety of businesses, and the value of those synergies changed in response to regulatory, technological, and market conditions that evolved over time and across all firms. So what is then new about ecosystems that are promoted by a higher degree of digitalization?

In general, ecosystems hold different design options for companies regarding (1) the extent to which a company wants to control the value chain (vertical integration) or drive or be part of an ecosystem that delivers on the end customer's needs and (2) the extent to which they know about their end customer's goals (partial or complete) (Weill & Woerner, 2015, 29). According to this definition, specific characteristics of these ecosystems are that they (1) provide a branded platform, (2) ensure great customer experience, (3) plug and play third-party products, (4) extract customer knowledge from all data, (5) match customer needs with providers, and (6) extract "rents" from providers. Currently, most banks are primarily working in vertically integrated value chains covering the complete knowledge of end customer goals. But banks are increasingly evolving into digital ecosystems which are constructed of networks, customers, (non-)banks, and providers. This may also include the provision and/or (out)sourcing of services from companies from other industries which increasingly leads to blurring industry sector borders like the examples of the bigtechs have shown.

Currently, five of the world's top seven companies ranked by market capitalization are ecosystem companies. This includes Apple, Microsoft, Alphabet, Amazon and Meta (Saudi Aramco ranked third and Nvidia ranked fifth are non-ecosystem companies). But what characterizes an ecosystem? Such ecosystems can be broadly described as network configurations between hierarchy and market (Jacobides et al., 2018, 2261). More specifically, a "business ecosystem" is defined as an "economic community supported by a foundation of interacting organizations and individuals - the organisms of the business world. The economic community produces goods and services of value to customers, who are themselves members of the ecosystem. The member organisms also include suppliers, lead producers, competitors, and other stakeholders. Over time, they co-evolve their capabilities and roles and tend to align themselves with the directions set by one or more central companies. Those companies holding leadership roles may change over time, but the function of the ecosystem leader is valued by the community as it enables members to move toward shared visions of aligning their investments and finding mutually supportive roles" (Moore, 1996, 26). This definition leads to three questions, which an individual company might ask itself:

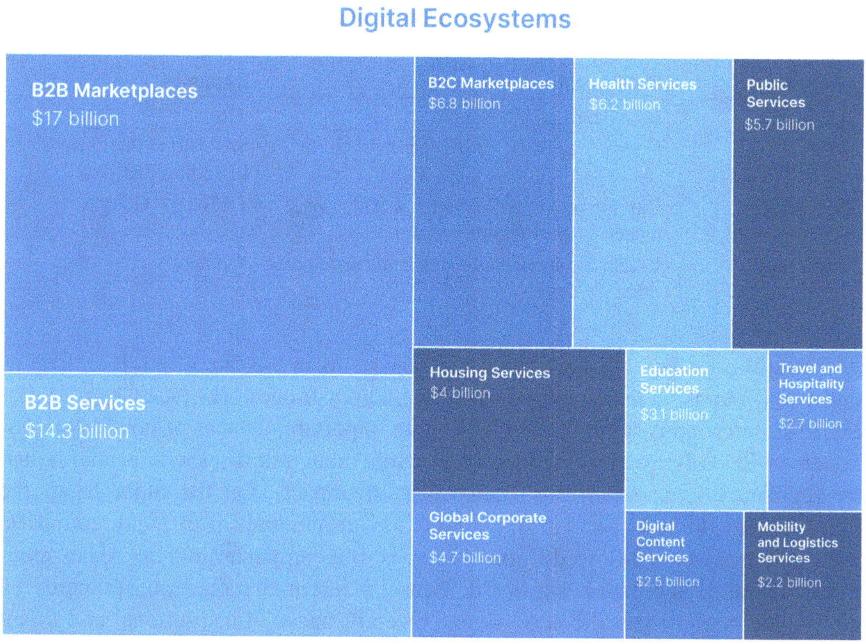

Fig. 5.11 Twelve emerging ecosystems until 2030 (modified according to Joshi et al., 2021)

1. *Why.* What value can ecosystems create for a company?
2. *What.* What is a company's role in each ecosystem it participates in and with whom does it partner with?
3. *How.* How does a company engage with each of these ecosystems and how does it set up the organization?

In general, multi-product and multi-actor ecosystems can be distinguished (Jacobides, 2022). While multi-product ecosystems focus on digitally linking services together around customer needs, multi-actor ecosystems are ecosystems in which various actors form ecosystems based on their competencies and production capabilities. Both types can occur at the same time. Based on this distinction in recent years 12 ecosystems have evolved which are predicted to comprise a total revenue of around $70 billion by 2030 and will by then account for around 25% of the entire global economy (see Fig. 5.11; Joshi et al., 2021).

For these emerging digital ecosystems, companies can apply four strategies: tabula rasa, head-on, unbundling, and enveloping (see Table 5.8). "Tabula rasa" ecosystems are ones which invent entirely new ecosystems (e.g., Apple's iOS), whereas "head-on" ecosystems establish new ones in competition to already existing ones (e.g., SAP Cloud Platform vs. Lightning Platform). The "unbundling" of services is a third strategy, where small niches are carved out of an existing ecosystem (e.g., TikTok vs. Google). Finally, a fourth strategy is "enveloping" which aims at the creation of an unassailable lock-in by enveloping other services (e.g., WeChat).

Table 5.8 Ecosystem strategies (Jacobides, 2022)

Digital ecosystem strategies	Description	Examples
Tabula rasa	Ecosystem first movers in an industry	iOS
Head-on	Compete head-on with a rival ecosystem	SAP Cloud Platform vs. Lightning Platform
Unbundling	Carving out a smaller niche within a space owned by previous incumbent	TikTok vs. Google
Enveloping	Create an unassailable lock-in by enveloping other services	WeChat

It is still open how financial services ecosystems in the future will look like, as this also depends on the development of regulatory frameworks (see Chap. 4). For example, inter-industry regulation will be an important element of how these ecosystems will evolve (e.g., embedded finance into other industries where other industry regulators (e.g., retail, etc.) have also an impact). On the other hand, the internationalization of ecosystems contrasts with nationalism in many countries: WeChat for example followed Chinese tourists. But companies in other Asian countries like India and Indonesia could focus on internationalization strategies by developing country-specific ecosystems. Overall, financial institutions' and financial utilities' primary role as intermediaries and service providers between investors and borrowers is increasingly challenged by various other actors like fintech startups and bigtech companies that already entered this market and either compete or collaborate with the incumbent players. This is currently enabled by regulators opening 1:1 customer–bank relationships by "open banking" (application programming interfaces, APIs) which allow non-banks to access customer and product data from banks that were previously stored in banks' systems and not accessible for third parties. These open application programming interfaces (APIs) are the prerequisite for the emergence of digital ecosystems.

Open banking addresses the sharing of customer-permission data by banks with third parties. These approaches differ regarding the country in which they are developed (e.g., the EU has already passed the law while Switzerland has not yet drafted it, as the banks aim to follow a market-driven approach) and the type of data that is being shared by banks with third parties (e.g., the EU focuses on payments processing data while the UK includes further data elements like loan data, etc.) (BIS, 2019a). For example, today, price comparison websites must often obtain their data for an SME business loan either via proprietary APIs from the banks (e.g., very often via information collected by dedicated data capture agencies) or via a process called "screen scraping" that captures the data directly from the banks' web pages. But as this process is very complex and error-prone, a standard API would allow more third-party providers to provide applications that could target consumer markets in particular. The specification for such an API comprises different elements, such as information about the interest rates, the conditions for loan repayment, or product features. The UK Open Banking initiative, for example, specifies APIs not only for SME loans, but also for branches, accounts, customer data, ATMs, and credit cards. In addition to this technical specification, the UK also supports creating user experience standards (e.g., authentication), operational guidelines, an open banking directory, user dispute mechanisms, implementation support, and a monitoring function (Open Data Institute, 2019).

While open banking is an enabler of digital ecosystems, the question how future business models of both the financial institutions and utilities and the entrants based on digital ecosystems look like remains still vague. In general, these ecosystems connect providers with consumers through either direct connections (e.g., Airbnb) or indirect connections (e.g., YouTube music videos created by professional producers). In each of these connections, the provider and the consumer exchange (1) information and data, (2) goods or services, and (3) some form of currency (Parker et al., 2016). In this way, they are reconfiguring value creation, value consumption, and quality control:

- *Value creation.* By minimizing barriers for providers, value creation can be redefined. An example is 99designs, which has built up a large pool of professional designers that can be crowdsourced only for certain projects.
- *Value consumption.* Consumer behavior changes, as the examples of Uber (using strangers' cars as taxis), Turo (lending private cars to other consumers), or Feastly (eat in other consumers' private dining rooms) show.
- *Quality control.* New curation mechanisms are introduced by automation based on socially driven feedback loops (e.g., ratings of hotels on Booking.com).

While in the first phase of the early ecosystem approaches, startups mostly dominated the landscape, more and more incumbents are now entering the market. An example is the Mobility Open Blockchain Initiative (MOBI), a global nonprofit alliance of the world's largest vehicle manufacturers, along with startups, NGOs, transit agencies, insurers, toll road providers, smart city leaders, financial institutions, and tech companies. In this context, incumbents must consider novel ways of which processes can be outsourced, how partners can be engaged to create products and services, and how cooperation with competitors and enhancement of the value of goods and services by leveraging data can be organized. A very well-known example is Apple with its AppStore. The following case study shows how Standard Chartered uses digital ecosystems.

Case Study: Standard Chartered

- Standard Chartered (SC) invests more than half of its $1.6 billion in annual technology spending on strategic and digital enhancements. The goal of this strategy is to make the bank more:
  - *Adaptive.* Adaptivity enables SC to quickly reconfigure its business capabilities to capture future customer demands and create new growth opportunities like creating the nexus banking-as-a-service platform, which provides banking services to customers like in Indonesia via digital platforms like Bukalapak.

 - *Creative.* Technology fosters creativity by embracing innovation management principles. For this, in 2018, the bank created SC Ventures to invest in fintechs and promote the implementation of new business models.
 - *Resilient.* As SC operates in more than 60 countries and interfaces with at least as many regulators an effective and efficient approach to business resiliency and risk management are core tech topics.
 - *Rapid.* The pace of innovation is much slower in regulated banking. Therefore, partnerships with startups and tech firms that are not regulated can speed up innovation processes.

- These elements are the basis for the use of digital platforms. But SC has traditionally been relying on a relationship model. This model is based on the relationship of a customer (e.g., a CEO from a firm) and a bank professional (e.g., a local branch client advisor for SMEs). For example, a CEO from a local firm would call the local branch manager and paper forms would be filled in, to apply for a loan. This process usually required 15–60 days to be completed.
- In the platform model, the loan application is now entirely online based on existing data, which already considers individual data of the CEO and other risk data of the firm. The processing time is now around 2 days.
- The platform model requires fully integrated and digital processes covering the front-, middle-, and back office without or with only little human intervention.
- The new approach also requires new forms of leadership, as a platform not only involves hierarchical settings in vertically integrated firms but also co-operations with startups and even competitors.

Source: According to Forrester (2021)

A more specific view of how banks can participate in digital ecosystems knows at least four ways (Greer 2021; see Fig. 5.12):

- *Beyond finance.* Beyond finance refers to non-financial services and products that are delivered by a bank.
- *Financial platform/marketplace.* A financial platform/marketplace provides financial services and products which are delivered by a bank.
- *Embedded finance.* Embedded finance refers to the discovery and acquisition of tailored financial services and products at the point of customers' need within the digital experience curated by a non-bank third party.
- *Open banking.* Open banking provides financial services and products which are enabled by banks' data by a non-bank third party.

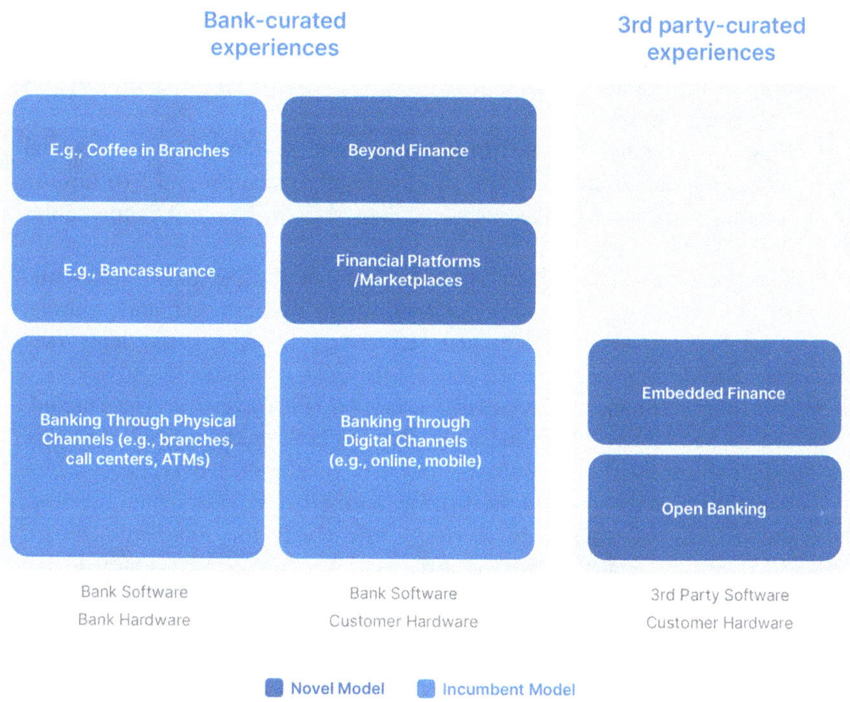

Fig. 5.12 Ecosystem models for banks (adapted from Greer 2021)

The implementation of these different models might differ from bank to bank and might also include fintech startups and bigtech companies. However, depending on these different strategies, digital ecosystems may generate benefits in at least five areas:

- *Broaden out offerings to be sticky.* Be part of bundles that customers (b2b / b2c) want.
- *Access key complementary capabilities.* As it's unlikely that a company has all services that customers may need, ecosystems ensure that it doesn't needlessly have to tie up capital to develop them itself.
- *Strategic necessity.* This refers to new distribution, storefront, perception space (e.g., Roblox or Sandbox in the Metaverse for b2c; e-procurement platforms for b2b; see Sect. 2.7).
- *Maintain visibility and growth orientation.* To end consumer and/or investors.
- *Co-create new value propositions.* With the support of orchestrators/complementors; enhance ability to innovate co-creating value and push the organization.

An example for a company, which provides/is part of six different digital ecosystems that are interconnected with each other, is Ping An.

Case Study: Ping An

- Ping An Insurance was founded in 1988 by Peter Ma Mingzhe in Shenzhen, China.
- Ping An Insurance (Group) Ltd, is a technology-enabled retail financial services group. With over 200 million retail customers and 516 million Internet users and with this one of the largest financial services companies in the world.
- The growth of the company is bolstered by its diverse group of revenue streams including insurance, banking, asset management, and Internet finance (such as telehealth and real estate services ecosystems (see Fig. 5.13).
- The Ping An financial services ecosystem provides diverse services including the facilitation of seamless connections between them. New and prospective customers are acquired through the development of six ecosystems, namely financial services, healthcare, auto services, real estate services, cloud tech, and smart city services. As a result, the company acquired 36.57 million new customers in 2019, 40.7% of whom were sourced from Internet users within the company's ecosystems.
- Ping An can receive and process data of the same people in multiple ways on a single platform. As a result, it allows them to understand its customers' dynamic behavior and needs. This capability has simplified customer journeys by allowing them to easily cross-buy multiple products across the company network.
- One of the bigger cases is OneConnect which provides a technology-as-a-service platform for financial institutions.

Source: According to Twimbit (2020)

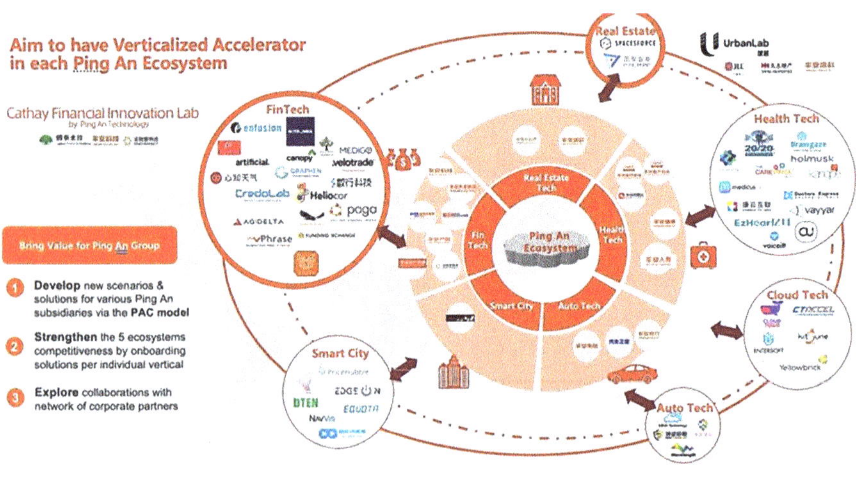

Fig. 5.13 Ping An's ecosystem

5.7 Sustainable Digital Finance

Sustainability is one of the so-called "grand challenges" and includes the decrease of health, poverty, inequality, climate change, and environmental degradation and the increase of prosperity which are comprehensively defined in the United Nations' 17 sustainability goals (SDGs) (George et al., 2016). In the past few years, the role of the financial system in achieving the SDGs has been intensively discussed in the mass media. Among the examples is the role of banks of which some still invest in companies that are harmful to climate change or in ones that pay workers poorly or rely on child labor (only 5%–25% of all assets were estimated globally to be invested sustainably until 2019) (Eccles & Klimenko, 2019). But how can the financial system facilitate this trade-off between economic, social, and environmental goals? The potential of promoting digital finance for sustainability lies in (1) the availability of cheaper and more trustworthy data, which enables greater transparency about firms and value chains; (2) cost reduction in financial intermediation through unbundling of financial services, which are provided by specialized firms; and (3) innovative products, services, and business models. With this, digitalization could, for example, help reduce global carbon emissions by 15% through innovative solutions in energy, agriculture, and transportation (Eckholm & Rockström, 2019). For example, similarly, the Carbon Trust and the mobile operators' association GSMA estimate that mobile technologies may enable carbon emission reductions in other sectors that are ten times greater than the direct emissions related to the technology itself (GSMA and Carbon Trust, 2019).

While only some large corporations have already begun to align the SDGs with their existing profit-driven business models, an increasing number of SDG-focused startups has emerged that effectively incorporate SDG objectives in their initial business models. They consider an SDG approach as their competitive advantage, which allows the pursuit of both business and sustainability benefits by the use of innovative technologies to implement them (Puschmann et al., 2020). Among the examples are novel, token-based financing platforms for startups in developing countries that do have only limited access to bank credits in their countries, new payment infrastructures based on digital currencies, and digital wallets for improving financial inclusion, waste management in smart cities, peer-to-peer trading platforms for renewable energy production and consumption, and DAOs based on blockchain for the governance of financing large (public) projects to prevent fraud and corruption.

In a global analysis, 531 startups were analyzed in detail to find common patterns and identify relevant trends (Puschmann & In, 2023). The analysis revealed that most of the identified startups are based in the USA (19.21%), followed by the UK (16.20%), Germany (11.86%), and Switzerland (11.11%), which collectively represent 58.38% of all startups in this field. The remaining startups are distributed among other countries, with France (5.08%), the Netherlands (4.71%), Sweden (3.95%) and Spain (3.58%), and Singapore (2.82%) being notable contributors, while the remaining 21.48% are from various other countries. Countries with well-established financial systems, such as the USA, Switzerland, the UK, and Singapore, have a higher concentration of startups, while others, such as Brazil, India, and Nigeria, have a lower representation. The analysis showed that startups not only provide services to the financial sector but also to other industries, such as the energy, technology, government/NGO, agriculture, and supply chain sector. This is because digital finance services often enable innovative services such as carbon accounting tools, emissions trading platforms, etc. Among the startups, 50.66% focus on supply chains, offering solutions such as ESG data provision, carbon emission analysis and reduction, blockchain platforms for green supply chains, and data for responsible consumption. 35.22% of the startups concentrate on the financial services industry, offering impact assessment, financing solutions for sustainability projects, and risk management solutions. The energy industry makes up 9.04% of startups, focusing on decentralizing and digitalizing energy management, emissions trading, and monitoring. 6.97% of the startups target governments and NGOs, providing sustainability-oriented innovations, web donation platforms, and novel financing and investment methods. The agriculture sector constitutes 5.08% of startups and focuses on financing farmers and providing crop insurance. 1.69% of the startups serve the technology sector with solutions related to carbon monitoring and carbon footprint reduction. And finally, 1.13% and 0.94% cater to the transportation and real estate sectors, respectively. Importantly, many startups provide services across multiple industries, rather than exclusively focusing on just one.

While these examples demonstrate the growing interest of startups in the private sector, the UN Sustainable Digital Finance Task Force aims at harnessing digitalization in advancing citizen-centric financial systems that have three major pillars: (1) inclusive international governance (e.g., considering the principles of the SDGs in digital finance regulation), (2) sustainable digital ecosystems (e.g., digital IDs, etc.), and (3) catalytic opportunities. While the first two mentioned action fields are based on shaping long-term policies, the catalytic opportunities provide very concrete examples for fostering the SDGs' success in various fields (see Table 5.9):

- *Channel domestic savings into development financing.* An example is Bangladesh, which has an infrastructure budget of $20 billion. Two-thirds of the budget come from international aid and borrowing. Considering that international capital is 15–20% more expensive than domestic capital, it becomes obvious that the $20 billion in domestic savings might be of interest, especially since only about 4% is used for infrastructure investment. These domestic micro savings are aggregated by digital wallets and managed by a mega fund specific to the SDGs. The citizens can themselves decide in which infrastructure projects the money is flowing (e.g., green energy projects, etc.). This solution shall be implemented in other countries as well.
- *Enhance financing for SMEs.* An example is the Zimbabwe stock exchange platform, jointly launched by UNCDF and Escrow Group. The aim is to bring a capital market infrastructure to solve the SME financing issue. For the listing of SMEs, draws on payments data and third-party sources data such as credit bureaus and financial institutions provide robust due diligence and credit ratings

Table 5.9 Catalytic opportunities of sustainable digital finance (UN, 2020)

Opportunities	Channel domestic savings into development financing	Enhance financing for small and medium-sized businesses (SMEs)	Digitize public financing and make public budgets and contracts transparent	Embed SDGs into decisions of financial and capital markets	Shape consumption decisions through improved information and choice architecture
Scale	Global savings pool has grown over two decades from $ 7.5 to 23.3 trillion	Potential to meet the $ 5.2 trillion a year for SME financing in developing countries	Governments in developing countries could gain $ 220 to 320 billion annually from digitalizing payments	The outstanding value of global equity and bond markets is $ 185 trillion	Annual global consumption expenditure is $ 47 trillion
SDGs	6, 7, 9, 11	1, 5, 8, 10	1, 3, 4, 16	7, 9, 11, 13	11, 12, 14, 15
Citizens as	Small savers and co-beneficiaries of sustainable infrastructure	Borrowers, entrepreneurs, employees	Taxpayers, voters, public service users	Savers, investors	Consumers, asset owners

for prospective SME listings on the stock exchange platform. This approach shall also be rolled out to other African countries.

- *Embed SDGs into decisions of financial and capital markets.* A project in Latin America in this domain focuses on natural capital preservation. For this, a novel valuation model was developed that defines a pricing model for the valuation of ecosystem services. These values are then securitized on a financial, blockchain-based platform for natural capital assets. The monitoring and reporting are done through digital technologies such as IoT and satellite data analysis, etc. The investments are then used for social development and nature preservation projects by connecting environmental preservation and community development. A similar approach is currently being piloted in Africa for some keystone species.
- *Shape consumption decisions through information and choice architecture.* This field focuses on rechanneling the annual global consumption expenditure to greener and more sustainable products and services, for example, by designing user experiences on "e-commerce" platforms by making the impact of consumer choices transparent to the buyers of these products and services. This data can then be linked to digital IDs, which then show network effects of these consumer choices in a broader context of certain communities.

The following case studies show how Pula uses insurtech and how Cardano leverages blockchain technology to promote sustainability in the financial system.

Case Study: Pula Scoops Crops and Livestock Insurtech

- Pula is an agricultural insurance and technology company that designs and delivers innovative agricultural insurance and digital products to help smallholder farmers endure yield risks.
- Pula's Yield Index Insurance (YII) covers the risks that affect yield. YII inssures the value of the purchased inputs against low yield and replaces the purchase to registered farmers at the end of the season. Under this cover, the country is divided into agro-ecological zones based on historical rainfall, temperatures, prior yields, etc., and average historical yield data is determined for each zone based on past data.
- At the end of the season, trained enumerators measure yield levels for each agro-ecological zone. With this information, farmers receive compensation if yields in a specific agro-ecological zone are below a determined trigger level.
- With this model Pula has insured \$1.1 billion by including more than five million farmers that farm three million hectares of land in 13 African countries.
- For example, Pula has worked over 3 years to provide crop insurance to farmers in Kitui, Kenya. Over the past 3 years, the program has grown from 1000 to about 10,000 insured farmers, and crop loss compensation amounting to \$766,000.
- In 2020, Pula worked with the Central Bank of Nigeria to insure about 543,000 farmers for the wet season. Of these, 196,301 were under the National Cotton Association of Nigeria (NACOTAN) and 235,907 were rice farmers under the Rice Farmers Association of Nigeria (RIFAN) and NIRSAL MFB.

Source: www.pula-advisors.com

Case Study: Cardano

- Cardano develops a financial and social operating system (see Fig. 5.14) which runs on a PoS consensus mechanism. Cardano's blockchain business model is based on a transaction-based model, where for each transaction a fee will be charged.
- Cardano's implementation roadmap is based on four phases: (1) participation in stake pools delegation and treasury-in, (2) utility with metadata, multi-currency, and smart contracts, (3) scalability with interoperability and sidechains, (4) governance with voting, treasury-out, and sustainability. The development path is to establish so-called Cardano Nations which are based on the Cardano platform standards (see Fig. 5.14).

- Cardano aims at focusing on sustainability challenges. For example, Veritree's global land restorations are powered by Cardano. With this, Veritree can solve some of the major challenges of deforestation: (1) double spending, (2) lack of transparency, (3) lack of community involvement, (4) non-standardized data, and (5) lack of data feedback loop. For each Ada (Cardano's digital token) donated one tree is planted. For each tree the donor receives one Veritree non-fungible verification token. This NFT is connected to the tree by geosatellite data. With this solution one million trees were already planted in Africa.
- In another use case in Kenya and Ethiopia, five million students are equipped with a blockchain-based identity solution. In these countries, an identity is often based on a transaction history rather than on a passport which is a fundamentally different understanding of identity than is the case, for example, in European and North American countries. But with this solution individuals can be reached for financial transactions in a way that was not possible before.

Source: Cardano

Fig. 5.14 Cardano's financial and social operating system development path

One specific focus area of sustainable digital finance is financial inclusion. In 2013, around 3.6 billion people were unbanked who accounted for more than half of the world's population at that time. This was for two major reasons: (1) They had no possibility to prove their identity (e.g., no papers, no address, no birth certificate) according to know-your-customer (KYC) processes and (2) banks usually have no interest in providing services to these mostly poor people. Today the number of unbanked fell to around 1.3 billion people because of the intense work of philanthropies like the Bill & Melinda Gates Foundation as well as public (e.g., World Bank) and private organizations (e.g., Mastercard). Around 400 million of these unbanked people live in Africa. But what can accelerate the second wave of innovation to reduce this number to zero until 2030 according to the SDGs? While from 2013 on the big countries like India and Brazil have advanced their efforts in financial inclusion, there are now a big number of smaller countries which need to include their people financially and which require to adapt to a much more diverse landscape of policies, regulations, cultures, and technological requirements. The following case study of the Level One Project gives an overview of how this could be achieved with a principle-based approach.

Case Study 1: Level One Project

- The Level One Project is focused on helping the public and private sectors develop pro-poor, digital financial services and markets. The initiative is based on a principle-based approach including:
  - The system is available to any licensed financial service provider in a certain country.
  - Payments are real-time and "push" only which removes many of the risks and costs inherent in batch processes and "pull" payment systems. Payments are irrevocable and have same-day settlement.
  - It includes pro-poor governance practices, such as equal ownership opportunities, and financial service provider engagement is supported and regulated by a government financial authority and leverages tiered KYC requirements.
  - It operates on a not-for-loss or cost-recovery-plus-investment basis where payments are a utility and takes into account the needs of women, poor, and other disadvantaged groups. It does not preclude financial service providers or other providers in the ecosystem from earning profits.
  - It provides a shared investment in fraud detection and other scheme and platform services. The compliance burden remains with the financial service providers, but they share a less costly more efficient fraud service.
- The Level One Project consists of two major elements to assist countries and regions to deploy, regulate, and operate:

  - Foundational identity platforms to onboard people. For example, India has onboarded 1.2 billion people by using a biometric concept with fingerprints and iris scans. This also gives people now access to other government services like voting, etc.
  - Instant inclusive and interoperable payment platforms to enable people to transact (p2p, p2m, g2p).
- The pioneering countries of the Level One Project are Kenya (M-PESA), Pakistan (Raast), India (Aadhaar, UPI), and Brazil (Pix). In the next phase, other countries shall be assisted with this approach.
- Launched in 2017, Mojaloop is a reference model of the Level One Project's core principles, which include interoperability between services, low fees for customers, and collaboration to lower costs and accelerate growth. Mojaloop together with the digital identity platform MOSIP is provided as an open-source platform for public institutions which provide (1) sovereignty and ownership of data, (2) full ownership of the solution, (3) benefits from early adopters, and (4) community-driven innovation. Both platforms are hosted by two independent foundations.

Source: Bill & Melinda Gates Foundation

Approaches like the Level One Project could evolve into so-called "digital public infrastructures" (DPIs). A DPI is defined as "(…) a set of shared digital systems that should be secure and interoperable and can be built on open standards and specifications to deliver and provide equitable access to public and/or private services at societal scale and are governed by applicable legal frameworks and enabling rules to drive development, inclusion, innovation, trust, and competition and respect human rights and fundamental freedoms" (UNDP, 2023, 3). DPIs focus on the four elements: digital identity, digital payments, consent-based data sharing, and other emerging ones like geospatial data or aggregation of data and content. The DPI is a catalyzer for coalitions (philanthropy, MDBs, institutional donors), governments, and central banks stakeholders as well as private sector and open-source communities (technical assistance, service, and support). DPIs might foster innovation for new financial services, consumer protection, and new forms of UI/UX (e.g., voice interaction for payments for illiterate people) as well as ownership of data and privacy. However, the replication of the existing financial instruments and methods like credit rating might be not suitable for DPIs in developing countries (what is often called "digital colonialism"). Additionally, there is a challenge that regulators allow non-banks to offer financial services (see Sect. Sect. 4)), as banks in most cases are not interested in offering services to these customer groups for profitability reasons.

The introduction of such DPIs must be reflected against regulatory requirements. For example, public service broadcasting was first pioneered in the UK in the 1920s which led (not only to the BBC but also) to a redefinition of the relationship between the government, media producers, and citizens and also motivated other countries to adopt such a model, too. In contrast, in the case of the Internet regulators acted many years after the introduction to correct market failures, an approach which could also be observed in the case of crypto assets in some parts of the world.

Chapter 6
Outlook

The financial system has been spurred by innovations in money and payments over the last decades and has accelerated over the last few years driven by the enormous IT developments. The globalization of the economy would not have been possible without the digitalization of the financial system but instead moving around large amounts of metal coins and towers of paper-based ledgers. IT served as a strong enabler for these developments and fintech brought another realm of digital innovations in the last decade driven by blockchain, AI, and other converging technologies. This has reduced information asymmetries and transaction costs to almost zero in several areas such as stock trading or payments. For example, AI can already solve many problems in banking and finance better than humans, such as collecting information about firms in publicly available online sources and databases or determining credit scores for individuals based on their payment behavior. It is estimated that around one third of back office jobs in finance could be replaced by IT. Although IT is evolving rapidly and shaping the financial system 2030 in its future contours, many questions remain unanswered. Among the examples are data correctness, ethical bias, or market manipulation. Therefore, in this increasingly technologized world, the human remains a key component. The human brain is (still) able to develop creative ideas better than computers and remains the benchmark for many manual tasks that are too complex to be solved by robots. However, as the DeFi world shows, in a world of fully digital financial systems, smart contract-based solutions promise to offer advantages in terms of improved accessibility, transparency, execution security, and democratization.

While the financial system has already undergone major transformations in the past centuries, we now stand at the cusp of the next major step: the full digitalization of money and other assets, often termed as "tokenization." Although the early crypto and DeFi adventures showed us the enormous potential of this reorganization of the financial system, they also demonstrated the risks that come along with it. As the bigtech companies are providing more and more financial services, digital

T. Puschmann, H. S. H. P. M. of Liechtenstein, *Financial System 2030*, Financial Innovation and Technology,
https://doi.org/10.1007/978-3-031-55700-2_6

ecosystems evolve, and DeFi is reducing the number of intermediaries, nation states prepare themselves by safeguarding their monetary sovereignty through introducing CBDCs, improving competitiveness by open banking, and renewing payment infrastructures. Finally, regulation across the world has stepped up to improve the conditions for startups and at the same time ensuring that consumers can still act in a safe environment. But the regulation of digital platforms, DeFi and crypto assets is not an easy path forward, since many regulatory approaches use an institutional approach instead of an activity-based one, which is hard to apply in an intermediary-free environment. In some cases, model laws or the application of enterprise law might serve as a good starting point for the redesign of the financial system.

This book outlined major developments at the intersection of digitalization and the financial system and structured them along the Vaduz Architecture of the Financial System (see Chap. 1), which lead to automation and innovation and disintermediation (IT), financial inclusion and sustainability (nation states), and innovation and protection (regulation) fostering digital money and digital ecosystems (see Fig. 6.1). By outlining different aspects of developments in all of these areas, the previous sections provide different scenarios for the future financial system. For example, there might be different combinations and integration scenarios of

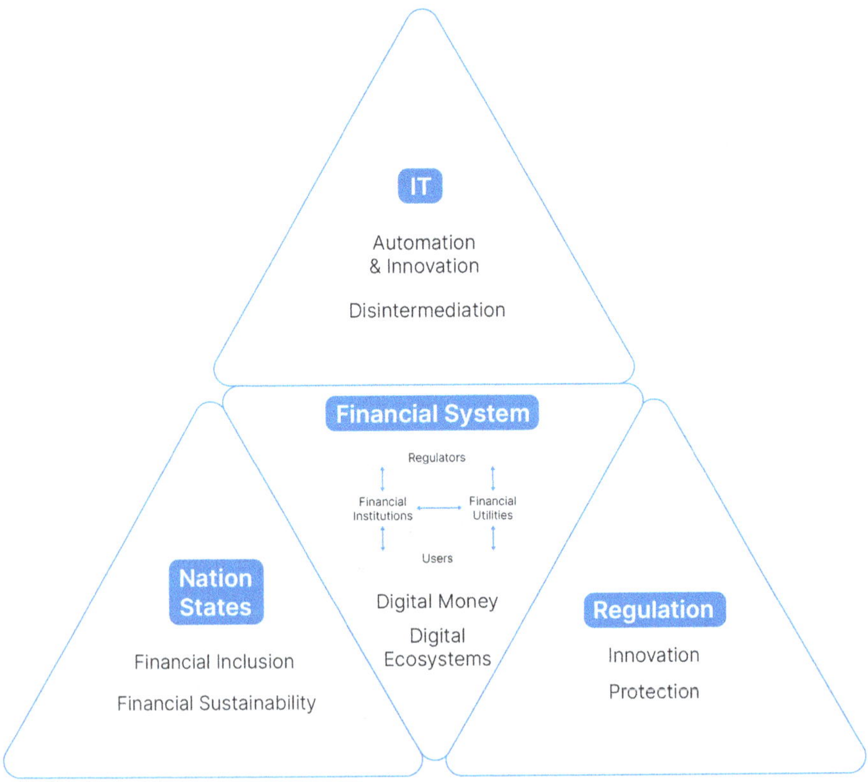

Fig. 6.1 Development lines toward the financial system 2030

centralized and decentralized finance models (e.g., the use of AMMs might make sense only in specific b2b processes) or different use cases for CBDCs depending on the country and its characteristics (e.g., a retail CBDC might not be introduced in some industrialized countries in the next few years due to their already very efficient payment systems while emerging economies might use them for reducing dollarization, increasing financial inclusion, etc. But what does this development hold for the financial system beyond 2030? Looking ahead, at least four lines of development might be relevant as future pathways: repositioning within the financial system 2030, maturity of the financial system 2030, globalization of the financial system 2030 and sustainability of the financial system 2030.

6.1 Repositioning Within the Financial System 2030

The financial system is not an end in itself. It is an enabler for economic transactions across various industries and countries. And "money" (at least until now) is its primary "glue." But it seems that money is currently changed in its fundamentals. Central banks have started to rethink "currencies" as "CBDCs." In addition, traditional, money-based economic transactions are complemented by new models of "sharing" and "swapping," creating a new system for "evaluation," where consumers can create their own digital "currencies." These developments pave the way for new actors which offer digital wallets, decentralized exchanges, and novel custodians. Some of those might be even more important in developing countries for financial inclusion or for novel products in green and sustainable fintech.

In parallel, the lines between established industry sectors are blurring and digitalization may lead to a redefinition of the well-established industries. Examples of such new cross-industry digital financial services are on-demand insurances for the sharing economy or payment services for cross-mobility services. Just as the Internet evolved from an Internet of information and Internet of services in the last few decades, the Internet of value will allow clients and organizations to exchange money and other values (e.g., digital assets, loyalty points, etc.). For this, trusted financial services will play an important role. While new players from the emerging blockchain and fintech space have already positioned themselves, banks need to do the same in this evolving new financial system. The financial system is engaging in these novel digital ecosystems through digital finance platforms, embedded finance, open banking, as well as beyond finance models, which allow financial institutions to extend their value creation in non-financial services domains. This is enabled by digital forms of money such as CBDCs and private forms of digital money like stablecoins, which give citizens and consumers a trustable instrument for economic transactions like trusted transaction stakeholders, etc. But as the many projects in Bhutan, Palau, Japan, etc. demonstrate, most of them are still in an early phase of development and are not live yet. Yet, the early movers may benefit just as the examples of the early Internet firms have shown (e.g., Cisco and Apple) while others like Napster failed. But there might not be one or the other model dominating in this competition. For example, the choice for decentralization and centralization is not black or white. Instead, hybrid models emerge. Lessons from the Internet 1.0 with intranets and the Internet demonstrated how permissioned and permissionless areas can exist side by side.

Despite the new opportunities, the global return on tangible equity (ROTE) of banks has come down to 10.5%, and even in emerging markets banks' ROTEs have sharply declined from 20% in 2013 to 14.1% in 2018 and 12.5% in 2022 (McKinsey & Company, 2019a, 2022). On the other side of the spectrum, the challengers like the fintechs and the bigtechs have sped up their activities and primarily focus on those financial products which represent almost half of the global revenues in banking (retail deposits and payments, consumer finance, wealth management, asset management) but leave out mortgages, commercial and transaction banking, as well as capital markets and investment banking. In addition, the number of fintech start-ups worldwide increased and the bigtech companies hired financial services experts from banks. But also, the incumbent banks have reacted by launching "digital attackers" like ABN Amro with the introduction of "New10" or Royal Bank of Scotland with "Mettle"; others foster partnerships like ING with Kabbage or JPMorgan Chase with Finicity. The incumbents' focus is on new digital ecosystems to extend their businesses. However, these digital businesses require fewer employees to achieve the same results with fewer resources. Google, for example, in 2023 had a revenue of $305.6 billion with approximately 182,500 employees (around $1.67 million per employee). In contrast, Bank of America had a revenue of $171.91 billion with around 213,000 employees ($807,089 per employee; other US banks have similar results with around $800,000 per employee). While this simple calculation leaves out other relevant factors like network effects and other industry-specific criteria which are relevant for an important service like finance in contrast to advertising business, the profitability of online businesses is clearly significantly higher.

All these developments have implications for the future of the financial system and pose general questions like (1) the intermediaries' landscape (e.g., the role of ecosystem platforms, the role of (central) banks, etc.), financial instruments (e.g., novel digital asset classes, cross-border transactions, etc.), transmission mechanisms (e.g., emergence of novel stock markets, etc.), etc. which touch all areas of the financial system's perspectives (institutional, intermediation, functional, systemic; see Chap. 1).

6.2 Maturity of the Financial System 2030

The financial system was first developed in the industrialized world with banks, stock exchanges, and other financial institutions and utilities as the major intermediaries. But this has led to a digital infrastructure which is currently tremendously challenged by IT leapfrogs in areas like AI and blockchain. While incumbent institutions still spend most of their budget on maintaining (very often old) systems, the fintech startups and the bigtechs could build their systems from scratch. Parallel, entirely new infrastructures emerge based on consortium blockchains and public blockchains. Until now it remains unclear which of those will win the battle and/or how they will be integrated with each other (interoperability). Countries of the developing world could have an advantage as they very often do not have to develop complex heterogeneous IT environments from scratch but could apply these novel technologies to introduce new financial infrastructures in their countries (e.g., Mojaloop in Africa). The many examples from Asia and Africa demonstrate that these regions leapfrogged the incumbent infrastructures and developed novel ones which are mobile by design. On the other hand industrialized countries started to modernize their existing IT infrastructures. All this has been made possible by recent IT developments which has served as a strong enabler of novel applications and business models.

IT promotes a new financial system that is made from digital money, digital assets, and a new digital financial market infrastructure which together connect the old and the new players. The first fintech developments are only the forerunners of this overall redesign. But the development of basic infrastructure elements driven by new IT developments, standards, and new services requires time and will not happen overnight. We tend to overestimate the speed of this development. But a closer look into open questions clearly shows a gap between the new world and the existing one. The development of standards, for example, is still at a very early stage. ISO launched its new working group on blockchain in 2016, and experiences from past developments show that this requires several more years. On the other hand, many technical questions are still unsolved. An example is the performance limitation of many blockchain solutions. The same applies to consensus mechanisms that consider that proof-of-work is not an acceptable solution for many application areas. And many of the web3 technologies are still at a very early stage. Additionally, AI is also confronted with serious challenges.

6.3 Globalization of the Financial System 2030

While globalization is currently being challenged by protectionism and other hurdles, the globalization of the financial system offers enormous opportunities. The globalization of the financial system is enabled by the ongoing digitalization. For example, digitalization leads to an abstraction of physical assets with digital representations via tokens. This allows for almost unlimited divisibility of assets across asset, investor, and country boundaries while at the same time facilitating decentralization of assets that can be traded through electronic marketplaces, sometimes even without intermediaries. This has implications for supranational regulation, which is only vaguely recognizable today and will require novel ways of cross-jurisdictional regulation. However, COVID-19 has led to an increasing focus on national borders leading to a more fragmented world. It has also demonstrated the vulnerability of global supply chains and hyper-connected just-in-time trading systems.

Before COVID-19, markets became international at the beginning of the late 1960s and global in the 1980s; domestic regulation became increasingly inadequate to address the challenges of cross-border global financial markets and institutions. Therefore, many new institutions evolved such as the Bank for International Settlements (BIS), the Basel Committee on Banking Supervision (Basel Committee), the Financial Action Task Force on Money Laundering (FATF), the Financial Stability Forum, and the Group of Seven (G-7) Industrialized Countries. We can observe the same trend today again with crypto assets, CBDCs, etc. which are treated differently in almost every jurisdiction. But although these institutions already started to entertain questions regarding a new blueprint of the future financial system, concrete steps remain still open. On the other side of the spectrum, the African continent aims to coordinate regional and cross-regional payment systems to increase financial inclusion and lower costs for remittances. Africa leapfrogged the branch-based payment systems by using mobile payment systems straight away.

Given the cross-industry and cross-jurisdictional nature of digital services, new international governance mechanisms might be needed. For example, the objectives and mandates of different relevant authorities (data protection, competition, cybersecurity, financial stability) interact in complex ways and may not always be compatible with each other. Various of these challenges address issues beyond the financial sector and thus the governance of the existing international financial institutions and coordination bodies like the FSB, BIS, IMF, etc. In addition, digital ecosystems are global by definition and thus are difficult to coordinate within national borders. Consequently, policy development must be coordinated on an international level across different industry sectors and across borders. An example are global stablecoins. Because of their potential global reach, they require a discussion of what form "money" can have, who can issue it, and how payments can be recorded and settled? As the scale and scope of such new digital ecosystems grow, so too do the benefits of network transactions in a more dynamic way (so-called "network externalities"). For example, a global stablecoin network may pose challenges to banks' business models as the migration to one or more global stablecoin networks may disintermediate the role of banks in payments and could have implications for the role of central banks and monetary policy. It may finally lead to the digital analogue of "dollarization."

As an answer to this development from the central banks, the introduction of various CBDCs could potentially lead to a more fragmented financial and business world due to a "splinter net." China, for example, has already introduced its CBDC, the e-CNY, while Europe is preparing the launch of the digital Euro later and the USA is still working on a conceptual stage. While the interoperability of a CBDC is of great benefit within one country, nations currently define virtual borders for the use of CBDCs. This means that the use of CBDCs outside a country is currently unclear or even out of scope and that a certain CBDC is converted into another CBDC when this CBDC crosses borders. Another example is multi-CBDC environments, where an exchange between different CBDCs is easily possible for consumers and financial institutions. However, there are clear political considerations which must be taken into account: it will be potentially easier for countries to substitute global reserve currencies when currencies are moving from physical cash to digital coins. However, the globalization of the financial system also requires global digital financial infrastructures and regulations, a challenge that is harder to achieve in times of fragmentation. For example, today the majority of all cross-border payments is organized by Swift. However, the Cross-border Interbank Payment System (Cips), the largest private sector US dollar clearing and settlement system, and the Clearing House Interbank Payments System (CHIPS) emerged as additional infrastructures.

6.4 Sustainability of the Financial System 2030

Sustainable finance has evolved as another key driver for the redesign of the financial system. However, definitions and taxonomies of what this means are either vague or very complex and often not interoperable. But given the fact that the financial sector is a major driver of innovation by allocating capital to sustainability projects, it has become a major element of governments' sustainability activities like the EU. This will strongly promote innovation in many areas like energy transition, sustainable value chains, financial inclusion, and the prevention of crime and fraud. An example is the tokenization of natural resources which enable investments in these resources by foundations, governments, and private investors. Today, natural resources can only be leveraged by extracting them (e.g., oil and gas), farming them (e.g., rain forests), or using them in other types of mostly non-sustainable ways. However, if these natural resources become directly investable because they are seen as more valuable if not being extracted or exploited, this might then lead to a scenario in which a country's currency is directly linked to the degree of digitally tokenized and protected natural resources. This may lead to a world where countries with a higher degree of tokenization of natural resources have a stronger currency compared to ones with a lower degree of tokenized resources. What in the past were precious metals or other backing instruments could in the future be natural resources.

However, currently, new technologies still contain many risks, such as surveillance and privacy concerns. But with the emergence of new services, built on standards like digital identities and other digital (governmental) services, the benefits for the society might dominate. A prominent example is machine readable regulations where the regulation text is digitally embedded in smart contracts and can be executed automatically. But there remains a "tech gap" between the public and the private sector due to one-sided skills. For consumers, it holds the potential of gaining digital sovereignty for the first time in the Internet era. But what would happen if someone would steal your private keys (e.g., through malware) or if voting could be influenced by cryptocurrency payments to manipulate voters to vote for specific candidates without being able to trace it back to individuals? In addition, web3 develops as the third version of the Internet and provides numerous modifications and novelties, such as DAOs. Nations states will be challenged by such DAOs, which offer a modern way to govern societies with smart contracts. This offers a unique opportunity, as DAOs allow delegating the governance of tokens to certain communities or NGOs for which these developments are critical, but (that) were so far not very much involved in the development of these platforms. But, as the discussion has also shown, the conversation about CBDCs and DAOs in Western democracies will take many years if not decades. The technologies of web3 point to the separation of money and state (just as the church and state centuries ago) by web3, however over the past decade the conjunction of both has emerged even stronger given the risks that private forms of money hold.

What approach could be beneficial looking to 2030 or even beyond? While in the past shared technology infrastructures were very often left to the private sector, this might be different this time due to the following reasons: (a) the existing financial infrastructure has some serious gaps (e.g., the payments infrastructure during COVID-19 in many countries showed its limitations), (b) there is a great focus on infrastructure in many countries at the moment (induced by COVID-19 and the war in Ukraine), (c) there are only a few cases, where governments have developed a world-class consumer facing digital system. The most likely solution is a hybrid approach, where the private sector develops novel systems guided by new regulatory and policy guardrails deployed by governments (e.g., DPIs). Just like natural ecosystems, the "financial system 2030" needs to be balanced in between sustainability and diversity and interconnectivity (Lietaer et al., 2010). The sustainability of any complex ecosystem, as the financial system obviously is, can be measured with a single metric: its structural diversity and interconnectivity which has its optimal balance in a small "window of viability" to be sustainable. Reducing diversity and interconnectivity automatically leads to monoculture and a collapse of the financial system due to brittleness. Too much diversity, however, leads to stagnation. This optimal window must be identified on different levels including currencies, institutions, regulations, etc. The "financial system 2030" should be centered around this optimal window of viability and balanced between efficiency and resilience. However, the identification of this optimal window is challenging in times of global (digital) transformation of the economy and the financial system paired with constantly changing geopolitical developments.

Literature

a16z. (2021). *How to win the future: An agenda for the third generation of the internet*. Whitepaper, Andreessen Horowitz, Menlo Park.

Alt, R. (2021). Electronic markets on the next convergence. *Electronic Markets, 31*(1), 1–9.

Alt, R., & Puschmann, T. (2012). The rise of customer-oriented banking - Electronic markets are paving the way for change in the financial industry. *Electronic Markets, 22*(4), 203–215.

Amler, H., Eckey, L., Faust, S., Kaiser, M., Sandner, P., & Schlosser, B. (2021) DeFi-ning DeFi: Challenges & pathway. In *17th IEEE international conference on intelligent computer communication and processing*, Romania.

Amstad, M. (2019) Regulating Fintech: Ignore, duck type, or code. In: *The economics of fintech and digital currencies*, Chapter 11.

Arner, D. W., Buckley, R. P., & Zetsche, D. A. (2018) *FinTech for financial inclusion: Designing infrastructure for financial transformation*. Working Paper. The University of Hong Kong, University of New South Wales and University of Luxemburg.

Azhar, A. (2021). *Exponential - How accelerating technology is leaving us behind and what to do about it*. Random House.

Bank of England. (2020). *Central Bank Digital Currency - Opportunities, challenges and design*. Bank of England.

Bank of England. (2022). *Machine Learning in UK Financial Services*. Source: https://www.bankofengland.co.uk/report/2022/machine-learning-in-uk-financial-services. Access: 22.4.24.

Bátiz-Lazo, B. (2015) A brief history of the ATM: How automation changed retail banking, an object lesson. *The Atlantic*. Source: https://www.theatlantic.com/technology/archive/2015/03/a-brief-history-of-the-atm/388547. Access: 22.4.24.

Bech, M., & Garrat, R. (2017). Central bank cryptocurrencies. *BIS Quarterly Review, 1709*, 55–80.

Benons, C. C. (2020). *Global payments*. Glenbrook Press.

Benston, G. J., & Smith, C. W. (1976). A transactions cost approach to the theory of financial intermediation. *Journal of Finance, 31*(2), 215–231.

BIS. (2019a). *Bank for international settlements, Report on open banking and application programming interfaces*. Basel.

BIS. (2019b). *Bank for international settlements, Investigating the impact of global stablecoins*. Basel.

BIS. (2020a). *Bank for international settlements, Enhancing cross-border payments: Building blocks of a global roadmap*. Basel.

BIS. (2020b). *Bank for international settlements, Central bank digital currencies: Foundational principles and core features*. Basel.

T. Puschmann, H. S. H. P. M. of Liechtenstein, *Financial System 2030*, Financial Innovation and Technology,
https://doi.org/10.1007/978-3-031-55700-2

BIS. (2020c). *Bank for international settlements, Project Helvetia: Settling tokenised assets in central bank money*. Basel.

BIS. (2021). *Bank for international settlements, Ready, steady, go? – Results of the third BIS survey on central bank digital currency*, Basel.

BIS (2023) *Bank for international settlements, Blueprint for the future monetary system: Improving the old, Enabling the New. Annual Economic Report*, Basel.

Blandin, A., Cloots, A. S., Hussain, H., Rauchs, M., Saleuddin, R., Allen, J. G., Zhang, B., & Cloud, K. (2021). *Global cryptoasset regulatory landscape study*. University of Cambridge.

Boaden, R., & Lockett, G. (1991). Information technology, information systems and information management: Definition and development. *European Journal of Information Systems, 1*(1), 23–32.

Bonde, D. O., & Pedersen, J. E .H. (2018). *Remaking banking for a world of bigtech ecosystems*. Working Paper, Copenhagen Business School.

Bonnet, D., Lange, K., & Dalsace, F. (2021). *Fuse soft skills and digital for customer centricity on steroids*. Source: https://iby.imd.org/technology/fuse-soft-skills-and-digital-for-customer-centricity-on-steroids/. Access: 22.4.24.

Boot, A. W. A., & Thakor, A. V. (1997). Financial system architecture. *The Review of Financial Studies, 10*(3), 693–733.

Bower, J. L., & Christensen, C. M. (1995). Disruptive technologies: Catching the wave. *Harvard Business Review, 73*(1), 43–53.

Braun, A., & Schreiber, F. (2017). *The current InsurTech landscape: Business models and disruptive potential*. Working Paper No. 62, Institute of Insurance Economics, University of St. Gallen.

Brummer, C., & Yadav, Y. (2017). Fintech and the innovation trilemma. *The Georgetown Law Journal, 107*, 235.

Brunnermeier, M., Niepelt, D. (2019) *On the equivalence of private and public money*, Working Paper. Princeton University and University of Berne.

Brunnermeier, M. K., James, H., & Landau, J.-P. (2019) *The digitalization of money*. Working Paper, Princeton University.

Buckley, R. P., Arner, D., Zetzsche, D. A., & Weber, R. H. (2020). The Road to RegTech: The (Astonishing) example of the European Union. *Journal of Banking Regulation, 21*(2020), 26–36.

Burns, N., Summers, L., Carter, A., Rosenbach, E., O'Sullivan, M.L., Kumar, A., & Verma, R. (2020). *Digital currency wars: A national security crisis simulation*. Report, Harvard Kennedy School, Belfer Center for Science and International Affairs, 2020. Source: https://www.belfercenter.org/sites/default/files/2020-01/DCW%20Simulation%20Recap.pdf. Access: 22.4.24.

Buterin, V. (2014). *A next generation smart contract & decentralized application platform*. Source: https://ethereum.org/en/whitepaper/?state={%22page_uri%22:%22javascript:alert(document.domain);%22}. Access: 22.4.24.

Casey, M. J., & Vigna, P. (2018). *The truth machine – The blockchain and the future of everything*. St. Martin's Press.

Casey, M. J., & Wong, P. (2017). Global supply chains are about to get better, thanks to blockchain. *Harvard Business Review, 13*(3), 2018.

Catalini, C., & Gans, J. S. (2019). *Some simple economics of the blockchain*. https://ssrn.com/abstract=2874598

CB Insights. (2015). Unbundling Wells Fargo, Citi and Bank of America. *Research Brief*. Source: https://www.cbinsights.com/research/disrupting-banking-fintech-startups/. Access. 17.4.2024.

Cecchetti, S. G. (2014). The future financial system. *Journal of Money, Credit and Banking, 46*(1), 137–141.

Cetorelli, N., et al. (2021). Mapping a sector's scope transformation and the value of following the evolving core. *Strategic Management Journal, 42*(12), 2294–2327.

Chaum, D. (1983). Blind signatures for untraceable payments. *Advances in Cryptology: Proceedings of Crypto '82, 82*(3), 199–203.

Chaum, D., & Moser, T. (2022). *How to issue a central bank digital currency*. SNB Working Papers No. 3/2021. Zurich: Swiss National Bank.
Chiu, I. (2021). *Regulating the crypto economy - Business transformations and financialisation*. Bloomsbury.
Clearing House. (2018). *Fintech apps and data privacy: New insights from consumer research*. Report, The Clearing House.
Cornelli, G., Frost, J., Gambacorta, L., Rau, R., Wardrop, R., & Ziegler, T. (2020) *Fintech and big tech credit: A new database. Bank for International Settlements, Working Paper No 887.*
Cornelli, G., Doerr, S., Gambacorta, L., & Merrouche, O. (2022) *Regulatory sandboxes and fintech funding: Evidence from the UK*. Bank for International Settlements, Working Paper No 901.
Deloitte. (2018). A journey through the FCA regulatory sandbox: The benefits, challenges, and next steps.
Dowd, K. (1998). *Money and the nation state - The financial revolution, government and the world monetary system*. Routledge.
Drucker, P. F. (1954). *The practice of management*. HarperCollins.
Duygun, M., & Xu, J. (2021) *Artificial intelligence and insurance: Application, roadmap and implications*. Working Paper, University of Nottingham.
Eccles, R. G., & Klimenko, S. (2019) The investor revolution. *Harvard Business Review*, May–June 2019.
Eckholm, B., Rockström, J. (2019) *Digital technology can cut global emissions by 15%. Here's how*. World Economic Forum: Geneva. Source: https://www.weforum.org/agenda/2019/01/why-digitalization-is-the-key-to-exponential-climate-action/. Access: 22.4.24.
Economist. (2023). Special report, Digital finance. May 15th, 2023.
English, S., & Hammond, S. (2016). *Cost of compliance 2016*. Thomson Reuters.
Euromoney. (2021). Markets on a war footing. *Euromoney*, October 2021. Source: https://faculty.fuqua.duke.edu/~charvey/Media/2001/EuromoneyOct01.pdf. Access 22.4.24.
European Financial Management Association (EFMA). (2017). *The rise of affluent millennials - How to stay relevant, Report*.
European Union. (2022). *Proposal for a regulation of the European Parliament and the Council on Markets in Crypto-Assets, and amending Directive (EU) 2019/1937*. Brussels, 2020.
Federal Reserve Board. (2023). *Joint statement on crypto-asset risks to banking organizations. Board of Governors of the Federal Reserve System, Federal Deposit Insurance Corporation, Office of the Comptroller of the Currency*. Source: https://www.federalreserve.gov/newsevents/pressreleases/files/bcreg20230103a1.pdf. Access: 22.4.24.
Financial Stability Board. (2019) . *BigTech in finance - Market developments and potential financial stability implications. Report*.
Financial Stability Board. (2020). The use of supervisory and regulatory technology by authorities and regulated institutions: Market developments and financial stability implications.
Financial Stability Board. (2021) . *Global monitoring report of non-bank financial intermediation 2021. Report*.
Financial Stability Board. (2022). *Review of the FSB high-level recommendations of the regulation, supervision and oversight of "Global Stablecoin" arrangements. Report*.
Financial Stability Board. (2023a). *High-level recommendations for the regulation, supervision and oversight of global stablecoin arrangements, Final Report*.
Financial Stability Board. (2023b). *High-level Recommendations for the Regulation, Supervision and oversight of crypto-asset activities and markets, Final Report*.
Forrester Research. (2021). *Case study: Standard chartered bank's future- Fit tech strategy. Report, 2021*.
Gambacorta, L., Huang, Y., Li, Z., Qiu, H., & Chen, S. (2020) *Data vs collateral*. Bank for International Settlements, Working Paper No. 881.
Gartner. (2023). Gartner Forecasts Worldwide Banking and Investment Services IT Spending to Reach $652 Billion in 2023. Source: https://www.gartner.com/en/newsroom/press-

releases/2023-06-21-gartner-forecasts-worldwidebanking-and-investment-services-it-spending-to-reach-652-billion-in-2023. Access: 17.4.2024.

Gartner Group. (2023). *Gartner forecasts worldwide banking and investment services IT spending to reach $652 billion in 2023*. Report, Stamford, CT.

Gąsiorkiewicz, L., & Monkiewicz, J. (2023). *Digital finance and the future of the global financial system - Disruption and innovation in financial services*. Routledge.

Gasser, U., Gassmann, O., Hens, T., Leifer, L., Puschmann, T., Zhao, L. (2018) *Digital banking 2025. Whitepaper*. Harvard University, University of St. Gallen, University of Zurich, Stanford University, University of Hong Kong.

Gassmann, O., Csik, M., & Frankenberger, K. (2014). *The business model navigator: 55 models that will revolutionise your business*. FT Press.

George, G., Howard-Grenville, J., Joshi, A., & Tihanyi, L. (2016). Understanding and tackling societal grand challenges through management research. *Academy of Management Journal, 59*, 1880–1895. https://doi.org/10.5465/amj.2016.4007

Gisiger, M., & Weber, W. (2005). Switzerland's financial infrastructure: Today and tomorrow. *Vierteljahrshefte zur Wirtschaftsforschung, 74*(4), 51–62.

Global Financial Innovation Network (GFIN). (2018). *Consultation Document*, UAE.

Gopalan, S., Jain, G., Kalani, G., & Tan, J. (2012). Breakthrough IT banking. *McKinsey Quarterly, 26*(2), 30–35.

Gorton, G., & Zhang, J. Y. (2021). Taming wildcat stablecoins. *University of Chicago Law Review, 90*.

Gray, M. L., & Suri, S. (2019). *Ghost work: How to stop silicon valley from building a new global underclass*. Houghton Mifflin Harcourt Publishing.

Greer, S. (2021). *Demistifying embedded finance: Promise and peril for banks, Celent*. Source: https://www.celent.com/insights/320916338. Accessed 21.11.2022.

GSMA and Carbon Trust. (2019). *The enablement effect: The impact of mobile communications technologies on carbon emission reductions*. Report.

Halaburda, H. (2018). Blockchain revolution without the blockchain? *Communications of the ACM, 61*(7), 27–29.

Harari, Y. (2019). *21 lessons for the 21st century*. Random House.

Heckel, M., & Waldenberger, F. (2022). *The future of financial systems in the digital age*. Springer.

Hellmann, T. F. et al. (2022). *The impact of the regulatory sandbox on the FinTech Industry*. Social Sciences Research Network. Source: https://papers.ssrn.com/sol3/papers.cfm?abstract_id=4187295. Access 14.3.2023.

Hens, T. (2020). Will the blockchain help to denationalize money? Working Paper: University of Zurich. In K. Leube (Ed.), *The state and its limits: The economic and politics of freedom for the third millennium: Essays in honor of Prince Hans-Adam II of Liechtenstein*. van Eck Publishers.

Hubbard, R. G., & O'Brien, A. (2018). *Money, banking, and the financial system* (3rd ed.). Pearson.

IMF. (2019). *International monetary fund. Fintech notes – The rise of digital money*. Report. Washington, DC.

IMF. (2020). *International monetary fund. Reserve currencies in an evolving international monetary system*. Report. Washington, DC.

IMF. (2023). *International monetary fund. Elements of effective policies for crypto assets*. Report. Washington, DC.

Jacobides, M. G., Cennamo, C., & Gawer, A. (2018). Towards a theory of ecosystems. *Strategic Management Journal, 39*(8), 2255–2276.

Jacobides, M. (2022). How to compete when industries digitize and collide: An ecosystem development framework. *California Management Review, 64*(3), 99–123.

Joshi, N. H., Khan, H., & Rab, I. (2021) *A design-led approach to embracing an ecosystem strategy*. Report. McKisney & Company.

Juniper Research. (2022). *Digital wallets: Market forecast, key opportunities and vendor analysis 2022-2026*. Report.

Kar, A. K., Ilavarasan, V., Gupta, M. P., Janssen, M., & Kothari, R. (2019). Moving beyond smart cities: Digital nations for social innovation & sustainability. *Information Systems Frontiers, 21*(3), 495–501.

Keynes, J. M. (1919). The Economic Consequences of the Peace. London: Macmillan & Co.

KPMG. (2023). *Pulse of Fintech H1 2023*, Report.

Kurzweil, R. (2001). *The law of accelerating returns.* https://www.kurzweilai.net/the-law-of-accelerating-returns. Access: 17.4.2024.

Kutler, J. (1993). Citibank is shedding individualistic image. *American Banker.* Source: https://www.americanbanker.com/opinion/friday-flashback-did-citi-coin-the-term-fintech. Access: 17.4.2024.

Law, J. (2018). *Oxford - A dictionary of finance and banking* (6th ed.). Oxford University Press.

Levine, R. (2005). Finance and growth: Theory and evidence. In P. Aghion & S. N. Durlauf (Eds.), *Handbook of economic growth* (Vol. 1, pp. 865–934). Elsevier.

Lietaer, B., Ulanowicz, R. E., Goerner, S. J., & McLaren, N. (2010). Is our monetary structure a systemic cause for financial instability? Evidence and remedies from nature. *Journal of Futures Studies, 14*(3), 89–108.

Mastercard. (2023). *Unlocking the potential of digital asset innovation: Building a mastercard multi-token network.* Whitepaper.

Matt, C., Hess, T., & Benlian. (2015). A. Digital transformation strategies. *Business & Information Systems Engineering, 57*(5), 339–343.

McAuley, D., & Weiner, S. (2015). *The millennial generation and the future of finance: A different kind of trust.* Report, Innotribe.

McKinsey & Company. (2018) *Banks in the changing world of financial intermediation.* Report.

McKinsey & Company. (2019a) *The last Pit Stop? Time for bold late-cycle moves.* Report.

McKinsey & Company. (2019b). *Amid sustained growth: Accelerating challenges demand bold actions.* Report.

McKinsey & Company. (2022). *McKinsey's global banking annual review.* Report.

McKinsey & Company. (2022). *Value creation in the metaverse: The real business of the virtual world, 2022.* Source: https://www.cbinsights.com/research/metaverse-market-map/?utm_source=CB+Insights+Newsletter&utm_medium=email&utm_campaign=newsletter_general_tues_2022_06_21&utm_term=block-1&utm_content=research-public. Access. 17.4.2024.

McKinsey & Company. (2023). *The 2023 McKinsey global payments report.* Report.

McMillan, J. (2014). *The end of banking: Money, credit, and the digital revolution.* Zero/One Economics.

Messias, J., Pahari, V., Chandrasekaran, B., Gummadi, K. P., Loiseau, P. (2023). *Understanding blockchain governance: Analyzing decentralized voting to amend defi smart contracts.* Research Paper. Source: https://arxiv.org/pdf/2305.17655.pdf. Access: 22.4.24.

Moor, J. (2006). The Dartmouth College Artificial Intelligence Conference: The next fifty years. *AI Magazine, 27*(4), 87–91.

Moore, J. F. (1996). *The death of competition: Leadership & strategy in the age of business ecosystems.* Harper Business.

Narula, N., Swartz, L., & Frizzo-Barker, J. (2023). *CBDC: Expanding financial inclusion or deepening the divide?* Working Paper, MIT Digital Currency Initiative and Maiden Labs, Cambridge, MA.

National Institute of Standards and Technology (NIST). (2016). *Report on post-quantum cryptography.* Source: https://csrc.nist.gov/publications/detail/nistir/8105/final. Access: 22.4.24.

Nilsson, N. J. (2010). *The quest for artificial intelligence: A history of ideas and achieve- ments.* Cambridge University Press.

Nora, S., & Minc, A. (1979). *Die Informatisierung der Gesellschaft.* Campus Verlag.

Office of Gas and Electricity Markets (Ofgem). (2018). *What is a regulatory sandbox?* Source: https://www.ofgem.gov.uk/sites/default/files/docs/2018/09/what_is_a_regulatory_sandbox.pdf. Access 8.12.23.

Open Data Institute. (2019). *Open banking – Preparing for lift off. Report*. Open Data Institute.
Orwell, G. (1984). *Nineteen eighty-four*. Secker & Warburg.
Palfrey, J., & Gasser, U. (2016). *Born digital: How children grow up in a digital age*. Revised Edition. Basic Books.
Parker, G. G., Van Alstyne, M. W., & Choudary, S. P. (2016). *Platform revolution: How networked markets are transforming the economy - and how to make them work for you*. Norton & Company.
Pazarbasioglu, C., Mora, A. G., Uttamchandani, M., Natarajan, H., Feyen, R., & Saal, M. (2020) *Digital financial services*. Report. .
Perrault, R., Shoham, Y., Brynjolfsson, E., Clark, J., Etchemendy, J., Grosz, B., Lyons, T., Manyika, J., Mishra, S., & Niebles, J. C. (2019). *The AI Index 2019 Annual Report*. Stanford University.
Pradhan, R. P., Arvin, M. B., Nair, M., Bennett, S. E., & Bahmani, S. (2019). Short-term and long-term dynamics of venture capital and economic growth in a digital economy: A study of European countries. *Technology in Society, 57*, 125–134.
Puschmann, T. (2017). Fintech. *Business and Information Systems Engineering, 59*, 69–76.
Puschmann, T., & Alt, R. (2016). Sharing economy. *Business & Information Systems Engineering, 58*(1), 93–99.
Puschmann, T., & In, S. Y. (2023). *Developing a research agenda for sustainable digital finance*. Working Paper, University of Zurich and Stanford University.
Puschmann, T. & Huang, M. (2024). *A taxonomy for decentralized finance*. International Review of Financial Analysis, 92, March 2024, 103083.
Puschmann, T., Hoffmann, C. H., & Khmarskyi, V. (2020). How green FinTech can alleviate the impact of climate change - The case of Switzerland. *Sustainability, 12*(24).
Rauchs, M., Blandin, A., Klein, K., Pieters, G. C., Recanatini, M., & Zhang, B. Z. (2018). *2nd Global cryptoasset benchmarking study*. University of Cambridge.
Ricardo, D. (1816) Proposals for an economical and secure currency. In: Sraffa, P. (Eds.), *The works and correspondence of David Ricardo* (pp. 72–73), 1951.
Ripple. (2019). *Blockchain adoption: The tipping point is near*. Report.
Ryll, L., Barton, M. E., Zhang, B. Z., & McWaters, J. (2020). *Transforming paradigms: A global AI in financial services survey report*. World Economic Forum & University of Cambridge.
Sanches, D. (2016). *The free-banking era: A lesson for today?* Federal Reserve Bank Philadelphia.
Schmidt, R., & Tyrell, M. (2003). *What constitutes a financial system in general and the German financial system in particular?* Working Paper No 111. Goethe University.
Serena, J. M. (2019). IFC survey on fintech data: Statistical initiatives to close data gaps. Presentation to Irving Fisher Committee on Central Bank Statistics.
Slonim, N., Bilu, Y., Alzate, C., Bar-Haim, R., Bogin, B., Bonin, F., et al. (2021). An autonomous debating system. *Nature, 591*, 379–384.
Sporny, M., Longley, D. (2016). A Web-based Ledger Data Model and Format. *World Wide Web Consortium (W3C)*. https://www.w3.org/2016/04/blockchain-workshop/interest/sporny-longley.html
Statista. (2023). *Number of Fintech startups worldwide from 2018 to 2023*. Source: https://www.statista.com/statistics/893954/number-fintech-startups-by-region. Access: 22.4.24.
Stephenson, N. (1993). *Snow crash*. Bantam Spectra.
Sundararajan, A. (2016). *The Sharing Economy: The End of Employment and the Rise of Crowd-Based Capitalism*. MIT Press: Cambridge (MA).
Sung, R. K. (2022). *How the cryptocurrency market is connected to the financial market*. Research Paper. Source: https://papers.ssrn.com/sol3/papers.cfm?abstract_id=4106815. Access 4.4.24.
Tallon, P. P. (2010). A service science perspective on strategic choice, IT, and performance in U.S. Banking. *Journal of Management Information Systems, 26*(4), 219–252.
Tapscott, D. (1996). *The digital economy: Promise and peril in the age of networked intelligence*. McGraw-Hill.
The Economist. (2019). *What comes after Bretton Woods II? The world's monetary system is breaking down*. August 15th 2019.

The Economist. (2020). *Free exchange – Change for the dollar*. August 8th 2020.

The Economist. (2021). *Govcoins: The digital currencies that will transform finance*. May 8th 2021.

The Economist. (2023). *Special report: Digital finance*. May 20th 2023.

The Economist. (2023) As payments systems go digital, they are changing global finance. *Special report digital finance*. May 5th 2023.

Thomson Reuters. (2022) *Cryptocurrency regulations by country*. Toronto.

Twimbit. (2020). *Widespread innovations in driving Ping An CX Aspirations*. Report. Source: https://cdn.twimbit.com/uploads/2020/12/25105105/PingAn-v1-1_compressed.pdf. Access: 22.4.24.

UK Finance. (2023). *UK payment markets summary 2023*. Report. Source: https://www.ukfinance.org.uk/system/files/2023-09/UK%20Finance%20Payment%20Markets%20Report%20 2023%20Summary.pdf. Access: 22.4.24.

UN. (2020). *United Nations. People's money: Harnessing digitalization to finance a sustainable future. The United Nations secretary general task force on digital financing the sustainable development goals. Final Report.*

UNDP. (2023). *United Nations Development Programme, Accelerating the SDGs through digital public infrastructure*. Report.

Van Niekerk, A. (2006). *A methodological approach to modern digital asset management: An empirical study* (Vol. 13, Issue 1). Proceedings of the Allied Academies International Conference. International Academy for Case Studies.

Von Hayek, F. A. (1976). *Denationalization of money*. Institute of Economic Affairs.

Weill, P., & Woerner, S. L. (2015). Thriving in an increasingly digital ecosystem. *MIT Sloan Management Review*, Summer 2015.

Weinberger, M. (2022). What is metaverse? A definition based on qualitative meta-synthesis. *Future Internet, 14*(11), 310.

Welfare. (2019). *Commercializing blockchain: Strategic applications in the real world*. Wiley.

World Economic Forum. (2022). *Decentralized autonomous organizations: Beyond the hype*. Source: https://www3.weforum.org/docs/WEF_Decentralized_Autonomous_Organizations_Beyond_the_Hype_2022.pdf. Access: 17.4.2024.

World Wide Web Consortium (W3C). (2019). *Decentralized Identifiers (DIDs) v1.0 - Core Data Model and Syntaxes*. W3C Credentials Community Group.

World Wide Web Consortium (W3C). (2022). *Decentralized Identifiers (DIDs) v1.0 - Core Data Model and Syntaxes*. W3C Credentials Community Group, Cambridge (MA).

Zetsche et al. (2020) *Digital finance platforms: Toward a new regulatory paradigm*. Research Paper. Source: https://papers.ssrn.com/sol3/papers.cfm?abstract_id=3532975. Access: 22.4.24.

Ziegler, T., Zhang, B. Z., Carvajal, A. F., Barton, M. E., et al. (2021). *The global COVID-19 FinTech market rapid assessment study*. University of Cambridge, World Bank Group and the World Economic Forum, Report.

Ziegler, T., Zhang, B. Z., et al. (2021). *The global COVID-19 FinTech market rapid assessment study*. University of Cambridge.

Index

T. Puschmann, H. S. H. P. M. of Liechtenstein, *Financial System 2030*, Financial Innovation and Technology,
https://doi.org/10.1007/978-3-031-55700-2

GPSR Compliance
The European Union's (EU) General Product Safety Regulation (GPSR) is a set of rules that requires consumer products to be safe and our obligations to ensure this.

If you have any concerns about our products, you can contact us on

ProductSafety@springernature.com

In case Publisher is established outside the EU, the EU authorized representative is:

Springer Nature Customer Service Center GmbH
Europaplatz 3
69115 Heidelberg, Germany

www.ingramcontent.com/pod-product-compliance
Lightning Source LLC
Chambersburg PA
CBHW061304161025
33954CB00070B/431
* 9 7 8 3 0 3 1 5 5 6 9 9 9 *